OECD/G20 Base Erosion and Profit Shifting Project

Limiting Base Erosion Involving Interest Deductions and Other Financial Payments Action 4 - 2016 Update

INCLUSIVE FRAMEWORK ON BEPS

OECD
BETTER POLICIES FOR BETTER LIVES

Please cite this publication as:
OECD (2017), *Limiting Base Erosion Involving Interest Deductions and Other Financial Payments, Action 4 - 2016 Update: Inclusive Framework on BEPS*, OECD/G20 Base Erosion and Profit Shifting Project, OECD Publishing, Paris.
http://dx.doi.org/10.1787/9789264268333-en

ISBN 978-92-64-26832-6 (print)
ISBN 978-92-64-26833-3 (PDF)

Series: OECD/G20 Base Erosion and Profit Shifting Project
ISSN 2313-2604 (print)
ISSN 2313-2612 (online)

Photo credits: Cover © ninog - Fotolia.com

Corrigenda to OECD publications may be found on line at: *www.oecd.org/about/publishing/corrigenda.htm*.

Foreword

The integration of national economies and markets has increased substantially in recent years, putting a strain on the international tax rules, which were designed more than a century ago. Weaknesses in the current rules create opportunities for base erosion and profit shifting (BEPS), requiring bold moves by policy makers to restore confidence in the system and ensure that profits are taxed where economic activities take place and value is created.

Following the release of the report *Addressing Base Erosion and Profit Shifting* in February 2013, OECD and G20 countries adopted a 15-point Action Plan to address BEPS in September 2013. The Action Plan identified 15 actions along three key pillars: introducing coherence in the domestic rules that affect cross-border activities, reinforcing substance requirements in the existing international standards, and improving transparency as well as certainty.

After two years of work, measures in response to the 15 actions were delivered to G20 Leaders in Antalya in November 2015. All the different outputs, including those delivered in an interim form in 2014, were consolidated into a comprehensive package. The BEPS package of measures represents the first substantial renovation of the international tax rules in almost a century. Once the new measures become applicable, it is expected that profits will be reported where the economic activities that generate them are carried out and where value is created. BEPS planning strategies that rely on outdated rules or on poorly co-ordinated domestic measures will be rendered ineffective.

Implementation is now the focus of this work. The BEPS package is designed to be implemented via changes in domestic law and practices, and via treaty provisions, with the negotiation for a multilateral instrument having been finalised in 2016 to facilitate the implementation of the treaty related measures. OECD and G20 countries also agreed to continue to work together to ensure a consistent and co-ordinated implementation of the BEPS recommendations and to make the project more inclusive. Globalisation requires that global solutions and a global dialogue be established which go beyond OECD and G20 countries.

As a result, the OECD has established an Inclusive Framework for BEPS implementation, bringing all interested and committed countries and jurisdictions on an equal footing in the Committee on Fiscal Affairs and all its subsidiary bodies. The Inclusive Framework will monitor and peer review the implementation of the minimum standards as well as complete the work on standard setting to address BEPS issues. In addition to BEPS Members, other international organisations and regional tax bodies are involved in the work of the Inclusive Framework, which also consults business and the civil society on its different work streams.

A better understanding of how the BEPS recommendations are implemented in practice could reduce misunderstandings and disputes between governments. Greater focus on implementation and tax administration should therefore be mutually beneficial to governments and business. Proposed improvements to data and analysis will help support ongoing evaluation of the quantitative impact of BEPS, as well as evaluating the impact of the countermeasures developed under the BEPS Project.

Table of contents

Part II
Elements of the design and operation of the group ratio rule

Part III
Approaches to address BEPS involving interest in the banking and insurance sectors

Figures

Tables

Box

Abbreviations and acronyms

BEPS	Base Erosion and Profit Shifting
BIAC	Business and Industry Advisory Committee
CFC	Controlled Foreign Company
CIV	Collective Investment Vehicle
EBIT	Earnings before interest and taxes
EBITDA	Earnings before interest, taxes, depreciation and amortisation
EU	European Union
GAAP	Generally Accepted Accounting Principles
IFRS	International Financial Reporting Standards
JV	Joint Venture
OECD	Organisation for Economic Co-operation and Development
PwC	PricewaterhouseCoopers
TFEU	Treaty on the Functioning of the European Union
USD	United States Dollar

Executive summary

It is an empirical matter of fact that money is mobile and fungible. Thus, multinational groups may achieve favourable tax results by adjusting the amount of debt in a group entity. The influence of tax rules on the location of debt within multinational groups has been established in a number of academic studies and it is well known that groups can easily multiply the level of debt at the level of individual group entities via intra-group financing. Financial instruments can also be used to make payments which are economically equivalent to interest but have a different legal form, therefore escaping restrictions on the deductibility of interest. Base Erosion and Profit Shifting (BEPS) risks in this area may arise in three basic scenarios:

- Groups placing higher levels of third party debt in high tax countries.
- Groups using intragroup loans to generate interest deductions in excess of the group's actual third party interest expense.
- Groups using third party or intragroup financing to fund the generation of tax exempt income.

To address these risks, Action 4 of the *Action Plan on Base Erosion and Profit Shifting* (BEPS Action Plan, OECD, 2013) called for recommendations regarding best practices in the design of rules to prevent base erosion through the use of interest expense. Part I of this report contains the text of the 2015 report *Limiting Base Erosion Involving Interest Deductions and Other Financial Payments* (OECD, 2015) which analyses several best practices and recommends an approach which directly addresses the risks outlined above. The recommended approach is based on a fixed ratio rule which limits an entity's net deductions for interest and payments economically equivalent to interest to a percentage of its earnings before interest, taxes, depreciation and amortisation (EBITDA). As a minimum this should apply to entities in multinational groups. To ensure that countries apply a fixed ratio that is low enough to tackle BEPS, while recognising that not all countries are in the same position, the recommended approach includes a corridor of possible ratios of between 10% and 30%. The report also includes factors which countries should take into account in setting their fixed ratio within this corridor. The approach can be supplemented by a worldwide group ratio rule which allows an entity to exceed this limit in certain circumstances.

Recognising that some groups are highly leveraged with third party debt for non-tax reasons, the recommended approach proposes a group ratio rule alongside the fixed ratio rule. This would allow an entity with net interest expense above a country's fixed ratio to deduct interest up to the level of the net interest/EBITDA ratio of its worldwide group. Countries may also apply an uplift of up to 10% to the group's net third party interest expense to prevent double taxation. The earnings-based worldwide group ratio rule can also be replaced by different group ratio rules, such as the "equity escape" rule (which compares an entity's level of equity and assets to those held by its group) currently in place in some countries. A country may also choose not to introduce any group ratio rule. If a country does not introduce a group ratio rule, it should apply the fixed ratio rule to entities in multinational and domestic groups without improper discrimination.

The recommended approach will mainly impact entities with both a high level of net interest expense and a high net interest/EBITDA ratio, in particular where the entity's ratio is higher than that of its worldwide group. This is a straightforward approach and ensures that an entity's net interest deductions are directly linked to the taxable income generated by its economic activities. An important feature of the fixed ratio rule is that it only limits an entity's net interest deductions (i.e. interest expense in excess of interest income). The rule does not restrict the ability of multinational groups to raise third party debt centrally in the country and entity which is most efficient taking into account non-tax factors such as credit rating, currency and access to capital markets, and then on-lend the borrowed funds within the group to where it is used to fund the group's economic activities.

The recommended approach allows countries to supplement the fixed ratio rule and group ratio rule with other provisions that reduce the impact of the rules on entities or situations which pose less BEPS risk, such as:

- A *de minimis* threshold which carves-out entities which have a low level of net interest expense. Where a group has more than one entity in a country, it is recommended that the threshold be applied to the total net interest expense of the local group.
- An exclusion for interest paid to third party lenders on loans used to fund public-benefit projects, subject to conditions. In these circumstances, an entity may be highly leveraged but, due to the nature of the projects and the close link to the public sector, the BEPS risk is reduced.
- The carry forward of disallowed interest expense and/or unused interest capacity (where an entity's actual net interest deductions are below the maximum permitted) for use in future years. This will reduce the impact of earnings volatility on the ability of an entity to deduct interest expense. The carry forward of disallowed interest expense will also help entities which incur interest expenses on long-term investments that are expected to generate taxable income only in later years, and will allow entities with losses to claim interest deductions when they return to profit.

The report also recommends that the approach be supported by targeted rules to prevent its circumvention, for example by artificially reducing the level of net interest expense. It also recommends that countries consider introducing rules to tackle specific BEPS risks not addressed by the recommended approach, such as where an entity without net interest expense shelters interest income.

Part II contains further guidance on elements of the design and operation of a group ratio rule based on the net interest/EBITDA ratio of a worldwide group, which was completed in 2016 and focuses on the calculation of net third party interest expense, the calculation of group EBITDA and approaches to address the impact of entities with negative EBITDA on the operation of the rule. This guidance does not alter anything recommended in Part I, but provides additional detail to assist countries implementing a rule.

Part I identifies features of banking and insurance businesses which indicate a different approach may be needed to deal with risks posed by entities in these sectors and proposes that further work should be conducted. The outcomes of this further work is contained in Part III, which explores factors that can impose constraints on the ability of banking and insurance groups to engage in BEPS involving interest, together with limits on these constraints. Overall, significant regulatory and commercial considerations reduce the risks posed by banking and insurance groups, but differences exist between countries and sectors. Each country should identify the specific risks it faces, taking into account the characteristics of banking and insurance groups and the requirements of regulators. Where no material risks are identified, a country may reasonably exempt banking and/or insurance groups from the fixed ratio rule and group ratio rule without the need for additional tax rules. Where BEPS risks involving interest are identified, a country should introduce rules which are appropriate to address these risks, taking into account the regulatory regime and tax system in that country. In all cases, rules to protect countries from BEPS should not weaken the effectiveness of capital regulation in providing protection against a future financial crisis.

The amount of intragroup interest and payments economically equivalent to interest is also affected by transfer pricing rules. Revisions to Chapter I of the Transfer Pricing Guidelines under Actions 8-10 of the BEPS Action Plan (OECD, 2013), contained in the OECD Report *Aligning Transfer Pricing Outcomes with Value Creation* (OECD, 2015), limit the amount of interest payable to group companies lacking appropriate substance to no more than a risk-free return on the funding provided and require group synergies to be taken into account when evaluating intragroup financial payments. Further work on the transfer pricing aspects of financial transactions will be undertaken during 2017.

A co-ordinated implementation of the recommended approach will successfully impact on the ability of multinational groups to use debt to achieve BEPS outcomes. To ensure the recommended approach remains effective in tackling BEPS involving interest, the implementation, operation and impact of the approach will be monitored over time, to allow for a comprehensive and informed review as necessary.

Part I

Limiting base erosion involving interest deductions and other financial payments

Part I contains the text of the 2015 report *Limiting Base Erosion Involving Interest Deductions and Other Financial Payments*, which formed part of the BEPS package of measures delivered to G20 Finance Ministers at their meeting on 8 October 2015 in Lima, Peru and to G20 Leaders at their summit on 15-16 November 2015 in Antalya, Turkey.

Introduction

Use of interest and payments economically equivalent to interest for base erosion and profit shifting

1. The use of third party and related party interest is perhaps one of the most simple of the profit-shifting techniques available in international tax planning. The fluidity and fungibility of money makes it a relatively simple exercise to adjust the mix of debt and equity in a controlled entity. Against this background, Action 4 of the *Action Plan on Base Erosion and Profit Shifting* (BEPS Action Plan, OECD, 2013) calls for the:

> [development of] recommendations regarding best practices in the design of rules to prevent base erosion through the use of interest expense, for example through the use of related-party and third-party debt to achieve excessive interest deductions or to finance the production of exempt or deferred income, and other financial payments that are economically equivalent to interest payments. The work will evaluate the effectiveness of different types of limitations. In connection with and in support of the foregoing work, transfer pricing guidance will also be developed regarding the pricing of related party financial transactions, including financial and performance guarantees, derivatives (including internal derivatives used in intra-bank dealings), and captive and other insurance arrangements. The work will be co-ordinated with the work on hybrids and CFC rules.

2. Most countries tax debt and equity differently for the purposes of their domestic law. Interest on debt is generally a deductible expense of the payer and taxed at ordinary rates in the hands of the payee. Dividends, or other equity returns, on the other hand, are generally not deductible and are typically subject to some form of tax relief (an exemption, exclusion, credit, etc.) in the hands of the payee. While, in a purely domestic context, these differences in treatment may result in debt and equity being subject to a similar overall tax burden, the difference in the treatment of the payer creates a tax-induced bias, in the cross-border context, towards debt financing. The distortion is compounded by tax planning techniques that may be employed to reduce or eliminate tax on interest income in the jurisdiction of the payee.

3. In the cross-border context, the main tax policy concerns surrounding interest deductions relate to the debt funding of outbound and inbound investment by groups. Parent companies are typically able to claim relief for their interest expense while the return on equity holdings is taxed on a preferential basis, benefiting from a participation exemption, preferential tax rate or taxation only on distribution. On the other hand, subsidiary entities may be heavily debt financed, using excessive deductions on intragroup loans to shelter local profits from tax. Taken together, these opportunities surrounding inbound and outbound investment potentially create competitive distortions between groups operating internationally and those operating in the domestic market. This has a negative impact on capital ownership neutrality, creating a tax preference for assets to be held by multinational

groups rather than domestic groups.[1] In addition, as identified in the BEPS Action Plan (OECD, 2013), when groups exploit these opportunities, it reduces the revenues available to governments and affects the integrity of the tax system. The use of interest deductions to fund income which is exempt or deferred for tax purposes, and obtaining relief for interest deductions greater than the actual net interest expense of the group, can also contribute to other forms of base erosion and profit shifting. These include the use of intragroup loans to generate deductible interest expense in high tax jurisdictions and interest income in low or no tax jurisdictions; the development of hybrid instruments which give rise to deductible interest expense but no corresponding taxable income; and the use of loans to invest in assets which give rise to a return that is not taxed or is taxed at a reduced rate. Box 1 below contains simple examples of how a multinational group can generate a benefit based on the location of its debt, in both outbound and inbound investment scenarios.

Box 1. Example of the impact of tax on the location of interest expense*

These examples assume no restriction on the ability of a group to obtain deductions for its interest expense, for example under transfer pricing or thin capitalisation rules.

Outbound investment

Consider a simple group structure, including two companies (A Co and B Co). A Co is resident in a country with a 35% rate of corporate income tax, which exempts foreign source dividends from tax. B Co is resident in a country with a 15% corporate tax rate.

B Co borrows USD 100 from a third party bank at an interest rate of 10%.** B Co uses these funds in its business and generates additional operating profit of USD 15. After deducting the USD 10 interest cost, B Co has a pre-tax profit of USD 5 and a post-tax profit of USD 4.25.

Alternatively, A Co could borrow the USD 100 from the bank and contribute the same amount to B Co as equity. In this case, B Co has no interest expense and its full operating profit of USD 15 is subject to tax. B Co now has a pre-tax profit of USD 15 and a post-tax profit of USD 12.75. Assuming A Co can set its interest expense against other income, A Co has a pre-tax cost of USD 10 and a post-tax cost of USD 6.50. Taken together, A Co and B Co have a total pre-tax profit from the transaction of USD 5 and a total post-tax profit of USD 6.25.

As a result of transferring the interest expense from B Co to A Co, the group is now subject to a negative effective rate of taxation (i.e. the group's post-tax profit exceeds its pre-tax profit).

Inbound investment

A similar result can also be achieved in an inbound investment context.

In this case, A Co is resident in a country with a 15% rate of corporate income tax and B Co is resident in a country with a 35% corporate tax rate.

B Co borrows USD 100 from a third party bank at an interest rate of 10%. B Co uses these funds in its business and generates additional operating profit of USD 15. After deducting the USD 10 interest cost, B Co has a pre-tax profit of USD 5 and a post-tax profit of USD 3.25.

A Co could also replace USD 50 of existing equity in B Co with a loan of the same amount, at an interest rate of 10% (the same rate as on the loan from the third party bank). In this case, B Co has a pre-tax and post-tax profit of nil. A Co has interest income on its loan to B Co, and has a pre-tax profit of USD 5 and a post-tax profit of USD 4.25. The group has reduced its effective tax rate from 35% to 15% by shifting profit from B Co to A Co.

Box 1. **Example of the impact of tax on the location of interest expense** *(continued)*

Taking this one step further, A Co could replace USD 100 of existing equity in B Co with a loan of the same amount. Assuming B Co can set its interest expense against other income, as a result of this transaction B Co now has a pre-tax loss of USD 5 and a post-tax loss of USD 3.25. A Co receives interest income from B Co, and has a pre-tax profit of USD 10 and a post-tax profit of USD 8.50. Taken together, A Co and B Co have a pre-tax profit of USD 5 and a post-tax profit of USD 5.25. As a result of thinly capitalising B Co and shifting profit to A Co, the group is now subject to a negative effective rate of taxation.

* The first part of this example is adapted from Graetz (2008).

** All monetary amounts in this example are denominated in United States dollars (USD). This is an illustrative example only, and is not intended to reflect a real case or the position in a particular country.

4. The ongoing existence of international debt shifting has been established in a number of academic studies which show that groups leverage more debt in subsidiaries located in high tax countries (Møen et al., 2011; Huizinga, Laeven and Nicodeme, 2008; Mintz and Weichenrieder, 2005; Desai, Foley and Hines, 2004). Debt shifting does not only impact developed countries, but is also an issue for developing countries which, according to academic research, are even more prone to these risks (Fuest, Hebous and Riedel, 2011). Academics have shown that thin capitalisation is strongly associated with multinational groups (Taylor and Richardson, 2013), and that foreign-owned businesses use more debt than comparable domestically-owned businesses (Egger et al., 2010). Additional debt is provided through both intragroup and third party debt (Møen et al., 2011), with intragroup loans typically used in cases where the borrowing costs on third party debt are high (Buettner et al., 2012). Academics have also looked at the effectiveness of thin capitalisation rules and illustrated that such rules have the effect of reducing the total debt of subsidiaries (Blouin et al., 2014; Buettner et al., 2012). Where thin capitalisation rules apply solely to interest deductions on intragroup debt, these rules are effective in reducing intragroup debt but then lead to an increase in third party debt, although this may not be to the same extent (Buettner et al., 2012).

5. The impact of interest limitation rules on investment has also been the subject of academic studies and the topic has been approached using both theoretical models and empirical analysis. Analysing the impact of interest limitation rules on investment from a theoretical standpoint, academics suggest that such rules would increase effective capital costs thus reducing real investment (Ruf and Schindler, 2012) The theoretical approach is supported by studies which suggest that certain countries set lenient thin capitalisation rules in order to protect foreign direct investment (Haufer and Runkel, 2012). The limited empirical analysis that has been done does not, however, support this theory. Two studies, both analysing the effect of German interest limitation rules on investment, find no significant evidence of a reduction of investment in relation to either thin capitalisation rules (Weichenrieder and Windischbauer, 2008) or interest barrier rules based on a ratio of interest expense to income (Buslei and Simmler, 2012).[2] This lack of empirical support may be due to a number of factors including the fact that multinational groups may avoid the application of the interest limitation rule by using loopholes in the legislation or by adjusting their capital structure (Ruf and Schindler, 2012). Therefore, there does not seem to be enough empirical evidence to reach conclusions on the actual impact of interest limitation rules on foreign investment.

6. Countries have introduced a wide range of rules to address issues of base erosion and profit shifting involving third party and intragroup interest. These include general interest limitation rules which put an overall limit on the level of interest deductions that an entity can claim, as well as targeted rules which address specific planning risks. Where general interest limitation rules have been used, in some countries they have focused on inbound investment situations only, while in others rules have attempted to address both inbound and outbound situations. The main types of rules applied by countries are considered later in this introduction. These approaches have been successful to varying degrees, but there is a sense that unilateral action by countries is failing to tackle some of the issues at the heart of this problem. Partly, this is because the fungibility of money and the flexibility of financial instruments have made it possible for groups to bypass the effect of rules and replicate similar benefits using different tools. This has led to countries repeatedly introducing new rules, or amending existing ones, creating layers of complexity without addressing the key underlying issues. There is also a concern that a robust approach to restrict interest deductions by a single country could adversely impact the attractiveness of the country to international business and the ability of domestic groups to compete globally.

7. It has therefore become increasingly apparent that a consistent approach utilising international best practices would be a more effective and efficient way of addressing concerns surrounding the use of interest in base erosion and profit shifting. This approach should encourage groups to adopt funding structures whereby: (i) the net interest expense of an entity is linked to the overall net interest expense of the group; and (ii) the distribution of a group's net interest expense should be linked to income-producing activities. Groups should also benefit from a consistent approach between countries. Similar rules based on the same principles should make the operation of rules more predictable, enabling groups to plan their capital structures with greater confidence. It could also make it possible to introduce group-wide systems and processes to produce required information, making compliance with rules in multiple countries simpler and cheaper. A consistent approach should remove distortions, reduce the risk of unintended double taxation and, by removing opportunities for base erosion and profit shifting, improve fairness and equality between groups.

BEPS Action Plan and interest expense

8. In 2012, the G20 called on the Organisation for Economic Co-operation and Development (OECD) to analyse the issue of base erosion and profit shifting and develop an action plan to address these issues in a co-ordinated and comprehensive manner. The BEPS Action Plan (OECD, 2013) was delivered by the OECD in July 2013 and contains 15 actions. Several of these address different aspects of base erosion and profit shifting using interest. Arrangements using hybrid financial instruments or hybrid entities to generate two tax deductions for the same payment, or payments which are deductible in the payer but are not taxed as ordinary income in the recipient, are addressed through model rules developed under Action 2 (Neutralise the effects of hybrid mismatch arrangements). Work under Action 3 (Strengthen CFC rules) has developed recommendations regarding the design of controlled foreign company (CFC) rules, which among other things should help to address the issue of interest income in controlled companies in low tax jurisdictions. Action 4 (Limit base erosion via interest deductions and other financial payments), which is the focus of this report, makes recommendations for best practices in the design of rules to address base erosion and profit shifting using interest and payments economically equivalent to interest, by aligning interest deductions with taxable economic activity. Action 4 also refers to the

development of transfer pricing guidance for related party financial transactions, which will be carried out as a separate project to be completed by 2017. This work should in no way impede countries from implementing the best practice approach contained in this report. Revisions to Chapter I of the Transfer Pricing Guidelines under Actions 8-10 (Intangibles; Risks and capital; and Other high risk transactions) limit the amount of interest payable to group companies lacking appropriate substance to no more than a risk-free return on the funding provided and require group synergies to be taken into account when evaluating intragroup financial payments.

9. Action 4 is focused on the use of third party, related party and intragroup debt to achieve excessive interest deductions or to finance the production of exempt or deferred income. A best practice approach to tackling these issues should apply to all forms of interest and payments equivalent to interest, to ensure that groups in an equivalent position are treated consistently and to reduce the risk of a rule being avoided by a group structuring its borrowings into a different legal form. Base erosion and profit shifting can arise from arrangements using third party debt (e.g. where one entity or country bears an excessive proportion of the group's total net third party interest expense) and intragroup debt (e.g. where a group uses intragroup interest expense to shift taxable income from high tax to low tax countries). It can also occur where payments are made to a lender outside a country or within the same country. For example, within a country base erosion and profit shifting may arise as a result of interest paid to a third party under a structured arrangement, or where interest is paid to a group entity in the same country which makes a corresponding payment to a foreign lender. In order to be effective in tackling base erosion and profit shifting, a best practice approach should therefore apply to all of these situations.

Existing approaches to tackle base erosion and profit shifting involving interest

10. The recommendations in this report are the result of significant work which explored the advantages and disadvantages of different types of rules. This included a review of countries' experiences as to how rules operate in practice and impacts on taxpayer behaviour. It also included an analysis of empirical data on the leverage of groups and entities in countries which do and do not currently apply rules to limit interest deductions, and the results of academic studies.

11. Rules currently applied by countries fall into six broad groups, with some countries using a combined approach that includes more than one type of rule:

1. Arm's length tests, which compare the level of interest or debt in an entity with the position that would have existed had the entity been dealing entirely with third parties.
2. Withholding tax on interest payments, which are used to allocate taxing rights to a source jurisdiction.
3. Rules which disallow a specified percentage of the interest expense of an entity, irrespective of the nature of the payment or to whom it is made.
4. Rules which limit the level of interest expense or debt in an entity with reference to a fixed ratio, such as debt/equity, interest/earnings or interest/total assets.
5. Rules which limit the level of interest expense or debt in an entity with reference to the group's overall position.
6. Targeted anti-avoidance rules which disallow interest expense on specific transactions.

12. An arm's length test requires consideration of an individual entity's circumstances, the amount of debt that the entity would be able to raise from third party lenders and the terms under which that debt could be borrowed. It allows a tax administration to focus on the particular commercial circumstances of an entity or a group but it can be resource intensive and time consuming for both taxpayers and tax administrations to apply. Also, because each entity is considered separately after arrangements are entered into, the outcomes of applying a rule can be uncertain, although this may be reduced through advance agreements with the tax administration. An advantage of an arm's length test is that it recognises that entities may have different levels of interest expense depending on their circumstances. However, some countries with experience of applying such an approach in practice expressed concerns over how effective it is in preventing base erosion and profit shifting, although it could be a useful complement to other rules (e.g. in pricing the interest income and expense of an entity, before applying interest limitation rules). In particular, countries have experience of groups structuring intragroup debt with equity-like features to justify interest payments significantly in excess of those the group actually incurs on its third party debt. Additionally, an arm's length test does not prevent an entity from claiming a deduction for interest expense which is used to fund investments in non-taxable assets or income streams, which is a base erosion risk specifically mentioned as a concern in the BEPS Action Plan (OECD, 2013).

13. Withholding taxes are primarily used to allocate taxing rights to a source country, but by imposing tax on cross-border payments they may also reduce the benefit to groups from base erosion and profit shifting transactions. Withholding tax has the advantage of being a relatively mechanical tool which is easy to apply and administer. However, unless withholding tax is applied at the same rate as corporate tax, opportunities for base erosion and profit shifting would remain. In fact, in some cases withholding taxes can drive base erosion and profit shifting behaviour, where groups enter into structured arrangements to avoid imposition of a tax or generate additional tax benefits (such as multiple entities claiming credit with respect to tax withheld). Where withholding tax is applied, double taxation can be addressed by giving credit in the country where the payment is received, although the effectiveness of this is reduced if credit is only given up to the amount of tax on net income. This can impose a significant cost on groups not engaged in base erosion and profit shifting, if an entity suffers withholding tax on its gross interest receipts, but is unable to claim a credit for this because its taxable income is reduced by interest expense. In practice, where withholding tax is applied the rate is often reduced (sometimes to zero) under bilateral tax treaties. It would also be extremely difficult for European Union (EU) Member States to apply withholding taxes on interest payments made within the European Union due to the Interest and Royalty Directive.[3] In addition, there are broader policy reasons why some countries do not currently apply withholding tax to interest payments, which could make the introduction of new taxes difficult. Taken together, these factors mean that in many situations withholding taxes would not be a suitable tool for completely tackling the base erosion and profit shifting risks which are the subject of this report. However, countries may still continue to apply withholding tax alongside the best practice.

14. Rules which disallow a percentage of all interest paid by an entity in effect increase the cost of all debt finance above any *de minimis* threshold. Therefore, entities with a relatively low leverage will be subject to the same proportionate disallowance as similar entities with very high levels of debt. This approach is likely to be more effective in reducing the general tax preference for debt over equity, than in targeting base erosion and profit shifting involving interest.

15. For the reasons set out above, the rules in groups 1 to 3, on their own, do not address all of the aims of Action 4 set out in the BEPS Action Plan (OECD, 2013). As such, they are not considered to be best practices in tackling base erosion and profit shifting involving interest and payments economically equivalent to interest if they are not strengthened with other interest limitation rules. However, these rules may still have a role to play within a country's tax system alongside a best practice approach, either in supporting those rules or in meeting other tax policy goals. Therefore, after introducing the best practice approach, a country may also continue to apply an arm's length test, withholding tax on interest, or rules to disallow a percentage of an entity's total interest expense, so long as these do not reduce the effectiveness of the best practice in tackling base erosion and profit shifting.

16. The best practice approach set out in this report is based on a combination of some or all of the rules in groups 4 to 6 above. A general limit on interest deductions would restrict the ability of an entity to deduct net interest expense based on a fixed financial ratio. This could be combined with a rule to allow the entity to deduct more interest up to the group's equivalent financial ratio where this is higher. If a country does not introduce a group ratio rule, it should apply the fixed ratio rule to entities in multinational and domestic groups without improper discrimination. These general rules should be complemented by targeted rules to address planning to reduce or avoid the effect of the general rules, and targeted rules can also be used to tackle specific risks not covered by the general rules. This approach should provide effective protection for countries against base erosion and profit shifting involving interest, but should not prevent businesses from raising the debt finance necessary for their business and commercial investments.

17. Rules which limit interest expense by reference to a fixed ratio are relatively easy to apply and link the level of interest expense to a measure of an entity's economic activity. These rules are currently applied by a number of countries. However, the way in which existing rules are designed is not always the most effective way to tackle base erosion and profit shifting. The majority of countries applying fixed ratio rules link interest deductibility to the level of equity in an entity, typically through thin capitalisation rules based on a debt/equity test. The main advantage of such a test is that it is relatively easy for tax administrations to obtain relevant information on the level of debt and equity in an entity and it also provides a reasonable level of certainty to groups in planning their financing. However, set against these advantages are a number of important disadvantages. A rule which limits the amount of debt in an entity still allows significant flexibility in terms of the rate of interest that an entity may pay on that debt. Also, an equity test allows entities with higher levels of equity capital to deduct more interest expense, which makes it relatively easy for a group to manipulate the outcome of a test by increasing the level of equity in a particular entity. An illustration of this is included as Example 1 in Annex I.D. It was therefore agreed by countries involved in this work that fixed ratio debt/equity tests should not be included as a general interest limitation rule within a best practice approach to tackle base erosion and profit shifting, although again this is not intended to suggest that these tests cannot play a role within an overall tax policy to limit interest deductions.

18. In recent years, countries have increasingly introduced fixed ratio tests based on an entity's interest/earnings ratio, which is a better tool to combat base erosion and profit shifting. In these tests, the measure of earnings used is typically earnings before interest, taxes, depreciation and amortisation (EBITDA). Most countries presently use a tax measure of EBITDA. However, there remains a general view that in many cases multinational groups are still able to claim total interest deductions significantly in excess of the group's actual third party interest expense. Available data, discussed in Chapter 6, shows that the majority of publicly traded multinational groups with positive EBITDA have a net

third party interest/EBITDA ratio below 10%, based on consolidated financial reporting information.

19. Rules which directly compare the level of interest expense or debt of an entity to that of its group are less common, but are applied by a small number of countries. These group ratio tests currently typically operate by reference to debt/equity ratios. However, in many cases the amount of equity in an entity may at best only be an indirect measure of its level of activity and as already mentioned can be subject to manipulation.

20. Targeted rules can complement a general interest limitation rule and are therefore a component of the best practice approach. Many countries have targeted anti-avoidance rules and these can be an effective response to specific base erosion and profit shifting risks. However, as new base erosion and profit shifting opportunities are exploited, further targeted rules may be required and so there is a tendency over time for more rules to be introduced, resulting in a complex system and increased administration and compliance costs. An approach which includes an effective general interest limitation rule should reduce the need for additional targeted rules, although some will be required to address specific risks. However, these targeted rules should operate consistently with the general interest limitation rules recommended in this report.

European Union law issues

21. Throughout this work, EU law requirements imposed on Member States of the European Union have been considered, and in particular the need for recommended approaches to be in accordance with EU treaty freedoms, directives and State aid regulations. Although countries outside the European Union are not required to comply with these obligations, the need for a consistent international approach outlined above means that any approach which cannot be fully implemented by the 28 EU Member States is unlikely to be effective in tackling the global issue of base erosion and profit shifting. Specific issues related to EU treaty freedoms, directives and State aid rules and possible approaches to deal with them are set out in Annex I.A of this report.

Notes

1. A domestic group is a group which operates wholly within a single country.

2. Weichenrieder and Windischbauer (2008) analysed the effect of the 1994 introduction and the 2001 tightening of Germany's former thin capitalisation rule. Buslei and Simmler (2012) analysed the effect of the introduction of Germany's current interest limitation rule in 2008.

3. Council Directive 2003/49/EC of 3 June 2003 on a common system of taxation applicable to interest and royalty payments made between associated companies of different Member States [2003] OJ L157/49.

Bibliography

Blouin, J. et al. (2014), "Thin Capitalization Rules and Multinational Firm Capital Structure", *IMF Working Paper*, No. 14/12, International Monetary Fund, Washington, DC.

Buettner, T. et al. (2012), "The impact of thin-capitalization rules on the capital structure of multinational firms", *Journal of Public Economics*, Vol. 96, Elsevier, Amsterdam, pp. 930-938.

Buslei, H. and M. Simmler (2012), "The impact of introducing an interest barrier – Evidence from the German corporation tax reform 2008", *DIW Discussion Papers*, No. 1215, DIW Berlin.

Desai, M.A., C.F. Foley and J.R. Hines (2004), "A Multinational Perspective on Capital Structure Choice and Internal Capital Markets", *The Journal of Finance*, Vol. 59, American Finance Association, pp. 2451-2487.

Egger. P. et al. (2010), "Corporate taxation, debt financing and foreign-plant ownership", *European Economic Review*, Vol. 54, Elsevier, Amsterdam, pp. 96-107.

Fuest, C., S. Hebous and N. Riedel (2011), "International debt shifting and multinational firms in developing economies", *Economic Letters*, Vol. 113, Elsevier, Amsterdam, pp. 135-138.

Graetz, M.J. (2008), "A Multilateral Solution for the Income Tax Treatment of Interest Expenses", *Bulletin for International Taxation*, Vol. 62, IBFD, pp. 486-493.

Haufler, A. and M. Runkel (2012), "Firms' financial choices and thin capitalization rules under corporate tax competition", *European Economic Review*, Vol. 56, Elsevier, Amsterdam, pp. 1087-1103.

Huizinga, H., L. Laeven and G. Nicodeme (2008), "Capital structure and international debt shifting", *Journal of Financial Economics*, Vol. 88, Elsevier, Amsterdam, pp. 80-118.

Mintz, J. and A.J. Weichenrieder (2005), "Taxation and the Financial Structure or German Outbound FDI", *CESifo Working Paper*, No. 1612.

Møen, J. et al. (2011), "International Debt Shifting: Do Multinationals Shift Internal or External Debt?", *University of Konstanz, Department of Economics Working Paper Series*, No. 2011-40.

OECD (2013), *Action Plan on Base Erosion and Profit Shifting*, OECD Publishing, Paris, http://dx.doi.org/10.1787/9789264202719-en.

Ruf, M. and D. Schindler (2012), "Debt Shifting and Thin Capitalization Rules – German Experience and Alternative Approaches", *Norwegian School of Economics, Bergen, NHH Discussion Paper RRR*, No. 06-2012.

Taylor, G. and G. Richardson (2013), "The determinants of thinly capitalized tax avoidance structures: Evidence from Australian firms", *Journal of International Accounting, Auditing and Taxation*, Vol. 22, Elsevier, Amsterdam, pp. 12-25.

Weichenrieder, A.J. and H. Windischbauer (2008), "Thin-capitalization rules and company responses – Experience from German legislation", *CESifo Working Paper*, No. 2456.

Chapter 1

Recommendations for a best practice approach

22. The critical objective of the work on Action 4 is to identify coherent and consistent solutions to address base erosion and profit shifting using interest and payments economically equivalent to interest. In constructing the best practice approach described in this report, a focus has been placed on the need for an approach that provides an effective solution to the risks countries face and which is robust against planning to avoid or reduce its application or effect. At the same time, this is balanced by the need for an approach to be reasonably straightforward for groups and tax authorities to apply. A short outline of the best practice approach is set out below. Detail on each element of the approach is included in later chapters.

23. The best practice approach is based around a fixed ratio rule which limits an entity's net interest deductions to a fixed percentage of its profit, measured using earnings before interest, taxes, depreciation and amortisation (EBITDA) based on tax numbers. This is a straightforward rule to apply and ensures that an entity's interest deductions are directly linked to its economic activity. It also directly links these deductions to an entity's taxable income, which makes the rule reasonably robust against planning. As described in Chapter 5,

Figure 1.1. **Overview of the best practice approach**

***De minimis* monetary threshold to remove low risk entities**
Optional
Based on net interest expense of local group

+

Fixed ratio rule
Allows an entity to deduct net interest expense up to a benchmark net interest/EBITDA ratio
Relevant factors help a country set its benchmark ratio within a corridor of 10%-30%

+

Group ratio rule
Allows an entity to deduct net interest expense up to its group's net interest/EBITDA ratio, where this is higher than the benchmark fixed ratio
Option for a country to apply an uplift to a group's net third party interest expense of up to 10%

Option for a country to apply a different group ratio rule or no group ratio rule

+

Carry forward of disallowed interest/unused interest capacity and/or carry back of disallowed interest
Optional

+

Targeted rules to support general interest limitation rules and address specific risks

+

Specific rules to address issues raised by the banking and insurance sectors

although EBITDA is the recommended measure of earnings to be used, the best practice allows a country the flexibility to introduce rules based on earnings before interest and taxes (EBIT). In limited cases, a country may apply a fixed ratio rule based on asset values rather than earnings. Chapter 6 includes factors which a country should take into account in setting the benchmark ratio for a fixed ratio rule, within a corridor of 10% to 30%.

24. A fixed ratio rule provides a country with a level of protection against base erosion and profit shifting, but it is a blunt tool which does not take into account the fact that groups operating in different sectors may require different amounts of leverage, and even within a sector some groups are more highly leveraged for non-tax reasons. If a benchmark fixed ratio is set at a level appropriate to tackle base erosion and profit shifting, it could lead to double taxation for groups which are leveraged above this level. Therefore, countries are encouraged to combine a robust and effective fixed ratio rule with a group ratio rule which allows an entity to deduct more interest expense in certain circumstances. A group ratio rule may be introduced as a separate provision from the fixed ratio rule, or as an integral part of an overall rule including both fixed ratio and group ratio tests.

25. Chapter 7 includes a description of a group ratio rule, which allows an entity that exceeds the benchmark fixed ratio to deduct interest expense up to the net third party interest/EBITDA ratio of its group, where this is higher. In calculating the group's ratio, a country may also apply an uplift of up to 10% to the group's net third party interest expense (i.e. its third party interest expense after deducting third party interest income). Under this approach, only net interest expense which takes an entity's net interest/EBITDA ratio above the higher of the benchmark fixed ratio and the group's ratio is disallowed. This rule should complement the fixed ratio rule and provide a robust response to base erosion and profit shifting involving interest expense. However, countries may also apply different group ratio rules, including those using asset-based ratios, so long as these rules only permit an entity to exceed the benchmark fixed ratio where it is able to demonstrate that a relevant financial ratio is in line with that of its group. A country may also decide to apply a fixed ratio rule in isolation. Where a country does not apply a group ratio rule, it should apply the fixed ratio rule consistently to entities in multinational and domestic groups, without improper discrimination. In all cases, under the best practice approach a country should implement the fixed ratio rule using a benchmark ratio which is sufficiently low to address base erosion and profit shifting.

26. In order to remove entities which pose the lowest risk from the scope of a general interest limitation rule, a country may apply a *de minimis* threshold based on a monetary value of net interest expense. Entities falling below this threshold may deduct interest expense without restriction. Where a group has more than one entity in a country, the threshold should take into account the total net interest expense of the entire local group, including all entities in that country. Where a rule is applied at the level of an individual entity, a country should consider including anti-fragmentation rules to prevent a group avoiding the application of an interest limitation rule by establishing a number of entities, each of which falls below the threshold.

27. Rules which link interest deductions to EBITDA raise issues where an entity's interest expense and earnings arise in different periods. This may be the result of volatility in earnings which means the ability of an entity to deduct interest changes from year to year, or because an entity has incurred interest expense to fund an investment which will give rise to earnings in a later period. To reduce the effect of these issues, a country may permit entities to carry forward disallowed interest expense or unused interest capacity for use in future periods, or carry back disallowed interest expense into earlier periods. It is suggested countries consider imposing limits on these carry forwards and carry backs.

28. A fixed ratio rule and group ratio rule should provide an effective framework to tackle most base erosion and profit shifting involving interest and payments economically equivalent to interest. These general interest limitation rules should be supplemented by targeted rules, which protect the integrity of the general interest limitation rules and deal with specific base erosion and profit shifting risks which remain.

29. Particular features of the banking and insurance industries mean that the fixed ratio rule and the group ratio rule set out in this report are unlikely to be effective in addressing base erosion and profit shifting involving interest in these sectors. As discussed in Chapter 10, further work will be conducted, to be completed in 2016, to identify targeted rules to deal with the base erosion and profit shifting risks posed by banks and insurance companies.

30. It is recommended that, as a minimum, the best practice approach in this report should apply to all entities that are part of a multinational group. Countries may also apply the best practice approach more broadly to include entities in a domestic group and/or standalone entities which are not part of a group. In certain cases countries may be required to do so. In this regard, Annex I.A includes a summary of EU law issues, including factors that should be taken into account by EU Member States.

31. The best practice approach set out in this report should provide an effective solution to base erosion and profit shifting involving interest and payments economically equivalent to interest. However, countries are free to apply stricter rules than those set out in this report either for the purposes of combating base erosion and profit shifting or to achieve other tax policy goals. For example, the best practice approach may be supplemented by additional general or targeted interest limitation rules which a country has identified as appropriate to address the risks it faces. It is also recognised that a country may have interest limitation rules that carry out broader policy aims, such as reducing the tax bias in favour of debt finance, and that it will want to retain these, or a country may introduce rules to achieve such aims. An illustration of how the best practice approach may be combined with other interest limitation rules is included as Example 2 in Annex I.D. Finally, when implementing a best practice approach, each country will need to take into account any obligations under its constitution (such as the equal treatment of taxpayers), as well as the specific features of its overall tax system. This may impact, for example, the application of a *de minimis* threshold, the operation of a fixed ratio rule and group ratio rule, and the use of carry forwards. How the fixed ratio rule and group ratio rule may be applied by countries with separate entity taxation or group taxation systems is considered in Chapter 11.

32. The remainder of this report discusses the structure and operation of the best practice approach in more detail, focusing on the following aspects:

- interest and payments economically equivalent to interest
- who a best practice approach should apply to
- applying a best practice approach based on the level of interest expense or debt
- measuring economic activity using earnings or asset values
- a fixed ratio rule
- a group ratio rule
- addressing volatility and double taxation
- targeted rules
- applying the best practice approach to banking and insurance groups
- implementing the best practice approach.

Chapter 2

Interest and payments economically equivalent to interest

33. Interest cost is treated as a tax deductible expense in most countries, but each country applies its own approach to determine what expenses are treated as interest and therefore deductible for tax purposes. It is not the aim of this report to recommend a definition of interest that is applied by all countries for all tax purposes. Differences will continue to exist between countries as to the items treated as deductible interest expense and countries will continue to use their own definitions of interest for other tax purposes, such as for withholding taxes. However, in identifying best practices for the design of rules to address base erosion and profit shifting, there are benefits in countries taking a broadly consistent approach to the items that should be covered by such rules, improving certainty for business and ensuring a coherent approach to tackling the issue across countries. This chapter therefore sets out the items which should be the subject of a best practice rule to tackle base erosion and profit shifting.

34. At its simplest, interest is the cost of borrowing money. However, if a rule restricted its focus to such a narrow band of payments,[1] it would raise three broad issues:

- It would fail to address the range of base erosion and profit shifting risks that countries face in relation to interest deductions and similar payments.
- It would reduce fairness by applying a different treatment to groups that are in the same economic position but use different forms of financing arrangements.
- Its effect could be easily avoided by groups re-structuring loans into other forms of financing arrangement.

35. To address these issues, rules to tackle base erosion and profit shifting using interest should apply to interest on all forms of debt as well as to other financial payments that are economically equivalent to interest. Payments that are economically equivalent to interest include those which are linked to the financing of an entity and are determined by applying a fixed or variable percentage to an actual or notional principal over time. A rule should also apply to other expenses incurred in connection with the raising of finance, including arrangement fees and guarantee fees. This chapter includes a non-exhaustive list of examples of the types of payment that should be covered by a rule, but it is left to each country to determine how this should be reflected within its domestic law, taking into account existing definitions of interest and other payments. In deciding whether a payment is economically equivalent to interest, the focus should be on its economic substance rather than its legal form.

36. A best practice rule to address base erosion and profit shifting using interest expense should therefore apply to: (i) interest on all forms of debt; (ii) payments economically equivalent to interest; and (iii) expenses incurred in connection with the raising of finance. These should include, but not be restricted to, the following:

- payments under profit participating loans
- imputed interest on instruments such as convertible bonds and zero coupon bonds
- amounts under alternative financing arrangements, such as Islamic finance
- the finance cost element of finance lease payments
- capitalised interest included in the balance sheet value of a related asset, or the amortisation of capitalised interest
- amounts measured by reference to a funding return under transfer pricing rules, where applicable
- notional interest amounts under derivative instruments or hedging arrangements related to an entity's borrowings
- certain foreign exchange gains and losses on borrowings and instruments connected with the raising of finance
- guarantee fees with respect to financing arrangements
- arrangement fees and similar costs related to the borrowing of funds.

37. It is recognised that foreign exchange gains and losses on instruments to hedge or take on a currency exposure connected with the raising of finance are not generally economically equivalent to interest. A country may however wish to treat some or all foreign exchange gains and losses on these instruments as economically equivalent to interest, in line with local tax rules and to reflect the economics of the currency exposure.

38. Throughout this report, references to interest should also be taken to include amounts economically equivalent to interest, unless the context clearly requires otherwise. Similarly, where the report refers to a group's or entity's interest income, this includes receipts of amounts economically equivalent to interest based on the definition and examples in this chapter.

39. The best practice approach does not apply to payments which are not interest, economically equivalent to interest or incurred in connection with the raising of finance. Therefore in general, the rules set out in this report should not limit deductions for items such as:

- foreign exchange gains and losses on monetary items which are not connected with the raising of finance
- amounts under derivative instruments or hedging arrangements which are not related to borrowings, for example commodity derivatives
- discounts on provisions not related to borrowings
- operating lease payments
- royalties
- accrued interest with respect to a defined benefit pension plan.

40. However, any payment (including those listed above) may be subject to limitation under the best practice approach where they are used as part of an arrangement which, taken as a whole, gives rise to amounts which are economically equivalent to interest.

41. An illustration of how this definition could be applied in practice is included as Example 3 in Annex I.D.

42. Where a country has a rule which grants a deemed deduction by applying a specified percentage to the equity capital of an entity, these deemed deductions are not treated as being interest or a payment economically equivalent to interest for the purposes of this report. These rules and rules having similar effect should be considered further by the OECD in separate work.

Note

1. Throughout this report, references to payments also include accruals of income or expense.

Chapter 3

Who a best practice approach should apply to

43. Base erosion and profit shifting arise in a range of scenarios, including within a group, with related parties outside a group and through the use of structured arrangements with third parties.[1] The best practice approach addresses the risks posed by each of these scenarios, although different rules may be used to address different types of risk. For the purposes of considering which entities these rules should apply to, entities have been categorised into three types: entities which are part of a multinational group; entities which are part of a domestic group; and standalone entities which are not part of a group. It is recommended that, as a minimum, the best practice approach in this report should apply to all entities that are part of a multinational group. Countries may also apply the best practice approach more broadly to include entities in a domestic group and/or standalone entities which are not part of a group.[2]

Entities which are part of a multinational group

44. As set out in the BEPS Action Plan (OECD, 2013), the deductibility of interest can raise base erosion and profit shifting concerns in both inbound and outbound investment scenarios. Therefore, it is recommended that as a minimum a fixed ratio rule as described in Chapter 6 should apply to all entities which are part of a multinational group.

45. An entity is part of a group if the entity is directly or indirectly controlled by a company, or the entity is a company which directly or indirectly controls one or more other entities. A group is a multinational group where it operates in more than one jurisdiction, including through a permanent establishment.

46. Where a country applies a group ratio rule alongside the fixed ratio rule, it may wish to use a consistent definition between both rules to reduce the risk that an entity subject to the fixed ratio rule is unable to apply the group ratio rule. In this case, the country may instead determine that an entity is part of a group where: (i) the entity is included on a line-by-line basis in the consolidated financial statements of any company; or (ii) the entity would be included on a line-by-line basis in the consolidated financial statements of any company, if that company prepared consolidated financial statements in accordance with any of the accounting standards accepted by the country in applying the group ratio rule (as described in Chapter 7).

47. Where a group has more than one entity in a particular country, the country may apply the fixed ratio rule and group ratio rule to the position of each entity separately, or to the overall position of all group entities in the same country (i.e. the local group).[3] Applying a rule to the overall position of the local group would avoid the scenario where a highly leveraged entity incurs an interest disallowance even though the interest expense of the local group as a whole falls within the limit permitted.

48. If the benchmark fixed ratio is set at an appropriate level, a fixed ratio rule should to a large extent address base erosion and profit shifting concerns involving payments by entities which are part of a multinational group. To ensure the fixed ratio rule is effective in tackling base erosion and profit shifting, it is recommended that all entities which are subject to the fixed ratio rule are also subject to targeted provisions which address planning to reduce the impact of the rule. However, there may be specific risks which are not dealt with by the fixed ratio rule and it is recommended that countries consider introducing targeted rules to deal with these risks. The role of targeted rules within the best practice is discussed in Chapter 9.

Entities which are part of a domestic group

49. Entities in multinational groups pose the main base erosion and profit shifting risk. Therefore, it may be appropriate for a country to restrict the application of a fixed ratio rule to these entities. However, a country may choose to apply a fixed ratio rule more broadly, to include entities in domestic groups (i.e. groups which operate wholly within a single country). This may be part of a broad approach to tackle base erosion and profit shifting in all types of entity, or may be in order to meet other policy goals, such as to avoid competition issues between domestic and multinational groups, to reduce the general tax bias in favour of funding with debt over equity, or to comply with constitutional obligations for the equal treatment of taxpayers. In particular, countries which are EU Member States would need to take into account EU law considerations in designing their domestic rules, to ensure they are compliant with EU law.

50. Where a country applies a fixed ratio rule and a group ratio rule to entities which are part of a domestic group, it may apply the rules either to each entity individually or to the overall position of the domestic group. In either case, the fixed ratio rule should to a large extent address base erosion and profit shifting concerns involving interest. However, there may be specific risks which are not dealt with by the fixed ratio rule and it is recommended that countries consider introducing targeted rules, discussed in Chapter 9, to address these risks.

51. Where a country does not apply a fixed ratio rule to entities in a domestic group, it will be exposed to base erosion and profit shifting risks, in particular involving interest paid to related parties and third parties under structured arrangements. In this case, a country should consider addressing these risks using targeted rules as described in Chapter 9.

Standalone entities which are not part of a group

52. A standalone entity is any entity which is not part of a group. The fact that a standalone entity is not part of any group means that the nature and level of base erosion and profit shifting risk that a standalone entity poses is often different to that posed by entities in a group. In many cases standalone entities are small entities, owned directly by an individual, where there are no other entities under common control. In these cases, due to the entity's small size and lack of related parties, the risk of base erosion and profit shifting involving interest is likely to be relatively low. However, in other cases, standalone entities may be large entities held under complex holding structures involving trusts or partnerships, where there are a number of entities under the control of the same investors. In these cases the level of base erosion and profit shifting risk may be similar to that posed by a group structure. In both scenarios, where base erosion and profit shifting involving interest does occur, it will arise as a result of payments to related parties and third parties.

53. A country should apply rules to address base erosion and profit shifting risks posed by standalone entities. A country may apply the fixed ratio rule to standalone entities or, recognising the differences between the risks posed by entities in groups and standalone entities, it may tackle risks posed by standalone entities using different rules. In either case, standalone entities should be subject to targeted rules to address specific risks, discussed in Chapter 9. EU Member States would need to take into account EU law considerations in designing their domestic rules, to ensure they are compliant with EU law. Such considerations should be taken into account when designing domestic rules in order to limit their possible negative impact on situations not involving base erosion or profit shifting.

De minimis threshold

54. While the main policy goal of the best practice approach set out in this report is to address base erosion and profit shifting using interest, it is recognised that certain entities may pose a sufficiently low risk that excluding them from a fixed ratio rule and group ratio rule would be appropriate. Excluding these entities from the fixed ratio rule and group ratio rule would mean that a best practice approach can focus on entities which pose material base erosion and profit shifting risk, reducing compliance costs for other entities. Reducing the number of entities covered would also reduce the costs of administering a rule and would allow a tax authority to focus its resources on entities which pose the greatest risk.

55. Countries may therefore introduce a *de minimis* threshold to exclude low risk entities from the scope of the fixed ratio rule and group ratio rule. It is recommended that such a threshold should be based on the total net interest expense of all entities in the local group. Where a country wishes to apply a threshold based on the net interest expense of each entity separately, it is important that these rules are not abused. Therefore, a country should consider introducing anti-fragmentation rules to prevent a group avoiding an interest limitation rule by establishing multiple entities, each of which falls below the threshold.

56. A *de minimis* threshold based on net interest expense should be relatively simple to apply and would ensure that highly-leveraged entities are required to apply a general interest limitation rule regardless of their size. A country should set the level of a *de minimis* threshold to reflect a number of factors, including the local economic and interest rate environment, as well as relevant tax or legal considerations. This may be reviewed and updated periodically to reflect changes in these factors.

Notes

1. The terms “related party” and “structured arrangement” are defined in Chapter 9.

2. There may be cases where a country is required to apply the fixed ratio rule more broadly, for example to entities in domestic groups. For instance, countries may need to take into account any constitutional issues which could have a direct impact on interest limitation rules. In addition, Annex I.A includes a summary of EU law issues, including factors that should be taken into account by EU Member States.

3. Chapter 11 includes a summary of different approaches that a country may use in applying a fixed ratio rule to a local group, depending upon the structure of its tax system.

Bibliography

OECD (2013), *Action Plan on Base Erosion and Profit Shifting*, OECD Publishing, Paris, http://dx.doi.org/10.1787/9789264202719-en.

Chapter 4

Applying a best practice approach based on the level of interest expense or debt

57. A key cause of base erosion and profit shifting is the ability of a group to artificially separate taxable income from the underlying activities that drive value creation. Therefore, one of the aims of the best practice approach set out in this report is to link the amount of interest deductions in an entity to the level of its taxable economic activity.

Applying the best practice approach to limit the level of interest expense or debt in an entity

58. A general interest limitation rule may operate directly, by restricting the amount of interest an entity may deduct for tax purposes, or indirectly, by restricting the amount of debt with respect to which an entity may claim deductions for interest. In considering which approach to include in the best practice recommendation, a number of factors have been taken into account. These include the following:

- Base erosion and profit shifting using interest is driven by the level of tax deductible expense incurred by an entity. A rule which directly limits the level of interest deductions an entity may claim addresses this.
- A rule which limits the level of debt in an entity will not necessarily address base erosion and profit shifting risks where an excessive rate of interest is applied to a loan. Therefore, such a rule would need to have a further mechanism to identify the maximum interest on the permitted level of debt. This could be done by applying an arm's length test or apportioning an entity's actual interest expense, but these approaches add a step to the operation of a rule and increase complexity.
- A best practice approach should apply to base erosion and profit shifting involving interest and payments economically equivalent to interest. However, for some payments economically equivalent to interest, there may be no existing requirement for an entity to separately recognise a debt linked to the payment. It should therefore be easier for entities and tax authorities to identify and value the payments of interest (and economically equivalent payments) for which tax relief is being claimed.
- The level of debt in an entity may vary throughout a period, which means that the amount of debt on a particular date, or even an average for the period, may not be representative of an entity's true position. On the other hand, the level of interest expense in an entity will reflect all changes in borrowings throughout the period. This is therefore likely to give a more accurate picture of the entity's actual position over the period.

- A rule based on the level of debt in an entity could take into account the fact that two entities with the same amount of debt may for commercial reasons be subject to different rates of interest (e.g. taking into account the currency of borrowings and credit risk). This could also be done under a rule that directly limits an entity's interest expense (e.g. by taking a group's actual level of interest expense into account).
- The level of debt in an entity is under the control of the entity's management and so is generally predictable. The amount of interest expense, however, may vary reflecting changes in interest rates. This means that a rule that directly limits the level of interest expense could make it difficult for an entity to enter into long-term borrowings if there is a risk that interest rates could increase and it would suffer an interest disallowance in future periods.

59. Taking these factors into account, and given the key policy objective is to tackle base erosion and profit shifting involving interest and payments economically equivalent to interest, the best practice set out in this report includes rules which directly limit the level of interest expense that an entity may deduct for tax purposes. It also includes features, such as the group ratio rule, which should address some of the possible issues this raises. For example, if a group represents a greater credit risk and is required to pay a higher rate of interest on its third party debt, a group ratio rule will take this into account in setting a limit on tax deductions for entities within the group. As set out in the Introduction, a country may continue to apply an arm's length test alongside the best practice approach. For example, this could ensure that the amount of interest expense claimed by an entity is in accordance with the arm's length principle, but this amount is then subject to limitation under the best practice approach in this report.

Applying the best practice approach to limit an entity's gross interest expense or net interest expense

60. Another key question is whether a general interest limitation rule should apply to the interest an entity incurs on its borrowings without any offset for interest income (gross interest expense) or after offsetting the interest income it receives (net interest expense).

61. A gross interest rule has the benefit of simplicity and is also likely to be more difficult for groups to avoid through planning. However, a gross interest rule could lead to double taxation where each entity is subject to tax on its full gross interest income, but part of its gross interest expense is disallowed.

62. A net interest rule would reduce the risk of double taxation, as an entity's interest income would be set against its interest expense before the interest limitation is applied. It would also allow an entity to raise third party debt and on-lend borrowed funds within its group, without the entity incurring a disallowance of part of its gross interest expense. Taking into account these considerations, the general interest limitation rules contained in this report apply to an entity's net interest expense paid to third parties, related parties and intragroup, after offsetting interest income.[1] Rules should apply to all of an entity's net interest expense, as discussed in Chapter 2, to ensure that a broad range of base erosion and profit shifting risks are addressed, including where excessive third party interest expense is incurred in a high tax country.

63. However, the fact that an entity has a relatively low net interest expense does not mean that base erosion and profit shifting is not taking place. For example, an entity with net interest income could use interest expense to shelter this income from tax. An entity may also disguise other forms of taxable income as interest income, reducing the level

of net interest expense to which the rule can apply. Therefore, it is recommended that countries supplement the general interest limitation rules with targeted provisions which disallow gross interest expense in specific situations identified as posing base erosion and profit shifting risk. This is discussed in Chapter 9. Rules which apply to limit an entity's net interest expense will also have no impact on entities which, because of their business model, are typically receivers of net interest income. This arises in particular in the banking and insurance sectors, which are discussed in Chapter 10.

An option to exclude certain public-benefit projects

64. The best practice approach set out in this report places a general limit on the level of net interest expense that an entity may deduct for tax purposes. The fixed ratio rule should be applied consistently to all interest paid to third parties, related parties and group entities. However, as an exception to this general principle, a country may choose to exclude interest expense incurred on specific third party loans meeting the conditions set out below from the scope of the fixed ratio rule and group ratio rule. Except as set out in this report, other exclusions should not be applied.

65. In some countries, privately-owned public-benefit assets may be large-scale assets financed using a high proportion of debt. However, because of the nature of the assets and the close connection with the public sector, some such financing arrangements present little or no base erosion or profit shifting risk.

66. Taking account of the specific circumstances of the public sector, a country may exclude certain amounts with respect to third party loans linked to specific assets when calculating an entity's net interest expense which is subject to limitation under the best practice approach. To ensure this approach is tightly targeted only on those projects which do not pose a base erosion or profit shifting risk, the following conditions must be met:

- An entity (the operator) establishes a project to provide (or upgrade), operate and/or maintain assets on a long-term basis, lasting not less than 10 years, and these assets cannot be disposed of at the discretion of the operator.
- A public sector body or a public benefit entity (the grantor),[2] contractually or otherwise obliges the operator to provide goods or services in which there is a general public interest.[3] This provision must be subject to specific controls or a regulatory framework in addition to rules applying generally to companies or other commercial entities within a jurisdiction.
- Interest is payable by the operator on a loan or loans obtained from and owed to third party lenders on non-recourse terms, so that the lender only has recourse to and a charge over the assets and income streams of the specific project. Arrangements involving recourse to other assets, guarantees from other group companies or which otherwise seek to offer recourse beyond the project assets would not qualify for the exclusion.
- The loan or loans made to the operator do not exceed the value or estimated value of the assets at acquisition or once constructed, unless additional investment is made to maintain or increase their value. Subject to minimal and incidental lending to a third party (such as a bank deposit), none of the funds should be on-lent.
- The operator, the interest expense, the project assets and income arising from the project are all in the same country, where the income must be subject to tax at ordinary rates.[4] Where the project assets are held in a permanent establishment,

the exclusion will only apply to the extent that income arising from the project is subject to tax at ordinary rates in the country applying the exclusion.

- Similar projects of the operator or similar projects of other entities of the operator's group are not substantially less leveraged with third-party-debt, taking into account project maturities.

67. Countries making use of the exclusion may impose additional rules before allowing an exclusion to apply, in order to prevent the exclusion being used by businesses not engaged in projects which deliver public benefits. These might include a requirement that obtaining the exclusion is not a main purpose of structuring the financing arrangements to meet the other conditions of the exclusion. Countries making use of the exclusion should publish full information about the scope of domestic legislation and the circumstances in which it can be used, and should also introduce mechanisms to provide for spontaneous exchange of information relating to the entities benefiting from the exclusion and investors in these with all relevant jurisdictions. The framework in Chapter 5 of the OECD Report *Countering Harmful Tax Practices More Effectively, Taking into Account Transparency and Substance* (OECD, 2015) would be used to determine the jurisdictions with which to spontaneously exchange such information. Countries adopting the exclusion should monitor its operation with a view to assisting in the review referred to below. Such countries should require taxpayers to clearly disclose any use of this exclusion.

68. Where this exclusion applies, a country applying the exclusion should also take steps to ensure that the project earnings and assets, and related interest expense, are not used to permit further interest deductions for the entity or other group entities in the country. Therefore, the country should adjust the operation of the fixed ratio rule and group ratio rule, so that where an entity benefits from this exclusion:

- Any earnings arising from the project (and/or the project assets) are excluded from the calculation of earnings or asset values under the fixed ratio rule and group ratio rule.

- The interest expense which has been excluded from limitation should not be included in the group's net third party interest expense when applying the group ratio rule.

69. There is also a risk that interest which benefits from this exclusion will be used to increase the level of net interest deductions for group entities in other countries in which a group ratio rule is applied. Therefore, in applying the group ratio rule, a country may exclude any third party interest expense which benefits from an exclusion in any other country. Similarly, project earnings and assets may be excluded from the calculation of group earnings or asset values. Countries may obtain information on whether the exclusion has been applied using the exchange of information provisions contained in applicable international agreements. A country may also choose not to require the adjustments in this paragraph, in order to minimise complexity.

70. The design and operation of this exclusion will be included in the initial review of the best practice, to be conducted by no later than the end of 2020. This will include consideration of how the exclusion is being used, to ensure it is not giving rise to base erosion or profit shifting risks. Following this review, the exclusion may be revised or removed.

71. EU law issues are considered in Annex I.A.

Notes

1. The term "related party" is defined in Chapter 9.
2. A public benefit entity will typically be an entity whose primary objective is to provide goods or services for the general public, community or social benefit and where any equity is provided with a view to supporting the entity's primary objectives rather than to provide a financial return to equity holders. The definition of a public benefit entity used by a country may be contained in law or a relevant applicable accounting standard.
3. Assets that provide goods and services in which there is a general public interest would generally refer to assets that are public goods.
4. Countries which are Member States of the European Union would need to take into account EU law considerations in designing their domestic rules.

Bibliography

OECD (2015), *Countering Harmful Tax Practices More Effectively, Taking into Account Transparency and Substance*, OECD Publishing, Paris, http://dx.doi.org/10.1787/9789264241190-en.

Chapter 5

Measuring economic activity using earnings or asset values

72. Fixed ratio rules and group ratio rules restrict the ability of an entity to deduct interest expense based on an objective measure of its economic activity. Work to develop a best practice approach has focused on earnings and asset values, as the measures which most clearly reflect the level of activity and value creation within a multinational group.

Measuring economic activity using earnings

73. As highlighted in the previous chapter, a goal of the BEPS project is to address practices that artificially separate taxable income from the activities that generate it. For most entities it is expected that there should be a clear correlation between earnings and taxable income. Therefore, measuring economic activity using earnings should be the most effective way to ensure that the ability to deduct net interest expense is matched with the activities that generate taxable income and drive value creation. In addition, depending upon the definition of earnings used, this is a useful indicator of an entity's ability to meet its obligations to pay interest, and therefore is one of the key factors used in determining the amount of debt an entity is able to borrow.

74. Another benefit of an earnings-based approach is that it makes a general interest limitation rule more robust against planning. Where the level of deductible interest expense in an entity is linked to earnings, a group can only increase net interest deductions in a particular country by increasing earnings in that country. Similarly, any restructuring to move profits out of a country will also reduce net interest deductions in the country. On the assumption that an increase in earnings will also give rise to an increase in taxable income, it is unlikely that the level of earnings will be manipulated in order to increase the interest deductions in a country.

75. The BEPS Action Plan (OECD, 2013) specifically requires the development of rules to address base erosion and profit shifting using interest expense to fund tax exempt or tax deferred income. A third important benefit of an approach using earnings is that the definition of earnings can be adapted to exclude income which is subject to favourable tax treatment. An obvious example would be dividend income, which in many countries is exempt from tax or is taxed at a reduced rate (subject to conditions such as a minimum holding requirement).

76. The main disadvantage of earnings as a measure of economic activity is that an entity's earnings may be relatively volatile and there is a limit to the extent this can be controlled by a group. This means that under an earnings-based rule it may be hard for an entity to anticipate the level of net interest expense that will be permitted from year to year. This could make it difficult for an entity to calculate a cost of debt for long term projects, without knowing the extent to which its interest cost will be deductible. To an extent, these

issues may be addressed in the design of a best practice approach, for example by allowing an entity to measure economic activity using the average earnings over a number of periods or by permitting an entity to carry forward disallowed interest expense and unused capacity to deduct interest. These approaches are discussed in Chapter 8.

77. A particular aspect of earnings volatility is the possibility that an entity may be in a negative earnings (i.e. loss-making) position. Under an earnings-based approach, an entity with negative earnings will be unable to deduct its net interest expense in the current period. In principle, this could mean that an entity with losses could be required to pay taxes as a result of an interest disallowance. However, this risk could be reduced depending upon the definition of earnings used, and whether this is based on tax or accounting information. Other mechanisms, such as the carry forward of disallowed interest expense, should enable a loss-making entity to retain the benefit of interest deductions and claim relief once it returns to profit.

Definition of earnings

78. In terms of the definition of earnings to be used, earnings before interest, taxes, depreciation and amortisation (EBITDA) and earnings before interest and taxes (EBIT) are both possible options. In either, non-taxable income such as branch profits or dividend income that benefit from a participation exemption should not be included in the calculation of earnings. Appropriate adjustments should also be made for taxable branch profits and dividend income to the extent that they are shielded from tax by foreign tax credits, in order to address the base erosion and profit shifting issues which are the subject of this report.[1] EBITDA is the most common measure of earnings currently used by countries with earnings-based tests. By excluding the two major non-cash costs in a typical income statement (depreciation of fixed assets and amortisation of intangible assets), EBITDA is a guide to the ability of an entity to meet its obligations to pay interest. It is also a measure of earnings which is often used by lenders in deciding how much interest expense an entity can reasonably afford to bear. On the other hand, using EBITDA potentially favours entities operating in sectors with high levels of fixed asset investment. This is because EBITDA does not include the write-down of capitalised costs such as investment in plant and machinery, whereas it does take into account revenue costs which are the majority of the cost base for entities in other sectors. Data suggests that, across all industry sectors, average gross interest/EBIT ratios based on information taken from consolidated financial statements are approximately 40% higher than average gross interest/EBITDA ratios, although there can be significant variation between different industry sectors.

Measuring economic activity using asset values

79. The main benefit of an assets-based approach to measuring economic activity is that in general asset values are typically more stable (except in the case of revaluations and write-downs, and assets which are carried at fair value under accounting rules). This means that using asset values as a basis for measuring economic activity within a group should give rise to a relatively steady and predictable limit on the level of interest relief that can be claimed. This would improve certainty for groups and could also reduce compliance costs. In addition, an approach based on asset values would mean that entities with losses would still be able to deduct an amount of net interest expense, which may not be possible under an earnings-based approach.

80. In order to provide an accurate measure of an entity's economic activity, an assets-based rule should take into account the value of those assets which drive the creation of value for the group. These would include assets such as land and buildings, plant and equipment, intangible assets, and financial assets which give rise to income other than interest, but excluding assets which give rise to non-taxable income (such as equity holdings which give rise to tax exempt dividends). However, a key issue surrounding an assets-based approach for the purposes of applying a fixed ratio rule is achieving a consistent and acceptable model for valuing each of these classes of assets. In terms of tangible assets, such as land and buildings and plant and equipment, a requirement to use market values of assets would be impractical and impose an excessive compliance burden on groups. However, an amortised historic cost valuation could give rise to inconsistencies depending upon the age of assets and is subject to influence by decisions of management, for instance on depreciation periods and the timing of revaluations and write downs. Historic cost is also unlikely to represent the actual value an asset contributes to a group's economic activity. Intangible assets including trademarks and patents can be a group's most valuable assets. However, accounting standards often impose stringent requirements on groups before they are able to recognise an intangible asset on their balance sheet, particularly where the asset has been internally created. This means that for a number of large groups, an approach to limiting interest deductions based on asset values for accounting purposes will not directly take into account the group's most valuable assets (although intangible assets may be indirectly reflected to the extent they give rise to earnings which are not distributed and so are included in retained earnings within equity). A specific area of difference in the treatment of assets under accounting standards is in the recognition of financial assets including derivative balances, and in particular the ability of groups to report positions on a gross or net basis. This can result in a significant difference in the value of a group's total assets and under some accounting standards is left to the discretion of a group's management, subject to conditions being met. These issues are in particular a problem in applying a fixed ratio rule based on asset values as in these cases a fixed benchmark ratio is applied to asset values which can vary significantly based on the accounting standards and policies applied by different groups. Concerns over the recognition and valuation of assets may be less of an issue in applying a group ratio rule, so long as a consistent approach is taken at entity and group level.

Proposed approach

81. On balance and taking into account the above factors, it appears that for a fixed ratio rule earnings is the most appropriate measure of economic activity, for groups operating in the majority of sectors and in different countries. In applying a group ratio rule, the differences between an earnings-based and an assets-based approach are less significant. This is reflected in the best practice approach set out in this report.

82. It is recommended that a fixed ratio rule should measure earnings using EBITDA. However, a country may apply a fixed ratio rule which measures earnings using EBIT, so long as the other elements of the rule are consistent with the best practice in this report. Where a country applies a fixed ratio rule based on EBIT, the benchmark net interest/EBIT ratio used should be equivalent to the appropriate benchmark net interest/EBITDA ratio described in Chapter 6, taking into account where the particular country would be placed within the corridor based on the factors in that chapter. In considering whether a benchmark net interest/EBIT ratio is equivalent to a net interest/EBITDA ratio, a country should take into account differences between average EBIT and EBITDA figures for the major sectors in its economy.

83. Where the economy of a particular country is highly reliant on heavily capitalised groups whose activities rely on tangible fixed assets with long depreciation periods, earnings should still be a suitable measure of economic activity for the purposes of applying a fixed ratio rule. However, in this case asset values may exceptionally be used as an acceptable alternative. Where a country applies a fixed ratio rule based on asset values, other elements of the rule should be consistent with the best practice approach. For example, the rule should apply to limit net interest expense payable to third parties and group entities located within the country and in other countries. The assets included in a valuation should include the main categories of assets which drive economic activity in a group but should exclude assets which give rise to non-taxable income such as dividends which qualify for a participation exemption. Asset values may be based on accounting or tax numbers, but this should be applied consistently. The benchmark net interest/assets ratio should be equivalent to the appropriate benchmark net interest/EBITDA ratio described in Chapter 6, taking into account where the particular country would be placed within the corridor based on the factors in that chapter. In considering whether a benchmark net interest/assets ratio is equivalent to a net interest/EBITDA ratio, a country may take into account the number of groups affected and the overall level of net interest expense disallowed.

84. Where a country applies a fixed ratio rule and group ratio rule both based on earnings, it is recommended that either EBITDA or EBIT be used for both rules. As described in Chapter 7, a country may also apply a fixed ratio rule based on earnings alongside a group ratio rule based on asset values, so long as the group ratio rule only permits an entity to exceed the benchmark fixed ratio where it is able to demonstrate that a relevant financial ratio (such as equity/total assets) is in line with that of its group.

Notes

1. Where branch profits benefit from a participation exemption, the entity's EBITDA or EBIT should be reduced by an amount equal to the EBITDA or EBIT of the branch. Where branch profits are taxed, an entity's EBITDA or EBIT should be reduced by an amount equal to part of the branch's EBITDA or EBIT, in proportion to the extent that the tax on branch profits is sheltered by tax credits. For example, under one possible approach, if 25% of the entity's tax liability on the branch profits is sheltered by tax credits, the entity's EBITDA or EBIT should be reduced by an amount equal to 25% of the EBITDA or EBIT of the branch.

Bibliography

OECD (2013), *Action Plan on Base Erosion and Profit Shifting*, OECD Publishing, Paris, http://dx.doi.org/10.1787/9789264202719-en.

Chapter 6

Fixed ratio rule

Aim of a fixed ratio rule

85. The premise underlying the fixed ratio rule is that an entity should be able to deduct interest expense up to a specified proportion of EBITDA, ensuring that a portion of an entity's profit remains subject to tax in a country. A fixed ratio rule can apply to all entities, including those in a multinational group, a domestic group and standalone entities. The underlying benchmark fixed ratio is determined by a country's government and applies irrespective of the actual leverage of an entity or its group. Interest paid to third parties, related parties [1] and group entities is deductible up to this fixed ratio, but any interest which takes the entity's ratio above this benchmark is disallowed.

86. The key advantage of a fixed ratio rule is that it is relatively simple for companies to apply and tax administrations to administer. On the other hand, a fixed ratio rule does not take into account the fact that groups operating in different sectors may require different amounts of leverage, and even within a sector groups may adopt different funding strategies for non-tax reasons. Applying a fixed ratio rule differently to groups in different sectors would inevitably make a rule more complex to administer, in particular where a sector cannot be easily defined or where a group has activities across more than one sector. The option to exclude interest funding certain public-benefit projects described in Chapter 4 may help to address these issues for some entities. However, in general, a country should apply the fixed ratio rule consistently, using the same benchmark fixed ratio, to groups in all sectors (with the exception of groups in the banking and insurance sectors, which are considered in Chapter 10, for which targeted rules are being considered).

87. However, groups in certain sectors may benefit from economic rent that means they are able to generate high levels of EBITDA, which under the general approach described in this report could give rise to relatively high levels of net interest deductions. A country may therefore choose to apply a fixed ratio rule more strictly to groups in these sectors. For example, groups in sectors which benefit from economic rents may be subject to a lower benchmark fixed ratio, or the calculation of entity EBITDA may be adjusted to strip out the effect of the economic rent.

Operation of a fixed ratio rule

88. Fixed ratio rules apply a predetermined benchmark fixed ratio to the earnings of an entity or a local group to calculate the maximum deductible interest expense.[2] Calculating the amount of any interest expense disallowance under a fixed ratio rule involves a three step process: firstly, calculating the appropriate measure of EBITDA; secondly, applying

the statutory benchmark fixed ratio to an entity's EBITDA to determine the maximum deductible interest expense; and thirdly, comparing this with the actual interest expense of the entity. The calculation of EBITDA should be based on values that are determined under the tax rules of the country applying the rule. The use of tax figures to calculate entity EBITDA has a number of advantages. Firstly, the rule should be reasonably straightforward to apply and audit. Secondly, using tax numbers reduces the risk that an entity with negative EBITDA is required to pay taxes as a result of an interest disallowance. Finally, linking interest deductions to taxable earnings means it is more difficult for a group to increase the limit on net interest deductions without also increasing the level of taxable income in a country.

Step 1: Calculating the measure of earnings

89. An entity's EBITDA should be calculated by adding back to its taxable income, the tax values for: (i) net interest expense and net payments equivalent to interest payments as defined in Chapter 2; and (ii) depreciation and amortization. Tax exempt income, such as exempt dividend income or foreign earnings that are tax exempt, should not form part of the entity's EBITDA figure. The rationale behind excluding exempt dividend income is to address concerns related to the outbound investment scenario as described in Action 4.

Step 2: Applying the statutory benchmark fixed ratio to earnings

90. Following the calculation of the entity's EBITDA, the statutory benchmark fixed ratio will be applied to the EBITDA figure. The result determines the maximum amount of interest expense that the entity is allowed to deduct for tax purposes.

Step 3: Comparing maximum deductible interest expense with actual interest expense

91. In the last step, the maximum amount that the entity is allowed to deduct for tax purposes is then compared with the entity's actual net interest expense.

92. Net interest expense in excess of the maximum allowable amount is disallowed. An illustration of how a fixed ratio rule might operate in practice is included as Example 4 in Annex I.D. This example also illustrates the potential advantages and disadvantages of applying a fixed ratio rule at the level of the local group.

Setting a benchmark fixed ratio

93. An effective fixed ratio rule requires a country to set the benchmark fixed ratio at a level which is appropriate to tackle base erosion and profit shifting. At the same time, it is recognised that countries differ in terms of both their economic environment and the presence of other targeted tax rules which specifically address base erosion and profit shifting risk involving interest. There are many factors which could affect the competitiveness of countries to attract investment, including the tax rate, composition of the tax base and interest deductibility rules. Therefore, without an agreed best practice approach, there is a risk that competitiveness concerns would drive countries to adopt benchmark fixed ratios at a high level which would allow more interest expense to be deducted and reduce the effectiveness of the rule in tackling base erosion and profit shifting.

A corridor of benchmark fixed ratios

94. In order to address base erosion and profit shifting risks, by co-ordinating the approach to setting a benchmark fixed ratio between countries and reduce the risk that countries will be driven to apply a ratio at a level which is too high to address base erosion and profit shifting risks, it is recommended that countries set their benchmark fixed ratio within a best practice range or "corridor".

95. In setting a best practice corridor, the key aim is to identify a range of benchmark fixed ratios which:

- allows the majority of groups to deduct an amount equivalent to their net third party interest expense (assuming net interest expense is spread around the group in accordance with accounting EBITDA)
- limits the extent to which groups can use intragroup interest expense to claim total net interest deductions in excess of their net third party interest expense.

96. Financial data provided to the OECD by BIAC/PwC[3] illustrates the proportion of publicly traded multinational groups with positive EBITDA that would in principle be able to deduct an amount equivalent to their net third party interest expense, if a benchmark fixed ratio is set at different levels. This assumes that a group's net interest expense is spread around the group in accordance with EBITDA. Groups with negative EBITDA are not included in this analysis, as the impact of a fixed ratio rule on an entity with negative EBITDA is the same irrespective of the level at which a benchmark fixed ratio is set. The numbers below are based on average figures over the period 2009 to 2013:[4]

- At a benchmark fixed ratio of 10%, 62% of these groups would in principle be able to deduct all of their net third party interest expense.
- At a benchmark fixed ratio of 20%, 78% of these groups would in principle be able to deduct all of their net third party interest expense.
- At a benchmark fixed ratio of 30%, 87% of these groups would in principle be able to deduct all of their net third party interest expense.
- At a benchmark fixed ratio of 40%, 91% of these groups would in principle be able to deduct all of their net third party interest expense.
- At a benchmark fixed ratio of 50%, 93% of these groups would in principle be able to deduct all of their net third party interest expense.

97. Once a benchmark fixed ratio exceeds 30%, the rate at which more groups are able to deduct all of their net third party interest expense increases more slowly. However, at this level, a significant proportion of groups may have an incentive to increase the level of intragroup debt in order to claim net interest deductions in excess of their net third party interest expense. For example, based on the financial data referred to in the paragraph above, around half of publicly traded multinational groups with positive EBITDA have a net third party interest/EBITDA ratio of 5% or below. Therefore, at a benchmark fixed ratio of 30%, there is a risk that these groups could deduct up to six times their actual net third party interest, assuming there are no impediments to the use of intragroup debt. This risk increases if a benchmark fixed ratio is set above this level. On the basis of this analysis, and balancing the goals of allowing most groups to deduct their net third party interest expense and limiting the risk that groups will deduct more than this amount, it is recommended that countries applying a fixed ratio rule based on a net interest/EBITDA ratio set their benchmark fixed ratio within a corridor of 10% to 30%. As set out in Chapter 11, this corridor may be revised

following an initial review of the best practice, to be completed by no later than the end of 2020.

98. Within the best practice corridor, a majority of groups with positive EBITDA should in principle be able to deduct all of their net third party interest expense. A country could also include other elements of the best practice approach to enable entities in groups with a net third party interest/EBITDA ratio above the benchmark fixed ratio to deduct more net interest expense, where they pose a low risk of base erosion and profit shifting. For example, a group ratio rule may be used to allow an entity which exceeds the benchmark fixed ratio to deduct more net interest expense up to the level of the group's net third party interest/EBITDA ratio where this is higher. A country may also apply a *de minimis* threshold to exclude from the scope of a fixed ratio rule and group ratio rule entities with low net interest expense.

Factors to assist countries in setting a benchmark fixed ratio

99. It is recommended that countries set their benchmark fixed ratio within the corridor of 10% to 30%. However, it should be recognised that countries differ in terms of their legal framework and economic circumstances and, in setting a benchmark fixed ratio within the corridor which is suitable for tackling base erosion and profit shifting, a country should therefore take into account a number of factors, including the following:

1. A country may apply a higher benchmark fixed ratio if it operates a fixed ratio rule in isolation, rather than operating it in combination with a group ratio rule.
2. A country may apply a higher benchmark fixed ratio if it does not permit the carry forward of unused interest capacity or carry back of disallowed interest expense.
3. A country may apply a higher benchmark fixed ratio if it applies other targeted rules that specifically address the base erosion and profit shifting risks to be dealt with under Action 4.
4. A country may apply a higher benchmark fixed ratio if it has high interest rates compared with those of other countries.
5. A country may apply a higher benchmark fixed ratio, where for constitutional or other legal reasons (e.g. EU law requirements) it has to apply the same treatment to different types of entities which are viewed as legally comparable, even if these entities pose different levels of risk.
6. A country may apply different fixed ratios depending upon the size of an entity's group.

100. These factors are considered in more detail below.

A country may apply a higher benchmark fixed ratio if it operates a fixed ratio rule in isolation, rather than operating it in combination with a group ratio rule

101. Where a country operates a fixed ratio rule alongside a group ratio rule, an entity which exceeds the fixed ratio may be able to deduct more net interest expense up to the relevant financial ratio of its group. The country is therefore able to apply a benchmark fixed ratio at a lower level, relying on the group ratio rule to moderate the impact of this on entities in groups which are highly leveraged. On the other hand, where a country introduces a fixed ratio rule without a group ratio rule, it may apply a higher benchmark fixed ratio.

A country may apply a higher benchmark fixed ratio if it does not permit the carry forward of unused interest capacity or carry back of disallowed interest expense

102. Unused interest capacity is the amount by which an entity's net interest expense is below the maximum amount permitted under the fixed ratio rule. As discussed in Chapter 8, where a country permits unused interest capacity to be carried forward, this could give rise to a tax asset which may be monetised by increasing the entity's net interest expense or by reducing its EBITDA. As these behaviours should not be encouraged by a rule to tackle base erosion and profit shifting, a country which allows the carry forward of unused interest capacity should apply a lower benchmark fixed ratio to reduce this incentive. Similarly, a country which permits the carry back of disallowed interest expense, which gives rise to the same risk, should also apply a lower benchmark fixed ratio. The weight which should be attached to this factor would depend upon the extent to which a country incorporates the restrictions discussed in Chapter 8. A country which does not allow either a carry forward of unused interest capacity or a carry back of disallowed interest expense may apply a higher benchmark fixed ratio.

A country may apply a higher benchmark fixed ratio if it applies other targeted rules that specifically address the base erosion and profit shifting risks to be dealt with under Action 4

103. Action 4 focuses on the development of best practices in the design of rules to prevent base erosion and profit shifting through the use of third party, related party and intragroup interest, including payments economically equivalent to interest, to achieve excessive interest deductions or finance the production of exempt or deferred income. The recommended best practice approach includes the fixed ratio rule described in this chapter, but it is recognised that other targeted interest limitation rules may also be effective in tackling some of these risks. For example, a country may have a targeted rule which disallows all interest expense used to fund tax exempt income. Where a country has targeted rules which specifically address the base erosion and profit shifting risks to be dealt with under Action 4, and it applies these rules in practice, these may reduce pressure on the fixed ratio rule meaning that a higher benchmark fixed ratio could be applied. The extent to which this factor supports a higher benchmark fixed ratio depends upon the extent to which the specific base erosion and profit shifting risks involving interest and targeted by Action 4 are addressed. Where a country does not have other rules which specifically deal with the base erosion and profit shifting risks targeted by Action 4, it should apply a lower benchmark fixed ratio.

A country may apply a higher benchmark fixed ratio if it has high interest rates compared with those of other countries

104. The net interest/EBITDA ratio of entities which raise third party debt locally can be impacted by a number of factors, including the level of a country's interest rates. Where a country's interest rates are high relative to those in other countries, the country may recognise this by applying a higher benchmark fixed ratio. This is not intended to favour entities operating in a high interest rate country, but simply recognises the fact that these entities are likely to be subject to a higher cost of funds. The extent to which this factor supports a higher benchmark fixed ratio depends upon the extent to which interest rates are higher than those in other countries. However, a country with high interest rates may still apply a low benchmark fixed ratio. For example, where a country applies the same benchmark fixed ratio to all entities, including those in large groups which are less likely

to be exposed to differences in interest rates between countries, it may decide that it is not appropriate for its high interest rate to be taken into account when setting the ratio. Where a country has low interest rates compared with other countries, it should apply a lower benchmark fixed ratio. In comparing its interest rates with those of other countries, a country may take into account one or more relevant rates, such as the central bank rate, the long-term government bond rate and the average corporate bond rate for entities with a good credit rating (for example, equivalent to a credit rating of "A" or above). Whether a particular interest rate is high or low must be judged in comparison with other countries and will change over time as interest rates move. Currently, it is suggested that a long-term government bond rate that is above 5% may be considered to be high.

A country may apply a higher benchmark fixed ratio, where for constitutional or other legal reasons (e.g. EU law requirements) it has to apply the same treatment to different types of entities which are viewed as legally comparable, even if these entities pose different levels of risk

105. As set out in Chapter 3, the main base erosion and profit risk involving interest is posed by entities in multinational groups. Therefore, within the best practice approach, a country may restrict the application of the fixed ratio rule to these entities. However, in some cases, constitutional or legal requirements mean that a country is also required to apply the fixed ratio rule to other entities which are seen as legally comparable, including entities in domestic groups and/or standalone entities which may pose less risk of base erosion and profit shifting involving interest. In this case, because the country is required to apply the same treatment to entities which are legally comparable, including those which pose less base erosion and profit shifting risk, the country may apply a benchmark fixed ratio at a higher level within the corridor. In such situations, a country may alternatively decide to apply a lower ratio in order to ensure that base erosion and profit shifting involving interest is addressed, even though this would also be applied to entities which pose less risk.

A country may apply different fixed ratios depending upon the size of an entity's group

106. In general, entities in large groups are in a different position to other entities when raising third party debt. For example, large groups are more likely to raise third party debt centrally, they may have better access to global capital markets, and they may have greater bargaining power with lenders. Large groups also often have sophisticated treasury functions to manage the financial position of the group, including its interest cost. This has two important implications for the application of a fixed ratio rule to entities in large groups compared with other entities:

- Firstly, the analysis of financial data provided to the OECD during the public consultation on Action 4 indicates that large groups tend to have lower net third party interest/EBITDA ratios compared with other groups. For example, a benchmark fixed ratio of 30% would allow around 95% of publicly traded multinational groups with market capitalisation of USD 5 billion or above and with positive EBITDA to deduct all of their net third party interest expense, compared with around 85% of groups of all sizes. Therefore, to create a level playing field, a country may apply one benchmark fixed ratio to entities in large groups, and a higher benchmark fixed ratio to other entities.
- Secondly, because large groups are more likely to raise third party debt centrally, they are less likely to be exposed to differences in interest rates in the countries

in which they operate. Therefore, in setting a benchmark fixed ratio to apply to entities in large groups, a country should not take into account whether its interest rate is higher or lower than those in other countries (i.e. factor 4 above should not be taken into account).

107. Where a country applies a different benchmark fixed ratio to entities in large groups compared with other entities, the definition of a large group should be based on the position of an entity's worldwide group and not only the local group including entities in the country. Although the data referred to above defined a large group based on market capitalisation, it is not recommended that this definition be used to set a benchmark fixed ratio. For privately held groups, a definition based on market capitalisation could not be applied. For publicly held groups, market capitalisation depends on many factors other than the group's level of economic activity. It is therefore suggested that a country's definition of a large group should be based on group consolidated revenue or group assets. Information on a group's consolidated revenue or assets may be obtained from the group's consolidated financial statements or directly from entities in the group where consolidated financial statements are not prepared. Information provided for the purposes of Country-by-Country reporting (*Transfer Pricing Documentation and Country-by-Country Reporting* (OECD, 2015)) may be used as a risk assessment tool to identify groups which may exceed this threshold, although this information should not be used by itself in order to apply a lower benchmark fixed ratio. Where a country applies different benchmark fixed ratios to entities in large groups and to other entities, it should include provisions to accommodate groups which cross the threshold, for example through a merger or divestiture. Such transitional provisions should be available for at most three years, to give groups an opportunity to adjust their capital structures.

Other factors that may be taken into account

108. When setting a benchmark fixed ratio within the corridor of 10% to 30%, countries may also take into account other relevant factors in addition to those set out above. For example:

- A country may apply a higher ratio within the corridor where data shows that there are high levels of net interest expense or debt due to economic or business policies and not due to base erosion and profit shifting.
- A country may apply a higher ratio within the corridor where it applies a macro-economic policy to encourage third party lending not related to base erosion and profit shifting, to increase investment (e.g. in infrastructure).
- A country may apply either a higher ratio or a lower ratio within the corridor where this is justified by local data on the external gearing of its domestic groups or the worldwide gearing of multinational groups operating in the country. This local data may for instance be based on tax rather than accounting figures.
- A country may apply a lower ratio within the corridor where it wishes to apply a stricter approach to tackling base erosion and profit shifting involving interest.

109. However, a country should not take into account any factor which is inconsistent with this report, which introduces competition issues or which fails to take into account the level of base erosion and profit shifting risk involving interest in that country. For example:

- A country should not apply a higher ratio where it has high levels of net interest expense or debt compared to those in other countries, which does not have a non-tax justification.

- A country should not apply a higher ratio due to a policy of attracting international investment into a country through lenient interest limitation rules.

Applying factors to set a benchmark fixed ratio within the best practice corridor

110. It is recommended that a country uses the factors in this chapter, along with other relevant factors, to set its benchmark fixed ratio within the recommended corridor. A country may develop its own approach as to how to apply the factors in setting a ratio, including applying a different weighting to each factor depending upon the extent to which it applies. In all cases, a country is able to choose to apply a lower benchmark fixed ratio within the corridor.

111. Illustrations of ways in which a country could use the factors to set its benchmark fixed ratio within the recommended corridor are included as Example 5 in Annex I.D. These are intended to illustrate possible ways in which a country could apply the factors in this chapter, but are not exhaustive and a different approach may be used.

Changes over time

112. Interest rates change over time and given interest rates are currently at a low level compared with long term averages, it may be necessary for a benchmark ratio to reflect changing interest rate environments. At the same time, however, countries need to consider that an entity's capacity to serve its interest payments is independent of the interest rate environment and that an increase in interest rates should typically result in reduced levels of debt. In this context, academic studies have found that corporate taxpayers issue more debt when interest rates are at a low level compared with historically higher rates (Barry et al., 2008).

113. Countries are therefore not expected to change the benchmark fixed ratio over time, but they may choose to change the ratio where there is a significant change in interest rates. For example, academic studies suggest that a country's credit rating, which influences the interest rates a country has to pay, has a significant impact on the credit rating for corporate bonds (Borensztein, Cowan and Valenzuela, 2007). This suggests that where a country's credit rating undergoes a significant change the benchmark fixed ratio may also be adjusted. However, to provide taxpayers with stable benchmark fixed ratios, countries should consider making changes only on an exceptional basis.

114. Additionally, where a country opts to make adjustments to the benchmark fixed ratio the country should ensure that the ratio moves down as well as up. For example, say a country operates an interest/EBITDA fixed ratio rule with a benchmark fixed ratio of 15%. As a result of an economic crisis domestic interest rates increase sharply, increasing the interest rates for local businesses. To reflect this increase the government raises the benchmark fixed ratio from 15% to 20%. At the same time, the government makes provision that when the interest rates return to pre-crisis levels the benchmark fixed ratio will automatically drop down to 15%.

Notes

1. The term "related party" is defined in Chapter 9.
2. Chapter 11 includes a summary of different approaches that a country may use in applying a fixed ratio rule to a local group, depending upon the structure of its tax system.
3. On 18 December 2014, the OECD released a Public Discussion Draft on Action 4 (see Public Discussion Draft – BEPS Action 4: Interest deductions and other financial payments (www.oecd.org/ctp/aggressive/discussion-draft-action-4-interest-deductions.pdf). As part of their response, BIAC provided financial data based on an analysis performed by PricewaterhouseCoopers (PwC) of net interest/EBITDA ratios for public companies (see "Comments received on Public Discussion Draft – BEPS Action 4: Interest deductions and other financial payments – Part 1" page 179 www.oecd.org/ctp/aggressive/public-comments-action-4-interest-deductions-other-financial-payments-part1.pdf). Following the public consultation PwC provided updated figures, included in Annex I.B.
4. See Table I.B.3 in Annex I.B.

Bibliography

Barry, C.B. et al. (2008), "Corporate debt issuance and the historical level of interest rates", *Financial Management*, Vol. 37, Financial Management Association International, pp. 413-430.

Borensztein, E., K. Cowan and P. Valenzuela (2007), "Sovereign Ceilings "Lite"? The Impact of Sovereign Ratings on Corporate Ratings in Emerging Market Economies", IMF Working Paper, No. 07/75, International Monetary Fund, Washington, DC.

OECD (2015), *Transfer Pricing Documentation and Country-by-Country Reporting*, OECD Publishing, Paris, http://dx.doi.org/10.1787/9789264241480-en.

Chapter 7

Group ratio rule

Aim of a group ratio rule

115. Under the recommended fixed ratio rule, an entity or local group can deduct net interest expense up to a fixed percentage of its EBITDA.[1] However, a fixed ratio rule does not take into account the fact that groups in different sectors may be leveraged differently and, even without a sector bias, some groups are simply more highly leveraged. Therefore, if a fixed ratio rule is introduced in isolation, groups which have a net third party interest/ EBITDA ratio above the benchmark fixed ratio would be unable to deduct all of their net third party interest expense. To reduce the impact on more highly leveraged groups, it is recommended that countries consider combining a fixed ratio rule as described in Chapter 6, with a group ratio rule. This would allow an entity in a highly leveraged group to deduct net interest expense in excess of the amount permitted under the fixed ratio rule, based on a relevant financial ratio of the worldwide group. This means that the benchmark fixed ratio can be kept low, in particular for entities in large multinational groups, making sure the fixed ratio rule is effective in combating base erosion and profit shifting, while the group ratio rule compensates for the blunt operation of such a rule.

116. A group ratio rule may be introduced as a separate additional provision, or as an integral part of an overall rule including a fixed ratio rule. For example, where a country applies an approach based on an entity's net interest/EBITDA ratio, a single rule could provide that an entity can deduct up to the higher of the benchmark fixed ratio and the group's ratio. The decision to implement the fixed ratio rule and group ratio rule separately or as parts of a single rule may depend upon how a country intends the different elements to operate. For example, a single rule with two parts may be easier to apply if a country determines that both the fixed ratio and group ratio elements should use the same calculation of entity EBITDA based on tax numbers, and the same carry forward/carry back provisions

117. This chapter contains a description of a best practice rule which allows an entity which exceeds the benchmark fixed ratio to deduct net interest expense up to its group's net third party interest/EBITDA ratio, if this is higher. Where the net interest/EBITDA ratio of an entity exceeds that of its group, the entity can claim deductions up to its group's ratio. Only net interest expense which exceeds both the benchmark fixed ratio and the ratio of its group should be disallowed. While a rule based on a net third party interest/EBITDA ratio should be effective in tackling base erosion and profit shifting, it is recognised that some groups are subject to legal or practical constraints that limit their ability to align net interest expense and EBITDA in each entity. For these groups, some of the elements within the best practice approach, such as applying an uplift to net third party interest expense (discussed in the section on *Calculation of net third party interest expense* below), and carry forward/carry back provisions (discussed in Chapter 8), may reduce the impact of

these constraints. Simple illustrations of how a group ratio rule in this form would allow an entity which exceeds the benchmark fixed ratio to deduct more interest expense up to its group's net third party interest/EBITDA ratio are included in Example 6 in Annex I.D. It is recognised that to date no country applies a group ratio rule based on this approach. Therefore, this report sets out a framework for a group ratio rule using a net third party interest/EBITDA ratio, but further technical work on the design and operation of such a rule will be undertaken and completed in 2016.

Option to apply different group ratio rules, or no group ratio rule

118. A number of countries currently apply a fixed ratio rule in combination with a group ratio rule using an assets-based ratio, such as equity/total assets. For example, under the "equity escape" rule applied in Finland and Germany (described in Annex I.C), the fixed ratio rule based on net interest/EBITDA does not apply if an entity can show that its equity/total assets ratio is equal to or exceeds that of its group (within a small tolerance). This approach has a stricter outcome for many groups as, where an entity is more highly leveraged than its group, it remains subject to the fixed ratio rule whereas, under the net third party interest/EBITDA rule described in this chapter, only net interest that exceeds both the benchmark fixed ratio and the group's ratio is disallowed. However, for a loss-making entity, the equity escape rule could be more generous, as the entity may still deduct its net interest expense if it can demonstrate that the requirements of the rule are met. Where a country applies a group ratio rule which differs from the net third party interest/EBITDA rule in this report, the country's rule is included in the best practice so long as it only permits an entity to exceed the benchmark fixed ratio based on a relevant financial ratio of its group (such as equity/total assets).

119. There will be cases where countries decide to apply a fixed ratio rule in isolation, without a group ratio rule. This could be because a country wishes to reduce the tax bias between funding using debt or equity for all entities; or where, for constitutional or other reasons, a country wants to apply the same benchmark fixed ratio to all entities, without reference to the leverage position of the wider group. Where a country does not apply a group ratio rule, it should apply the fixed ratio rule consistently to entities in multinational and domestic groups, without improper discrimination.

120. Whether a country applies the group ratio rule described in this chapter, a different group ratio rule, or no group ratio rule, in all cases, a best practice approach must include a fixed ratio rule with a benchmark fixed ratio set within the corridor and based on the factors described in Chapter 6.

Obtaining financial information on a group

121. The group ratio rule requires an entity to be able to determine the net third party interest/EBITDA ratio of its worldwide group. This means that an entity must obtain information on its group which can be audited by its local tax authority, reducing the need for the local tax authority to obtain information from tax authorities in other countries. Therefore, it is important that a best practice approach be designed with this need in mind, so that a rule can be reasonably simple to apply by groups and tax authorities. Where an entity is unable to obtain information on its group necessary to apply the group ratio rule, it can still apply the fixed ratio rule and deduct interest up to the benchmark fixed ratio.

122. Consolidated financial statements provide the most reliable source of financial information on a worldwide group. Therefore, where possible, the group information required to apply a group ratio rule should be taken from a group's consolidated financial statements. A national tax authority will typically not be in a position to confirm the accuracy of group financial data, and so it is recommended that consolidated financial statements should be audited by an independent regulated accountant. However, a country may allow unaudited financial statements to be used so long as these are subject to some form of reliable independent confirmation, or are reviewed by the tax authority.

123. It is recommended that, as a minimum, countries should accept consolidated financial statements prepared under local Generally Accepted Accounting Principles (GAAP) and the most common accounting standards used by large listed multinational groups (i.e. International Financial Reporting Standards (IFRS), Japanese GAAP and US GAAP). In order to enable non-listed groups to prepare a single set of consolidated financial statements for use in all countries in which they operate, countries should consider accepting consolidated financial statements prepared under other accounting standards, but it is left to each country to determine which accounting standards to accept (e.g. taking into account the geographical region and main sources of foreign investment).

124. For most listed groups and many unlisted groups, audited consolidated financial statements will be available from public sources including the group's website. In other cases, consolidated financial statements will need to be provided directly to the tax authority by entities in a group. In some cases, a tax authority may wish to use exchange of information provisions in applicable international agreements to confirm with the tax authority in the country of the group's parent company that the consolidated financial statements they have been provided with are the same as those provided by the parent, to ensure the group is using the same consolidated numbers in different countries.

Definition of a group

125. Given consolidated financial statements provide the most complete and objective source of financial information on multinational groups, a practical and workable definition of a group is one that is based on a consolidated group for financial accounting purposes. Therefore, for the purposes of applying a group ratio rule, a group includes a parent company and all entities which are fully consolidated on a line-by-line basis in the parent's consolidated financial statements.

126. In general, the parent should be the top level company in a holding structure. Where a group prepares consolidated financial statements at different levels (e.g. for local reporting or regulatory purposes), the group will be based on the consolidated financial statements prepared by the top level company (i.e. the highest level of consolidation). A group cannot be headed by an individual or entity other than a company. A group does not include entities which are included in the consolidated financial statements but are not fully consolidated on a line-by-line basis. In other words, it does not include entities which are included using equity accounting, proportionate consolidation or at fair value. In limited situations, an entity may be controlled by a company but not consolidated in that company's consolidated financial statements. This may arise for example where the company is an investment entity which makes investments for the purposes of capital appreciation and/or investment income, and may account for these investments at fair value. In these situations, even though the controlled entity is not the top level company in the holding structure, it may be the parent of a separate group (including itself and any entities that it includes in

its consolidated financial statements). Illustrations of how this definition would apply to groups in different scenarios are included as Example 7 in Annex I.D.

127. As set out in Chapter 9, a group ratio rule should be supported by a targeted rule to address the risk that a group ratio could be inflated using interest paid to a related party outside the group.[2] A targeted rule should be an effective solution to this risk, and also has the benefit that only groups which make interest payments to related parties would be required to make an adjustment under the rule. However, a country may choose to address this risk by including specified related parties, such as those under the common control of an individual or non-corporate entity, within the definition of a group. This approach is currently taken by some countries which apply a group ratio rule based on an equity/total assets ratio. A country may also address this risk by excluding all interest paid to related parties from the calculation of the group's net third party interest expense (as set out in the section *Calculation of net third party interest expense* below).

128. Where a country applies the best practice approach to the position of the local group rather than to each entity separately, attention will need to be paid to issues arising from differences between a group for financial reporting purposes (which in broad terms is based on a 50% control test) and a group for tax purposes (which is usually based on a higher level of control). A country's local group for the purposes of applying the group ratio rule may therefore include entities which are not included in a group for other tax purposes. Where this is the case, the interaction with, for example, tax consolidation, loss surrender and profit contribution rules may need to be considered. These issues are considered in Chapter 11.

Operation of a group ratio rule

129. Determining the amount of net interest expense deductible under a group ratio rule involves a two stage test.

1. Determine the group's net third party interest/EBITDA ratio

   Net third party interest expense / Group EBITDA = Group ratio

2. Apply the group's ratio to an entity's EBITDA

   Group ratio x Entity EBITDA = Limit on net interest deductions

Stage 1: Determine the group's net third party interest/EBITDA ratio

130. The first stage in applying the group ratio rule is to calculate the worldwide group's net third party interest/EBITDA ratio. To ensure that a rule is as straightforward as possible for a group to apply and for tax authorities to audit, this should be based on information which can be obtained from the group's consolidated financial statements.

Calculation of net third party interest expense

131. As described in Chapter 2, a best practice approach should address base erosion and profit shifting involving interest and payments economically equivalent to interest. Accounting standards vary in their treatment of a group's financial income and expenses, but most take a broad approach which includes interest and payments economically equivalent to interest. It is therefore recommended that when calculating a group's net third

party interest/EBITDA ratio, net third party interest expense should be based on financial accounting figures.

132. Within this approach, a group's net third party interest expense could be determined in three ways. These represent increasing degrees of accuracy but, at the same time, increasing degrees of complexity.

Approach 1: Using unadjusted financial reporting figures

133. The most straightforward approach to determining net third party interest expense would be to take income and expense figures directly from a group's consolidated financial statements without adjustment. Depending upon the accounting standards and policies applied, these may be described as interest income and expense, finance income and expense, or a similar term. This would be a simple approach to apply which in many cases should provide effective protection against serious base erosion and profit shifting. However, a risk remains as using unadjusted figures could mean that a group's net third party interest expense may be overstated or understated, resulting in a limit on an entity's net interest deductions which is too high (giving rise to possible base erosion and profit shifting) or too low (giving rise to double taxation). This approach would also mean that a group's net third party interest expense would vary depending on the accounting standards applied, and the ability for interest income or expense to be included in a different line of the group's income statement. For example, in some cases accounting standards allow flexibility for certain items of income and expense to be recognised in operating profit, in finance income and expense, or as a separate item on the face of the consolidated income statement. Finally, using unadjusted figures could result in significant volatility in a group's net third party interest expense, for example where a group preparing consolidated financial statements under IFRS includes fair value movements on financial assets and liabilities within finance income and expense.

Approach 2: Using financial reporting figures adjusted for certain amounts

134. Rather than using figures taken directly from a group's consolidated financial statements without adjustment, a country could require an entity to make adjustments to include or exclude certain payments. This would result in a slightly more complex rule, but one which addresses some of the differences between accounting standards and more accurately reflects the amounts described in Chapter 2. Possible adjustments which a country could require an entity to make in determining net third party interest expense include the following:

- **The removal of payments which are not economically equivalent to interest**. This could include (i) dividend income, (ii) gains and losses on the disposal of financial instruments, (iii) fair value gains and losses on financial instruments, and (iv) notional interest amounts which do not include actual payments of interest. In many cases these amounts may be identified in a group's consolidated financial statements.
- **The addition of capitalised interest.** Capitalised interest is included in the balance sheet valuation of an asset and is not included in the group's finance expense. The amount of interest capitalised in a year will often be identified in a group's consolidated financial statements. An adjustment for capitalised interest may be made in the period where the interest is incurred, or as it is amortised over the life of the related asset.

- **The addition of interest income or expense recognised within a different category of income or expense**. This could include interest income which is included within gross revenue, or interest expense which is included within cost of sales or in the tax line. In some cases these amounts may not be identified in a group's consolidated financial statements, and will need to be obtained from underlying financial information. Groups may be able to introduce processes to identify these payments more easily, in particular where this would mean an increase in total net third party interest expense.

135. Where a country applies this approach, it could require an entity to have the amount of each adjustment to be confirmed by an independent regulated accountant. Alternatively a tax authority may conduct its own enquiries to confirm the adjustments.

Approach 3: Using a financial reporting valuation of interest and other payments specified in Chapter 2

136. The most accurate, but potentially the most complex, approach would be to require an entity to provide a valuation of the amounts included in the definition of interest and payments economically equivalent to interest set out in Chapter 2, based on the amounts included in its group's consolidated financial statements.

137. In most cases this should give substantially the same value for net third party interest expense as under Approach 2. However, where there is a difference between the items included in a group's finance income and expense and those included in the definition contained in Chapter 2, which is not represented by adjustments set out above, this approach should give the more precise and targeted result. On the other hand, it may be more difficult for this value of net third party interest expense to be confirmed directly using a group's consolidated financial statements and so this approach should only be used if a country is confident that it is able to audit a group's underlying books and records.

Proposed approach

138. The calculation of net third party interest income should be based on figures taken from a group's consolidated financial statements. While the use of unadjusted figures is currently considered an acceptable approach, there are risks that net third party interest expense could be overstated or understated and it is likely that most countries will wish to make some adjustments to these figures, although in the interests of simplicity these adjustments should be kept to a minimum. Further work is required to assess the feasibility of each of the above approaches, how information may be obtained from financial statements prepared under different accounting standards and, where adjustments to financial reporting figures are to be made, what amounts should be included and excluded from net third party interest expense.

139. Under all three approaches, a country can choose to allow an uplift of net third party interest expense of up to 10%. This would reduce the risk that all of a group's actual net third party interest expense is not taken into account. It would also reduce the impact of constraints which mean that, even in the long term, a group may not be able to precisely align its net interest expense and EBITDA. An illustration of how an uplift could be applied is included in Example 6c in Annex I.D.

140. As discussed above in the section on *Definition of a group*, under a group ratio rule there is a risk that a group's net third party interest expense may be inflated using interest paid to related parties outside the group. This would have the effect of increasing the group's net third party interest/EBITDA ratio, and increase the limit on net interest

deductions applicable to each group entity. A country may address this risk by providing that net third party interest expense should exclude any payments made to related parties. Alternatively, where a country allows interest paid to related parties to be included in net third party interest expense, it should introduce targeted rules as described in Chapter 9 to ensure that these payments are not used to reduce the effectiveness of the rule in tackling base erosion and profit shifting.

Calculation of group EBITDA

141. EBITDA is an objective measure of economic activity in a group, which can be applied to groups operating in most sectors (with the exception of the banking and insurance sectors, which are considered in Chapter 10). EBITDA is not generally included on the face of a group's consolidated income statement, but for the purposes of applying a group ratio rule, it should be calculated using figures which are readily available from a group's consolidated financial statements.

142. Within a best practice, as a starting point group EBITDA should be profit before tax plus net third party interest expense, depreciation and amortisation (including impairment charges). To avoid double counting, where net third party interest expense has been adjusted to include capitalised interest (or the amortisation of capitalised interest), depreciation and amortisation should be adjusted to strip out any amounts that represent the amortisation of interest included in the value of capitalised assets. Further work will be conducted to refine the definition of group EBITDA, including for example whether or not it should exclude items such as dividend income (and whether this should be dependent on if the dividends would be taxable if received in the country applying the rule), other finance income and expense not included in net third party interest expense, one-off items resulting from restructurings and mergers, and the share of profit from associates and joint venture entities which are included in the consolidated financial accounts under equity accounting but are not part of the group for group ratio rule purposes.[3]

Stage 2: Apply the group's ratio to an entity's EBITDA

143. Once a group's net third party interest expense and EBITDA have been established, it is possible to calculate the group's net third party interest/EBITDA ratio. This ratio may then be applied to the EBITDA of an individual entity within a group to determine the limit on net interest deductions that may be claimed under a group ratio rule. Within the best practice, a country may provide for entity EBITDA to be calculated using either tax or accounting principles. A summary of how to determine an entity's tax EBITDA and accounting EBITDA under a best practice approach is set out below. More detail, including illustrations of how these approaches may give rise to different results, is included in Example 8 in Annex I.D.

Determining an entity's tax EBITDA

144. An entity's tax EBITDA is equal to its taxable profit after adding back tax values for net interest expense, depreciation and amortisation. These values are determined under the tax rules of the country applying the rule. Non-taxable income such as branch profits or dividend income that benefit from a participation exemption should not be included within tax EBITDA. Appropriate adjustments should also be made for taxable branch profits and dividend income to the extent that they are shielded from tax by foreign tax credits, to address the base erosion and profit shifting issues which are the subject of

this report. A group's net third party interest/EBITDA ratio can be applied to an entity's tax EBITDA to give a tax-based limit on net interest deductions. This limit is compared directly to the entity's net interest expense for tax purposes to determine the amount which may be deducted.

145. Determining EBITDA using tax principles is consistent with the approach recommended for calculating entity earnings under the fixed ratio rule. It is also straightforward for groups to apply and tax authorities to audit, and as an approach to tackle base erosion and profit shifting it has the benefit that an entity's interest deductions are linked to its level of taxable income. This means that where an entity's taxable income is higher than its accounting income, its ability to deduct interest expense will be correspondingly greater. Similarly, if an entity undertakes planning to reduce its taxable income, it will be able to deduct less net interest expense. Where a country applies the group ratio rule to the position of the local group, rather than to each entity separately, the local group's tax EBITDA should be reasonably straightforward to calculate, by aggregating the tax EBITDA of each entity (with adjustment where a local group includes entities which have different periods for tax purposes).

Determining an entity's accounting EBITDA

146. An entity's accounting EBITDA should be determined using the same formula as for group EBITDA. However, any income which is not subject to tax, such as dividends or branch profits which fall within a participation exemption, should be excluded. This is to ensure that an entity does not attract a higher level of interest capacity as a result of receiving tax exempt income, which could give rise to base erosion and profit shifting.

147. In principle, an entity's accounting EBITDA should be based on financial reporting figures prepared under the same accounting rules as used in the consolidated financial statements. However, for many groups this would impose a significant burden, as entity financial statements may only currently be prepared under local GAAP. Therefore, in light of the fact that for groups in most sectors the elements of EBITDA are recognised and valued in a broadly consistent way under the main accounting standards, countries should consider accepting entity EBITDA prepared under local GAAP as a practical alternative. In deciding whether to accept entity EBITDA prepared under local GAAP, a country may consider the extent to which local GAAP is aligned with IFRS and other major accounting standards.

148. In determining an entity's accounting EBITDA, it is also recommended that no adjustments should be made to strip out the profit or loss arising from intragroup transactions. This will mean that in some cases the aggregate EBITDA of the entities in a group may exceed the consolidated EBITDA of the group as a whole. This may arise, for example, where one entity in a group recognises the profit arising on the sale of goods to another group entity, but the purchase price is not included in the second entity's cost of sales as the goods have not yet been sold outside the group. However, this approach should ensure that the EBITDA of each entity reflects its level of economic activity, even where this is a result of dealing within its group. Where a country applies the group ratio rule to the position of a local group as a whole, the accounting EBITDA of the entities in the local group should be aggregated. In this case, to the extent intragroup transactions within the local group do not offset against each other, these may be eliminated.

149. A group's net third party interest/EBITDA ratio can be applied to an entity's accounting EBITDA to give an accounts-based limit on net interest expense. This limit could be compared directly to the entity's net interest expense for tax purposes, to determine how much may be deducted. Alternatively, the accounts-based limit may be adjusted to take into

account differences between the entity's net interest expense for accounting and tax purposes. A possible approach to achieve this is set out in Example 8c in Annex I.D.

Addressing the impact of loss-making entities on the operation of a group ratio rule

150. In general, under a group ratio rule an entity is able to claim deductions for interest expense up to the net third party interest/EBITDA ratio of its group. However there are two scenarios, both of which may arise as a result of the presence of loss-making entities within a group, which mean that this general approach needs to be limited.

151. The first scenario concerns a group which has a positive EBITDA, but this includes the results of a loss-making entity. The impact of this is that group EBITDA is reduced and the group's net third party interest/EBITDA ratio is increased. Under a group ratio rule, this would increase the capacity of profitable entities in the group to deduct interest expense, possibly to an extent that exceeds the actual net interest expense of the entire group. Where a carry forward of unused interest capacity is permitted, this interest capacity could be used to shelter interest deductions in future periods. This is illustrated by Example 9a in Annex I.D. This risk could be dealt with in part by a general principle that places an upper limit on the interest capacity of any entity applying the group ratio rule, equal to the net third party interest expense of the entire group. This upper limit should not mean that an entity's net interest deductions are lower than they would have been under the group ratio rule if group EBITDA had not been reduced by losses. This approach does not remove the risk that the total net interest deductions of all group entities could exceed the group's actual net third party interest expense. However, it should prevent an individual entity receiving a very high level of interest capacity that could be used for base erosion and profit shifting purposes. How this upper limit would operate is shown in Example 9b in Annex I.D.

152. The second scenario concerns groups which have negative EBITDA at a consolidated level, but which include some profitable entities. In this situation, it is not possible to calculate a meaningful net third party interest/EBITDA for the group, as the ratio will be negative. However, a profitable entity within the group is still making a positive contribution to the group's results, which should be recognised. In this case, under the best practice approach an entity with positive EBITDA which is part of a loss-making group could receive interest capacity equal to the lower of the entity's actual net interest expense and the net third party interest expense of the group. As shown in Example 9c in Annex I.D, this allows the entity to deduct its actual net interest expense, subject to an upper limit based on the actual net interest expense of its group. Given in these circumstances a group ratio cannot be calculated, this is the most straightforward way of linking an entity's interest deductibility to the position of its group.

153. An alternative approach would be to exclude loss-making entities from the calculation of a group's EBITDA. This would remove the risk that any entity would receive an excessive amount of interest capacity. However, in general it would not be possible to obtain information on loss-making entities within a group from the consolidated financial statements. It may be possible for an entity to provide this information directly to a country's tax authority, but it may be very difficult for the tax authority to confirm the accuracy of this information and ensure that all loss-making entities in a group have been identified and excluded. Illustrations of how this approach could operate in practice are shown in Examples 9d and 9e in Annex I.D.

154. Further work will be conducted on the impact of losses on the operation of a group ratio rule, and the feasibility of different approaches to address this impact. Issues surrounding the impact of losses on a group ratio rule only arise where the rule uses an earnings-based ratio. Where a different rule is applied such as one based on an equity/total assets ratio, there should be no need to have specific provisions to deal with the effect of losses.

Notes

1. Chapter 11 includes a summary of different approaches that a country may use in applying a fixed ratio rule to a local group, depending upon the structure of its tax system.
2. The term "related party" is defined in Chapter 9.
3. For financial reporting purposes, "associates" are entities over which a group has significant influence, but this influence is not sufficient for the group to exercise control. In broad terms, this is typically where a group controls between 20% and 50% of the voting power in the entity.

Chapter 8

Addressing volatility and double taxation

155. An important issue under a best practice approach which links net interest deductions to the level of an entity's EBITDA is how to deal with volatility in earnings which impacts an entity's ability to deduct its interest expense. Where earnings volatility or mismatches in the timing of interest expense and EBITDA result in an entity exceeding the benchmark fixed ratio under a fixed ratio rule, the group ratio rule described in Chapter 7 may provide a solution by allowing the entity to deduct net interest expense up to the group's net third party interest/EBITDA ratio where this is higher. This could also be achieved using a group ratio rule based on an equity/total assets ratio, such as an "equity escape rule" described in Annex I.C, which could also be used by an entity with negative EBITDA if it is able to demonstrate that the requirements of the rule are met. Otherwise, these issues may be addressed to an extent by using average EBITDA over a number of years or by permitting an entity to carry disallowed interest expense and unused interest capacity for use in earlier or later periods.

Measuring economic activity using average EBITDA

156. Rather than linking an entity's ability to deduct net interest expense to economic activity in a single year, the impact of short term volatility could be reduced through the use of average figures. For example, under a fixed ratio rule the ratio could be applied to the average of EBITDA in the current year and, say, the previous two years. In this case, the impact of a single year fall in EBITDA would be spread over a three year period, with the lower earnings in one year offset against higher earnings in other years. The use of averaging within a group ratio rule would be more complicated, as it would need to be used in calculating the EBITDA of the group as well as of each entity. This would give rise to additional issues that would need to be considered, such as how to deal with cases where the composition of a group changes during the period used for calculating the average. However, the use of averaging could reduce the impact of losses on the operation of a rule, in particular where an entity is only in a loss-making position for one or two years.

157. The use of averaging could provide an entity with some protection against short term volatility, but would provide no protection against longer term volatility outside of the period used for calculating an average. Averaging would also not help an entity which incurs interest expense to fund a project or investment that gives rise to EBITDA more than, say, two years later.

158. Overall, the use of averages is likely to make a rule more complex but it could help address volatility. Therefore, this is an option that countries may choose to apply under the best practice approach. However, to reduce the risk of arbitrage it is suggested that an election to use average figures should apply to all entities in a local group. An illustration of how three year averaging could be applied to a fixed ratio rule is included as Example 10 in Annex I.D.

Carry forward and carry back of disallowed interest and unused interest capacity

159. Where a payment of interest relates to a specific transaction intended to give rise to base erosion or profit shifting, or the entity consistently has a level of net interest expense in excess of the benchmark fixed ratio and group ratio, a permanent disallowance of net interest expense may be an appropriate result. However, there may be cases where the amount of interest expense in an entity exceeds that which is allowable merely as a result of a timing mismatch which will correct in a future period. This may arise, for example, where an entity incurs interest expense to fund a project or investment that will give rise to earnings in a future period. There may also be cases where an entity's EBITDA fluctuates for reasons outside of its control, for example as a result of changing market conditions, increasing or reducing the amount of net interest expense it may deduct for tax. In addition, under a group ratio rule, the amount of net interest expense that an entity can deduct may be impacted by volatility in EBITDA elsewhere in the group. In these cases, a permanent disallowance of interest expense would introduce a level of uncertainty for groups which could make long term planning difficult and which a country may view as undesirable. A permanent disallowance of interest expense may also result in double taxation, if the lender is taxed on the corresponding interest income.

160. Both a fixed ratio rule and a group ratio rule establish a limit on the ability of an entity to deduct net interest expense (i.e. its interest capacity). Except in cases where an entity's interest capacity precisely matches its net interest expense, the operation of a rule will result in an entity either incurring an interest disallowance (i.e. where its net interest expense exceeds the maximum permitted), or having unused interest capacity (i.e. where its net interest expense is below the maximum permitted). Allowing disallowed interest expense and unused interest capacity to be used in other periods through carry forward or carry back provisions would have clear benefits for entities, reducing the risk of a permanent disallowance of interest expense where interest expense and EBITDA arise in different periods. From a country's perspective, this could also support a policy that the level of an entity's net interest deductions should be linked to its level of earnings over time.

161. Under the best practice approach, there is no requirement for a country to allow an entity to carry forward or carry back disallowed interest expense or unused interest capacity. However, a country may choose to allow an entity:

- to carry forward disallowed interest expense only
- to carry forward disallowed interest expense and unused interest capacity
- to carry forward and carry back disallowed interest expense.

162. An entity's disallowed interest expense that may be carried forward or carried back under these provisions will generally be the deductible net interest expense that is in excess of the amount permitted under the fixed ratio rule and group ratio rule. Interest expense disallowed under targeted rules will generally relate to transactions or arrangements which give rise to specific base erosion and profit shifting risks, and should not be available for carry forward or carry back.

163. Where a country allows an entity to carry forward unused interest capacity, this may be limited to the amount by which an entity's net interest expense is below that permitted under the fixed ratio rule only. Alternatively, a country may allow the carry forward of unused interest capacity based on the level of net interest permitted under the group ratio rule. This would reduce the impact of volatility in group earnings on an entity's ability to deduct net interest expense, and is consistent with the principle of allowing a group to

deduct an amount equivalent to its net third party interest expense. In either case, a carry forward of unused interest capacity could allow an entity that has already deducted all of its net interest expense to build up a potentially significant carry forward.

164. Allowing disallowed interest expense and unused interest capacity to be carried forward or back and used in other periods does introduce potential base erosion and profit shifting risks. This is particularly the case for unused interest capacity, where a long or unlimited carry forward could give rise to a sizeable tax asset which can only be realised either by increasing the level of the entity's net interest expense, or by reducing the level of EBITDA in a future period, neither of which should be incentivised by a rule to tackle base erosion and profit shifting. Similar concerns exist with respect to carry backs of disallowed interest expense. On the other hand, a long or unlimited carry forward of disallowed interest expense could encourage an entity to increase its interest expense up to the maximum amount permitted, in the knowledge that if it exceeds the amount of interest allowed in a year, the surplus may be deducted in future periods. However, this risk is not judged to be as significant as the risks associated with a carry back of disallowed interest expense or carry forward of unused interest capacity, as these latter types of carry over provisions offer greater possibility of immediate monetisation.

165. Therefore, where carry forwards or carry backs are permitted, a country may consider imposing limits in terms of time and/or value. This is particularly important with respect to a carry forward of unused interest capacity and carry back of disallowed interest expense, which give rise to greater potential base erosion and profit shifting risks. Limits on carry forwards and carry backs could include the following:

- The number of years for which disallowed interest expense or unused interest capacity may be carried forward, or disallowed interest expense may be carried back, could be limited.
- The value of carry forwards could reduce over time (e.g. by 10% each year).
- The value of a carry forward or carry back could be capped at a fixed monetary amount.
- The amount of a carry forward or carry back that may be used in a single year could be limited (e.g. providing that no more than 50% of current net interest expense may be set against unused interest capacity carried forward from previous years).
- Carry forwards should be reset to zero in certain circumstances, following normal practice applied to loss carry forwards (e.g. where a company changes ownership and also changes the nature of its economic activity).

166. Where a country applies a fixed ratio rule in combination with a group ratio rule, it may apply a single carry forward provision to deal with disallowed interest under both rules. Alternatively, a country could impose different limits depending upon whether interest expense is disallowed under the fixed ratio rule or the group ratio rule. However, this approach is likely to be considerably more complex to apply and administer. For example, groups may be required to maintain a separate carry forward pool under each rule. The country would also need to consider how disallowed interest carried forward in each pool can be used (e.g. whether one pool should be used first, or whether interest disallowed under one rule may only be set against interest capacity arising under the same rule).

167. Where a country applies interest limitation rules to the position of the local group rather than each entity separately, it should also consider how this will impact any carry forward or carry back provisions (e.g. whether an entity should be able to utilise disallowed interest expense carried forward from a period prior to the time it joined the group).

Chapter 9

Targeted rules

Aim of targeted rules

168. Targeted interest limitation rules include any provisions which apply to restrict interest deductions on payments made under specific transactions or arrangements. These may be contrasted with general interest limitation rules, such as the fixed ratio rule and group ratio rule, which impose an overall limit on an entity's interest deductions. A number of countries do not currently apply any general interest limitation rule and rely solely on targeted rules. One benefit of such an approach is that it reduces the risk that a rule could negatively impact on entities which are already appropriately capitalised and also avoids any incentive for groups to increase the level of net interest expense of local entities up to the level allowed under a fixed ratio rule. The use of targeted rules also allows countries to address specific areas of concern, potentially minimising compliance costs for entities, in particular those which do not engage in base erosion or profit shifting. However, such an approach has drawbacks. Most importantly, to some extent targeted rules will always be a reactive response, requiring countries to be aware of specific base erosion and profit shifting risks as they emerge. There is a risk that some groups may consider all arrangements not covered by targeted rules to be acceptable, meaning that over time new targeted rules may be required. Targeted rules also require active application, meaning the tax administration must be able to recognise situations where a rule could apply, often as part of a complex transaction, and then engage with a group to determine the correct result. Overall, an approach based entirely on targeted rules may result in a large number of rules which will increase complexity, as well as increasing compliance and administrative costs. If the rules are not comprehensive then they are unlikely to deal with all base erosion and profit shifting risks. On the other hand, an approach which uses a general rule supplemented by targeted rules in key areas should provide countries with the comfort that the main risks posed by base erosion and profit shifting are addressed, while ensuring that groups are able to obtain relief for their real net third party interest expense.

169. While the best practice approach in this report recommends general interest limitation rules, it is recognised that targeted rules can also provide an effective solution to some base erosion and profit shifting risk. This chapter sets out a number of specific risks that may not be addressed by the fixed ratio rule and group ratio rule, where targeted rules may be required. Countries may also continue to apply existing targeted and general interest limitation rules, where these address specific risks. For example, a country may apply a thin capitalisation rule based on a fixed debt/equity ratio to disallow interest on excessive debt in addition to the fixed ratio rule and this could apply to disallow interest even where an entity does not exceed the level of net interest expense permitted under the fixed ratio rule.

170. The impact of a targeted rule applying to an arrangement will vary depending upon the nature of the arrangement and the risk the rule is intended to address. In some cases it may be appropriate for a rule to deny a deduction for a gross interest payment under a transaction. In other cases it may be more appropriate for a rule to apply to part of a payment, or to net interest payments after taking into account income under the same transaction. Where the result of a transaction is to increase the level of net third party interest expense under a group ratio rule, a rule may simply operate to disregard this increase, with no specific disallowance.

Targeted rules to prevent avoidance of the general rules

171. A best practice approach should be robust against attempts to avoid the effect of a rule. A fixed ratio rule (and group ratio rule where applied) should therefore be supported by targeted rules to counteract planning undertaken by groups to reduce the impact of these rules. To achieve this, it is recommended that countries also introduce targeted rules to address the following risks:

- An entity with net interest expense enters into an arrangement to reduce the net interest expense subject to the fixed ratio rule (e.g. by converting interest expense into a different form of deductible expense, or by converting other taxable income into a form which is economically equivalent to interest).
- An entity which is part of a group enters into an arrangement with a related party or third party in order to increase the level of net third party interest expense under the group ratio rule (e.g. by making a payment to a related party or to a third party under a structured arrangement, or by converting interest income into a different form).
- A group is restructured to place an unincorporated holding entity at the top of the structure, to create two groups. This may be to prevent a fixed ratio rule applying (e.g. in a country where the rule does not apply to standalone entities) or to separate the original group into two parts for group ratio rule purposes.

172. The above risks may be addressed by standalone rules, specific provisions within the fixed ratio rule and group ratio rule, or by other tax rules (such as, for example, a country's general anti-avoidance rule). These rules should be applicable to all entities which are subject to the fixed ratio rule, and group ratio rule where this applies. The terms "related party" and "structured arrangement" are defined below.

Targeted rules to address other base erosion and profit shifting risks

173. The fixed ratio rule and group ratio rule described in this report provide an effective solution to tackle most base erosion and profit shifting involving interest and payments economically equivalent to interest. However, as set out in Chapter 3, in certain situations, a country may restrict application of the fixed ratio rule and group ratio rule to entities in multinational groups. Therefore, targeted rules may be required to address base erosion and profit shifting risks posed by entities which are not subject to the general interest limitation rules. Even where the fixed ratio rule and group ratio rule apply, a number of specific base erosion and profit shifting risks remain. Therefore, it is recommended that countries consider introducing rules to address the risks listed below:

- An entity which would otherwise have net interest income enters into an arrangement which involves the payment of interest to a group entity outside the country or a related party to reduce the level of interest income subject to tax in the country.
- An entity makes a payment of interest on an "artificial loan", where no new funding is raised by the entity or its group.
- An entity makes a payment of interest to a third party under a structured arrangement, for instance under a back-to-back arrangement.
- An entity makes a payment of interest to a related party, which is excessive or is used to finance the production of tax exempt income.
- An entity makes a payment of interest to a related party, which is subject to no or low taxation on the corresponding interest income.

174. Rules to address the risks above should ideally be applicable to all entities, irrespective of whether they are also subject to the fixed ratio rule and group ratio rule. However, these rules are particularly important where an entity is not subject to a fixed ratio rule as described in Chapter 6.

Definition of "related parties" and "structured arrangements"

175. A number of the specific risks listed above refer to transactions with or payments made to a related party or to a third party under a structured arrangement.

Related parties

176. An entity which is part of a group may also be related to individuals or entities which are not part of the group, but where a significant relationship exists. For the purposes of this report, two persons (including individuals and entities) are related if they are not in the same group but they meet any of the following conditions:

- The first person has an investment that provides that person with effective control of the second person or there is a third person that holds investments which provide that person with effective control over both persons.
- The first person has a 25% or greater investment in the second person or there is a third person that holds a 25% or greater investment in both.
- They can be regarded as associated enterprises under Article 9.

177. A person will be treated as holding a percentage investment in another person if that person holds directly or indirectly through an investment in other persons, a percentage of the voting rights of that person or of the value of any equity interests of that person.

178. For the purposes of this related party definition, a person who acts together with another person in respect of the ownership or control of any voting rights or equity interests will be treated as owning or controlling all of those voting rights and equity instruments.

179. Two persons will be treated as acting together in respect of ownership or control of any voting rights or equity interests if they meet any of the following conditions:

- They are members of the same family.
- One person regularly acts in accordance with the wishes of the other person in respect of ownership or control of such rights or interests.

- They have entered into an arrangement that has material impact on the value or control of any such rights or interests.
- They each directly or indirectly hold debt in the entity in proportion to their voting rights or equity interests.
- The ownership or control of any such rights or interests is managed by the same person or group of persons. In respect of any taxpayer that is a collective investment vehicle (CIV), if the investment manager can establish to the satisfaction of the tax authority from the terms of the investment mandate and the circumstances in which the investment was made that two funds were not acting together in respect of the investment, then the interests held by those funds should not be aggregated under this part of the "acting together" test.

180. For these purposes a CIV is any vehicle which is widely held, holds a diversified portfolio of securities and is subject to investor-protection regulation in the country in which it is established. It is left to countries to determine the types of vehicle which would meet this definition. For example, countries may consider certain types of CIVs to be widely-held if their shares or units are listed for quotation on a stock exchange or can be readily purchased or sold by the public (i.e. the purchase or sale of shares or units is not implicitly or explicitly restricted to a limited group of investors). However, a country may apply a different test to determine whether a CIV is widely held.

Structured arrangements

181. Targeted rules may also apply where an entity makes a payment of interest to a third party under a structured arrangement. A structured arrangement is any arrangement where the entity, its group and its related parties, taken together, do not bear the entire cost of the interest payment.

182. An example of a structured arrangement would be a "back-to-back" arrangement whereby an entity makes a payment of interest to a third party in circumstances where the third party also makes a payment to the entity, a member of the entity's group or a related party of the entity. This second payment may be in a form other than interest.

Chapter 10

Applying the best practice approach to banking and insurance groups

183. In developing a best practice approach to combat base erosion and profit shifting involving interest, a number of particular features of groups in the banking and insurance sectors need to be taken into account.

184. An important consideration is that the role interest plays in a banking or insurance business is different to that in other sectors. Banks and insurance companies hold financial assets and liabilities as an integral part of their main business activities. In addition, financial sector businesses in most countries are subject to strict regulations which impose restrictions on their capital structure. In 2011, Basel III introduced a leverage ratio standard intended to constrain leverage in the banking sector, helping to mitigate risks which in the past have damaged the financial system and the economy.[1] The Solvency II Directive introduces a similar system for insurers in the European Union.[2] It should be noted however that, although banking and insurance groups are subject to regulation, not all entities within a group are subject to the same obligations and the treatment of branches in particular must be taken into account.

185. Despite the restrictions imposed by regulatory requirements, a number of studies have found that the leverage of banks is influenced on average by corporate taxes to the same extent as for groups in other sectors. The influence of tax on leverage is reduced where a bank is capital constrained, but in practice many groups hold a buffer of capital above the minimum amount required by regulations (Heckemeyer and de Mooij, 2013; Keen and de Mooij, 2012).

186. Base erosion and profit shifting by banking and insurance groups could potentially take a number of forms. These include: regulated entities holding a regulatory capital buffer (including a debt component) above the level required to support existing business; routing regulatory capital and ordinary debt issued within a group through intermediate entities in low tax countries, placing excessive interest deductions in branches, which do not need to be separately capitalised for regulatory purposes, and in non-regulated entities; using deductible interest expense to fund assets which are tax exempt or taxed on a preferential basis; and the use of hybrid financial instruments and hybrid entities.

187. Banks and insurance companies typically hold buffers of regulatory capital above the minimum level required, and there are significant commercial drivers to maintain these buffers (e.g. connected to credit rating and cost of capital). Holding capital above the minimum required by regulations allows a group to accommodate changing capital needs, but also provides some opportunities for base erosion and profit shifting.

188. The fixed ratio rule and group ratio rule set out in this report are unlikely to be effective in addressing these base erosion and profit shifting risks for a number of reasons. In particular, banking and insurance groups are important sources of debt funding for

groups in other sectors and as such many are net lenders by a significant margin. This means that the main operating companies in these groups, and the groups overall, will often have net interest income rather than net interest expense. As the fixed ratio rule and group ratio rule apply to limit the level of an entity's net interest expense, these rules would have no impact on important entities within banking and insurance groups. In addition, the fact that interest income is a major part of a bank or insurance company's income means that EBITDA would not be a suitable measure for economic activity across a group in these sectors. Finally, the financial statements of banking and insurance groups typically differ from those of groups in other sectors, which in particular could impact the operation of a group ratio rule. As a fixed ratio rule and group ratio rule in this report are unlikely to address base erosion and profit shifting in the banking and insurance sectors, countries may consider excluding entities in groups operating in these sectors from the scope of these rules, in which case they should introduce targeted rules addressing base erosion and profit shifting in these sectors (as discussed below).

189. Any exclusion should not apply to treasury companies, captive insurance companies or other non-regulated entities which carry out quasi-banking or other financial activities where there are no regulatory restraints, or to investment vehicles whether or not regulated. These entities should remain subject to the rules contained in the best practice approach.

190. It is not intended that entities operating in the banking and insurance sectors, or regulated banking or insurance entities within non-financial groups, should be exempted from the best practice approach to tackle base erosion and profit shifting involving interest. Instead, in order to tackle base erosion and profit shifting by groups in all sectors, it is essential that a best practice approach includes rules which are capable of addressing risks posed by different entities. Further work will therefore be conducted to be completed in 2016, to identify best practice rules to deal with the potential base erosion and profit shifting risks posed by banks and insurance companies, taking into account the particular features of these sectors. This will include work on regulated banking and insurance activities within non-financial groups (such as groups operating in the manufacturing or retail sector). In particular, it is crucial that any recommended interest limitation rules do not conflict with or reduce the effectiveness of capital regulation intended to reduce the risk of a future financial crisis. Where a country applies the fixed ratio rule set out in this report to entities in banking and insurance groups, the country should still apply the specific best practice rules to be designed to address the base erosion and profit shifting risks posed by these sectors.

Notes

1. The Third Basel Accord is a comprehensive set of reform measures, agreed upon by members of the Basel Committee on Banking Supervision, to strengthen the regulation, supervision and risk management of the banking sector (www.bis.org/bcbs/index.htm?m=3%7C14, accessed on 3 September 2015).

2. Directive 2009/138/EC of the European Parliament and of the Council of 25 November 2009 on the taking-up and pursuit of the business of Insurance and Reinsurance (Solvency II) [2009] OJ L335/1.

Bibliography

Heckemeyer, J. and R. de Mooij (2013), "Taxes and Corporate Debt: Are Banks any Different?", *IMF Working Paper*, No. 13/221, International Monetary Fund, Washington, DC.

Keen, M. and R. de Mooij (2012), "Debt, Taxes and Banks", *IMF Working Paper*, No. 12/48, International Monetary Fund, Washington, DC.

Chapter 11

Implementing the best practice approach

Implementation and co-ordination

191. This report includes recommendations for a best practice approach to tackle base erosion and profit shifting involving interest. As set out in Chapter 1, a country may supplement this approach with other general or targeted interest limitation rules, either to address base erosion and profit shifting risks it faces or to achieve wider tax policy aims.

192. Further work will be conducted on particular areas of the best practice approach for instance guidance on the detailed operation of the group ratio rule. Work will also be conducted on the design of special rules to address base erosion and profit shifting in the banking and insurance sectors, taking into account the specific issues that groups operating in these sectors face. This work will be completed in 2016.

193. The design and content of the best practice approach set out in this report, including the corridor for setting a benchmark fixed ratio and the optional exclusion for interest funding certain public-benefit projects, will initially be reviewed by countries involved in the BEPS Project by no later than the end of 2020. This review will include consideration of the experience of countries which have introduced rules in accordance with the best practice and the impact on the behaviour of groups. The review will also consider any additional available data that could assist in assessing the effectiveness of the agreed corridor. To this end, countries are encouraged to collect tax data on the level of net interest expense and EBITDA of entities and local groups in that country, as well as those of multinational groups operating in the country where available. Following this review, elements of the best practice may be revised.

Transitional rules

194. The best practice approach set out in the report should address base erosion and profit shifting involving interest. However, it is recognised that any rule to limit tax deductions for an entity's interest expense could involve a significant cost for some entities. Therefore, it is expected that a country introducing a fixed ratio rule and group ratio rule would give entities reasonable time to restructure existing financing arrangements before the rules come into effect.

195. A country may also apply transitional rules which exclude interest on certain existing loans from the scope of the rules, either for a fixed period or indefinitely. In this case it is recommended that these transitional rules are primarily restricted to interest on third party loans entered into before the rules were announced. Interest on any loans entered into after the announcement of the new rules should not benefit from any transitional provisions. Alternatively, a country may apply no transitional rules.

Separate entity and group taxation systems

196. Countries currently apply corporate tax systems which include different types of group taxation and separate entity taxation. The best practice approach described in this report should be compatible with any system, although in some cases specific provisions within the best practice approach may require adjustment.

Countries applying separate entity taxation systems

197. Where a country taxes each entity within a group separately, the fixed ratio rule and group ratio rule may be applied in any of the following three ways at the discretion of the country:

- The fixed ratio rule and group ratio rule may be applied separately to each entity based on its EBITDA.
- The country may treat entities within a tax group as a single entity for the purposes of applying the fixed ratio rule and group ratio rule. For example, the benchmark fixed ratio would be applied to the tax group's total tax EBITDA. Interest capacity would then be allocated within the tax group in accordance with rules developed by the country, which may include allowing a group to determine the allocation of interest capacity between entities. To prevent abuse, transactions within the tax group which do not net off may be stripped out of the tax group's "entity EBITDA". Under this option, entities which are in the same financial reporting group, but which are not part of the same tax group, would continue to be treated as separate entities and would apply the fixed ratio rule and group ratio rule independently.
- The country may treat all entities in the country which are part of the same financial reporting group as a single entity for the purposes of applying the fixed ratio rule and group ratio rule. Transactions within the financial reporting group which do not net off may be excluded from "entity EBITDA" to prevent abuse. This option may be particularly relevant for a country with a group ratio rule, which applies to entities in a financial reporting group. However, as this could in effect allow the transfer of interest capacity between entities which are not in a tax group, the country may need to consider whether this raises any policy concerns (such as inconsistency with existing loss surrender, profit contribution or similar rules). The operation of other provisions such as carry forwards and carry backs would need to be considered, for example whether an entity should be able to benefit from attributes carried forward from a period before it joined the financial reporting group.

Countries applying group taxation systems

198. Where a country taxes entities on a group or consolidated basis, the fixed ratio rule and group ratio rule may be applied in any of the following ways at the discretion of the country:

- The country may treat entities within the consolidated tax group as a single entity for the purposes of applying the fixed ratio rule and group ratio rule. For example, the benchmark fixed ratio would be applied to the consolidated tax group's total tax EBITDA, and the amount of interest capacity applied to calculate the permitted net interest deductions for the consolidated tax group as a whole. Under this option, entities which are in the same financial reporting group, but which are not part of the same consolidated tax group, would continue to be treated as separate entities and would apply the fixed ratio rule and group ratio rule independently.

- The country may treat all entities in the country which are part of the same financial reporting group as a single entity for the purposes of applying the fixed ratio rule and group ratio rule. Transactions within the financial reporting group which do not net off may be excluded from "entity EBITDA" to prevent abuse. This option may be particularly relevant for a country with a group ratio rule, which applies to entities in a financial reporting group. However, as this could in effect allow the transfer of interest capacity between a consolidated tax group and an entity outside of that group, the country may need to consider whether this raises any policy concerns. The operation of other provisions such as carry forwards and carry backs would need to be considered, for example whether an entity should be able to benefit from attributes carried forward from a period before it joined the financial reporting group.

Interaction of the best practice approach with hybrid mismatch rules under Action 2

199. Where a country has introduced a fixed ratio rule, the potential base erosion and profit shifting risk posed by hybrid mismatch arrangements is reduced, as the overall level of net interest deductions an entity may claim is restricted. However, this risk is not eliminated. Within the limits imposed by a fixed ratio rule, there may still be significant scope for an entity to claim interest deductions in circumstances where a hybrid financial instrument or hybrid entity is used to give rise to a double deduction or deduction/no inclusion outcome. Where a group ratio rule applies, there is also a risk that hybrid mismatch arrangements could be used to increase a group's net third party interest expense, supporting a higher level of net interest deductions across the group. In order to address these risks, a country should implement all of the recommendations under Action 2, alongside the best practice approach in this report.

200. Rules to address hybrid mismatch arrangements should be applied by an entity before the fixed ratio rule and group ratio rule to determine an entity's total net interest expense. Once this total net interest expense figure has been determined, the fixed ratio rule and group ratio rule should be applied to establish whether the full amount may be deducted, or to what extent net interest expense should be disallowed.

201. The OECD Report, *Neutralising the Effects of Hybrid Mismatch Arrangements* (OECD, 2014) stated that rules which grant deemed interest deductions for equity capital, or have similar effect, would not be considered under Action 2, but should be considered further either separately or in the context of Action 4. As set out in Chapter 2, deemed deductions which are calculated by applying a specified percentage to the equity capital of an entity are not treated as being interest or a payment economically equivalent to interest for the purposes of this report. However, these rules should be considered further by the OECD in separate work.

Interaction of the best practice approach with controlled foreign company rules under Action 3

202. The fixed ratio rule and group ratio rule should be effective in addressing base erosion and profit shifting involving excessive interest deductions and interest used to finance the production of tax exempt income. A country may also introduce controlled foreign company (CFC) rules in accordance with the recommendations under Action 3 (*Designing Effective Controlled Foreign Companies Rules* (OECD, 2015)), to address situations where an entity makes an interest payment which is deductible under the fixed

ratio rule and group ratio rule, but the payment is made to a CFC which is subject to a low rate of tax.

203. Where a country applies CFC rules alongside interest limitation rules, CFC income which is subject to tax on the parent company may be included in the calculation of the parent's EBITDA when applying the fixed ratio rule and group ratio rule. Where this CFC income includes interest income or expense, the country should consider including the interest in the calculation of the parent's net interest expense and excluding that interest from the calculation of the parent's EBITDA.

204. The best practice approach in this report should also reduce the pressure on a country's CFC rules, by encouraging groups to spread net interest expense between group entities so that there is a greater link to taxable economic activity. This should reduce the level of net interest income arising in CFCs, as groups are likely to reduce the level of intragroup interest payments, and increase the alignment of net interest expense and EBITDA within the group.

Interaction of the best practice approach with other rules to limit interest deductions

205. As described in this report, a country may apply the fixed ratio rule and group ratio rule together with targeted rules to tackle specific base erosion and profit shifting risks, including the risks discussed in Chapter 9 as well as other risks identified by the country. A country may also apply other general interest limitation rules, such as arm's length rules, rules to disallow a percentage of all interest expense and thin capitalisation rules.

206. It is suggested that in most cases, these targeted and general interest limitation rules should be applied before the fixed ratio rule and group ratio rule. However, the ultimate decision as to the order in which to apply interest limitation rules is left to countries, taking into account the design of its rules and the risks they are intended to address.

Interaction of the best practice approach with withholding taxes

207. Withholding tax on interest is typically imposed in order to allocate taxing rights over income to a source country, although it is recognised that an effect of withholding taxes may be to reduce the benefits to groups of base erosion and profit shifting involving interest. Where a country applies withholding tax to payments of interest, this should in no way be impacted by the application of the fixed ratio rule, group ratio rule or targeted rules described in this report. Where the best practice approach limits an entity's net interest deductions, leading to an interest disallowance, there is no intention that the interest expense disallowed should be re-characterised for any other purpose. Therefore, to the extent a payment would be subject to withholding tax under a country's tax law, this would continue to apply. Where a country currently re-characterises disallowed interest, for example as a dividend payment, it may continue to apply this treatment but this is not part of the best practice approach in this report.

208. Where an entity receives interest net of withholding tax, and the country of the recipient allows a credit for this tax, the entity will typically be subject to tax on a gross amount of interest income including an amount representing the tax withheld. This treatment is not changed as a result of any aspect of the best practice approach. Therefore, where an entity would currently be able to claim credit for withholding tax on its interest income, this should not change following the introduction of the fixed ratio rule and group ratio rule.

Bibliography

OECD (2015), *Designing Effective Controlled Foreign Companies Rules*, OECD Publishing, Paris, http://dx.doi.org/10.1787/9789264241152-en.

OECD (2014), *Neutralising the Effects of Hybrid Mismatch Arrangements*, OECD Publishing, Paris, paragraph 4, http://dx.doi.org/10.1787/9789264218819-en.

Annex I.A

European Union Law issues

209. This annex includes a brief outline of EU law issues that EU Member States should take into account in implementing the best practice approach in this report.

EU treaty freedoms

210. The treaty freedoms that need to be considered in the context of interest limitation rules are the freedom of establishment, and the free movement of capital. The freedom of establishment applies to cases where the shareholder would be able to exercise a significant influence over the entity,[1] while the free movement of capital applies to cases where the shareholder acquired the shares for the sole purpose of making a financial investment without participating in the decision making process of the entity. In addition, the freedom to provide services, which also has to be analysed from the perspective of both the service provider and recipient, may also need to be considered.

211. The scope of an interest limitation rule determines which freedom applies and there are a number of approaches that the countries involved in this work have discussed in order to avoid any restriction of EU treaty freedoms. In this respect, consideration should also be given to the circumstances in which EU Member States could justify a restriction of EU treaty freedoms, for example:

- the need to preserve the balanced allocation between EU Member States of the power to impose taxes
- the need to prevent tax avoidance and to combat artificial arrangements.

EU directives

212. There are two EU directives with relevance to interest deduction limitation rules within the European Union: the Parent Subsidiary Directive[2] and the Interest and Royalty Directive.[3] The Parent Subsidiary Directive eliminates cross-border withholding taxes on dividend payments made by a subsidiary to a parent company and also eliminates double taxation of such income at the level of the parent company. The directive may be relevant in cases where excessive interest is re-qualified as a dividend. In such cases, the re-qualified interest should be granted the benefits of the Parent Subsidiary Directive.

213. The Interest and Royalty Directive provides that interest and royalty payments arising in an EU Member State shall be exempt from any taxes imposed on those payments in that State, whether by deduction at source or by assessment. Disallowing a deduction for excessive interest could be considered as taxation of interest and, thus, fall within the scope of the directive. However, the Court of Justice of the European Union clarified that the directive only concerns the tax position of the interest creditor.[4] It seems to follow

that the deductibility of interest expenses at the level of the debtor entity may therefore be restricted.

EU State aid

214. EU State aid issues may arise if interest deductibility rules include specific exceptions for particular entities or sectors. The relevant treaty provision considers "any aid granted by a Member State or through State resources in any form whatsoever which distorts or threatens to distort competition by favouring certain undertakings or the production of certain goods shall, in so far as it affects trade between Member States" as being in conflict with the treaty.[5]

215. The European Commission has provided guidance on how it will apply the State aid provisions in relation to direct business taxation.[6] According to this guidance an exception to a specific tax rule without any justification is considered State aid. However, the EU treaty provides EU Member States with options to introduce exceptions to the State aid provisions, for instance categories of State aid may be specified as being deemed compliant with the treaty.[7]

Notes

1. So far the Court of Justice of the European Union has not provided clarity on what significant influence means. In *Beker* (Case C-168/11) the court highlighted that shareholding below 10% does not give a significant influence, and in *Itelcar* (Case C-282/12) and *Kronos* (Case C-47/12) the court pointed out that shareholding above 10% does not necessarily imply that the holder exerts significant influence. In this respect, attention should also be given to other case law referred to in these decisions.

2. Council Directive 2003/123/EC of 22 December 2003 amending Directive 90/435/EEC on the common system of taxation applicable in the case of parent companies and subsidiaries of different Member States [2003] OJ L007/41.

3. Council Directive 2003/49/EC of 3 June 2003 on a common system of taxation applicable to interest and royalty payments made between associated companies of different Member States [2003] OJ L157/49.

4. *Scheuten Solar Technology* (Case C-397/09).

5. Art 107 Treaty on the Functioning of the European Union (TFEU).

6. Commission notice on the application of the State aid rules to measures relating to direct business taxation [1998] OJ C384/3.

7. Art 107(3)(e) TFEU.

Annex I.B

Data on companies affected by a benchmark fixed ratio at different levels

Table I.B.1. **Tabulations for multinational and non-multinational companies, excluding companies with negative EBITDA, 2009-13**

Percentage of companies affected by interest deduction limitation

Percent of EBITDA limit on net interest deductibility	2009		2010		2011		2012		2013	
	Non-MNC	MNC	Non-MNC	MNC	Non-MNC	MNC	Non-MNC	MNC	Non-MNC	MNC
5%	59%	56%	57%	51%	57%	52%	57%	54%	56%	53%
10%	47%	41%	44%	35%	44%	37%	45%	39%	43%	38%
15%	37%	30%	34%	25%	35%	27%	36%	29%	34%	29%
20%	29%	23%	27%	19%	28%	20%	29%	23%	28%	23%
25%	24%	18%	22%	14%	23%	16%	25%	18%	22%	18%
30%	20%	14%	17%	11%	19%	13%	20%	15%	19%	14%
35%	16%	12%	14%	9%	16%	11%	17%	12%	16%	12%
40%	13%	9%	12%	7%	13%	9%	14%	11%	13%	10%
45%	11%	8%	9%	6%	11%	7%	12%	9%	11%	8%
50%	9%	7%	8%	5%	9%	6%	11%	8%	10%	7%
55%	8%	6%	7%	4%	8%	5%	9%	7%	9%	6%
60%	7%	5%	6%	4%	7%	4%	8%	6%	7%	6%
65%	6%	5%	5%	3%	6%	4%	7%	5%	7%	5%
70%	6%	4%	5%	3%	5%	4%	6%	5%	6%	5%
75%	5%	4%	4%	3%	5%	3%	5%	5%	6%	4%
80%	5%	3%	4%	2%	5%	3%	5%	4%	5%	4%
85%	4%	3%	4%	2%	4%	3%	5%	4%	5%	4%
90%	4%	3%	3%	2%	4%	3%	4%	3%	5%	3%
95%	4%	3%	3%	2%	3%	2%	4%	3%	4%	3%
100%	3%	3%	3%	2%	3%	2%	4%	3%	4%	3%
Observations	**6 472**	**10 911**	**6 675**	**11 372**	**6 631**	**11 165**	**6 547**	**11 015**	**6 523**	**10 908**

Source: PwC calculations based on consolidated financial statement information from Standard & Poor's GlobalVantage database.

Table I.B.2. **Tabulations for multinational and non-multinational companies, excluding companies with negative EBITDA, average for 2009-13**

Percentage of companies affected by interest deduction limitation

Percent of EBITDA limit on net interest deductibility	Average 2009-13	
	Non-MNC	MNC
5%	57%	53%
10%	45%	38%
15%	35%	28%
20%	28%	22%
25%	23%	17%
30%	19%	13%
35%	16%	11%
40%	13%	9%
45%	11%	8%
50%	9%	7%
55%	8%	6%
60%	7%	5%
65%	6%	4%
70%	6%	4%
75%	5%	4%
80%	5%	3%
85%	4%	3%
90%	4%	3%
95%	4%	3%
100%	3%	3%

Source: OECD Secretariat calculations based on data in Table I.B.1.

Table I.B.3. **Tabulations for multinational and non-multinational companies, excluding companies with negative EBITDA, average for 2009-13**

Percentage of companies that would in principle be able to deduct an amount equivalent to their net third party interest expense

Percent of EBITDA limit on net interest deductibility	Average 2009-13	
	Non-MNC	MNC
5%	43%	47%
10%	55%	62%
15%	65%	72%
20%	72%	78%
25%	77%	83%
30%	81%	87%
35%	84%	89%
40%	87%	91%
45%	89%	92%
50%	91%	93%
55%	92%	94%
60%	93%	95%
65%	94%	96%
70%	94%	96%
75%	95%	96%
80%	95%	97%
85%	96%	97%
90%	96%	97%
95%	96%	97%
100%	97%	97%

Source: OECD Secretariat calculations based on data in Table I.B.1.

Table I.B.2 includes the companies affected by a particular fixed ratio. Table I.B.3 includes the companies that in principle are not affected. Taken together, numbers from these tables for a particular ratio should add to 100%.

Table I.B.3 assumes that net interest expense is spread around a group in accordance with EBITDA. In practice there may be barriers which prevent a group achieving this.

Table I.B.4. **Tabulations for large cap and small cap multinational companies, excluding companies with negative EBITDA, 2009-13**

Percentage of multinational companies affected by interest deduction limitation

Percent of EBITDA limit on net interest deductibility	2009		2010		2011		2012		2013	
	Small Cap	Large Cap	Small Cap	Large Cap	Small Cap	Large Cap	Small Cap	Large Cap	Small Cap	Large Cap
5%	57%	56%	51%	51%	52%	48%	54%	53%	53%	54%
10%	42%	35%	36%	27%	37%	27%	40%	27%	39%	28%
15%	32%	20%	26%	15%	28%	15%	30%	16%	30%	17%
20%	24%	13%	20%	9%	21%	8%	24%	10%	24%	10%
25%	19%	8%	15%	5%	17%	5%	19%	6%	19%	7%
30%	15%	6%	12%	3%	14%	3%	16%	4%	15%	4%
35%	12%	4%	10%	2%	11%	2%	13%	2%	12%	3%
40%	10%	3%	8%	2%	9%	1%	11%	2%	10%	2%
45%	9%	3%	6%	1%	8%	1%	10%	1%	9%	1%
50%	7%	2%	5%	1%	7%	1%	8%	1%	8%	1%
55%	6%	2%	5%	0%	6%	0%	7%	1%	7%	1%
60%	6%	1%	4%	0%	5%	0%	6%	1%	6%	1%
65%	5%	1%	3%	0%	4%	0%	6%	1%	6%	1%
70%	4%	1%	3%	0%	4%	0%	5%	1%	5%	0%
75%	4%	1%	3%	0%	4%	0%	5%	0%	5%	0%
80%	4%	1%	3%	0%	3%	0%	4%	0%	4%	0%
85%	4%	0%	2%	0%	3%	0%	4%	0%	4%	0%
90%	3%	0%	2%	0%	3%	0%	4%	0%	4%	0%
95%	3%	0%	2%	0%	3%	0%	4%	0%	3%	0%
100%	3%	0%	2%	0%	3%	0%	3%	0%	3%	0%
Observations	**8 745**	**872**	**9 453**	**1 018**	**9 765**	**949**	**9 794**	**1 050**	**9 635**	**1 157**

Source: PwC calculations based on consolidated financial statement information from Standard & Poor's GlobalVantage database.

Annex I.C

The equity escape rule

216. The equity escape rule is currently applied by a number of countries, including Germany and Finland. The description below is based on the rule applied by Germany.

217. Under this approach, the fixed ratio rule does not apply to entities that are part of a group, if the entity can demonstrate that its equity/total assets ratio is equal to (within a tolerance of two percentage points) or higher than the equivalent group ratio. Where an entity's ratio is lower than that of the group, the entity remains subject to the fixed ratio rule. Under this approach, an entity which is leveraged more highly than its group cannot deduct interest expense up to its group's ratio.

218. For these purposes, a group exists if an entity may be consolidated with other entities under IFRS, or the financial or business decisions of the entity may be controlled together with those of other entities. A group also exists where entities are held or controlled by an individual or unincorporated entity.

219. The equity escape test should be based on audited consolidated financial statements of a group prepared in accordance with IFRS. However, audited financial statements drawn up in accordance with the commercial law of an EU Member State or US GAAP may be used if no IFRS financial statements are prepared. The requirement to prepare audited consolidated financial statements applies even where the group comprises entities under the control of an individual or unincorporated entity.

220. Entity financial statements should be prepared under the same accounting rules as the consolidated financial statements. Otherwise, a reconciliation must be prepared of the entity financial statements to the accounting standards used by the group, and this must be reviewed by an accountant. For purposes of determining the entity's equity ratio, all assets and liabilities must be valued using the same method as in the consolidated financial statements.

221. Therefore, an entity's equity figure must also be adjusted for the following items:

- to add goodwill included in the consolidated financial statements to the extent attributable to the business enterprise
- to adjust the valuation of assets and debts (valued at the amounts reported in the consolidated financial statements)
- to deduct equity not carrying voting rights (with the exception of preference shares)
- to deduct equity investments in other group entities.

222. An entity's total assets figure is adjusted for the following items:

- to add goodwill included in the consolidated financial statements to the extent attributable to the business enterprise

- to adjust the valuation of assets and debts (valued at the amounts reported in the consolidated financial statements)
- to deduct equity investments in other group entities
- to deduct financial claims which are not included in the consolidated financial statements but which are matched by liabilities of at least the same amount.

223. Anti-avoidance rules in Germany also require that, in applying the rule, an entity's equity and total assets figures are adjusted to deduct contributions made over the last six months prior to the relevant balance sheet date to the extent these are matched by withdrawals or distributions during the first six months after the relevant balance sheet date.

224. Even where the requirements of the equity escape rule are met, an entity which is part of a group remains subject to the fixed ratio rule unless the entity can demonstrate that interest payments on related-party loans from shareholders outside the group do not exceed 10% of the group's total net interest expense. A loan is a related party loan if it is from (i) a 25% shareholder (including direct and indirect shareholdings), (ii) an entity related to a shareholder, or (iii) any entity where there is recourse to a 25% shareholder.

Annex I.D

Examples to Part I

Example 1 – Thin capitalisation rule based on a fixed debt/equity ratio

225. A simple group structure includes two companies, Parent and Subsidiary. Subsidiary is resident in a country which applies a thin capitalisation rule based on a fixed debt/equity ratio of 1.5/1. In Year 1, Subsidiary has total debt from Parent of USD 750 million and total equity of USD 375 million.[1] On the intragroup debt, Subsidiary pays interest at a rate of 2%, or USD 15 million. As Subsidiary's debt/equity ratio of 2/1 exceeds the benchmark fixed ratio of 1.5/1, Subsidiary will incur an interest disallowance of USD 3.75 million. Subsidiary therefore has total interest deductions of USD 11.25 million.

226. To avoid this disallowance recurring, in Year 2 Subsidiary issues additional equity of USD 125 million to Parent. Subsidiary uses the funds received to make a loan to Parent of USD 125 million. The loan is on a short term basis at an interest rate of 1% and Subsidiary receives interest income of USD 1.25 million. Subsidiary's debt/equity ratio is now in line with the benchmark fixed ratio of 1.5/1 and so Subsidiary does not incur any interest disallowance. Subsidiary now has total net interest deductions of USD 13.75 million.

227. In Year 3, Subsidiary issues a further USD 100 million of equity and USD 150 million of debt to Parent. The new debt is on a medium term and bears interest at 2%. Subsidiary makes a new loan of USD 250 million to Parent on a short term basis at a rate of 1%. Subsidiary's debt/equity ratio is in line with the benchmark fixed ratio and Subsidiary incurs no interest disallowance. Subsidiary now has total net interest deductions of USD 14.25 million.

228. Finally, in Year 4, Subsidiary restructures USD 450 million of its existing debt into a long term subordinated loan with an arm's length interest rate of 5%. Subsidiary's debt/equity ratio is in line with the benchmark fixed ratio and Subsidiary incurs no interest disallowance. Subsidiary now has total net interest deductions of USD 27.75 million.

229. Between Year 1 and Year 4, Subsidiary's net interest deductions have increased from USD 11.25 million to USD 27.75 million, with no increase in underlying economic activity. Between Year 2 and Year 4, Subsidiary was fully compliant with the thin capitalisation rule based on a fixed debt/equity ratio.

230. However, this type of arrangement may contravene the general anti-avoidance rule of a country.

Example 2: Combining the best practice approach with other interest limitation rules

231. As set out in Chapter 1, a country may apply other interest limitation rules alongside those recommended in this report, either to tackle specific base erosion and profit shifting risks, or to achieve other tax policy goals. This is just one example of the way in which a country may apply the best practice approach alongside other rules but this is not the only approach available to countries.

232. In this example, Country X decides that a comprehensive approach to limiting an entity's interest deductions should comprise four parts. The first three of these are aimed at addressing base erosion and profit shifting involving interest. The fourth is included to achieve broader tax policy goals:

1. A fixed ratio rule which limits an entity's net interest deductions to 20% of EBITDA. This rule applies to all entities which are part of a multinational group or a domestic group. In this particular case, Country X does not apply the fixed ratio rule to standalone entities (although as stated in Chapter 3, a country may also choose to apply the fixed ratio rule to all entities, including standalone entities).
2. A group ratio rule, which allows an entity which is subject to the fixed ratio rule to deduct net interest expense up to the net third party interest/EBITDA ratio of its group, where this is higher than 20%.
3. Targeted rules to address specific base erosion and profit shifting risks involving interest. These rules are used to tackle base erosion and profit shifting risks involving interest posed by standalone entities. Some targeted rules are also used to prevent abuse of the general interest limitation rules by entities which are part of a multinational group or a domestic group.
4. An upper limit on the net interest expense of all entities (including all group entities and standalone entities) of 30% of EBITDA. This additional rule is not aimed at tackling base erosion and profit shifting involving interest but is used to reduce the existing tax bias in favour of debt funding over equity.

233. This approach is summarised in Table I.D.1 below.

Table I.D.1. **How the best practice approach may be combined with other interest limitation rules**

	Entities in multinational groups	Entities in domestic groups	Standalone entities
Fixed ratio rule (20% of EBITDA)	✓	✓	-
Group ratio rule	✓	✓	-
Targeted rules to address specific risks	✓	✓	✓
Upper limit on net interest deductions (30% of EBITDA)	✓	✓	✓

234. The application of these rules by Country X to five example companies is set out in Table I.D.2.

Table I.D.2. **Application of the best practice approach and other interest limitation rules**

	A Co USD	B Co USD	C Co USD	D Co USD	E Co USD
EBITDA	100 million	100 million	100 million	100 million	100 million
Net interest expense	(15 million)	(28 million)	(33 million)	(30 million)	(35 million)
Group net third party interest/EBITDA ratio	10%	25%	35%	n/a	n/a

235. A Co is a company in a multinational group. A Co has net interest expense of USD 15 million and EBITDA of USD 100 million. Because A Co has a net interest/ EBITDA ratio of below 20%, it is able to deduct all of its net interest expense. No targeted rules apply.

236. B Co is a company in a multinational group. B Co has net interest expense of USD 28 million and EBITDA of USD 100 million. Because B Co has a net interest/ EBITDA ratio in excess of 20%, the fixed ratio rule would apply to restrict B Co's net interest deductions to USD 20 million. However, because B Co is part of a group which has a net third party interest/EBITDA ratio of 25%, B Co is able to apply the group ratio rule and deduct net interest expense of USD 25 million. USD 3 million of interest expense is disallowed. No targeted rules apply.

237. C Co is a company in a domestic group. C Co has net interest expense of USD 33 million and EBITDA of USD 100 million. Because C Co has a net interest/EBITDA ratio in excess of 20%, the fixed ratio rule would apply to restrict C Co's net interest deductions to USD 20 million. However, C Co is part of a group which has a net third party interest/EBITDA ratio of 35%, and so is able to apply the group ratio rule and deduct more net interest expense. Because the group ratio exceeds the upper limit on net interest deductions, C Co's net interest deductions are limited to 30% of EBITDA. Therefore, C Co can deduct net interest expense of USD 30 million. USD 3 million of interest expense is disallowed. No targeted rules apply.

238. D Co is a standalone entity and is not part of any group. D Co is controlled by an individual who owns 100% of the ordinary shares in the company. D Co has net interest expense of USD 30 million and EBITDA of USD 100 million. This net interest expense includes USD 5 million paid on an arrangement giving rise to base erosion and profit shifting (such as an "artificial loan" where no new funding is raised by D Co). Because D Co is a standalone entity, it is not subject to the fixed ratio rule. Instead, D Co is subject to targeted rules which deal with the specific base erosion and profit shifting risks posed by standalone entities and to the upper limit on net interest deductions of 30% of EBITDA. Therefore, D Co is able to deduct USD 25 million of its net interest expense. USD 5 million is disallowed.

239. E Co is a standalone entity and is not part of any group. E Co has net third party interest expense of USD 35 million and EBITDA of USD 100 million. Because E Co is a standalone entity, it is not subject to the fixed ratio rule. However, it is subject to targeted rules to address specific base erosion and profit shifting risks (although none of those apply in this situation) and is also subject to the upper limit on net interest deductions of 30% of EBITDA. Therefore, E Co is able to deduct USD 30 million of its net interest expense. USD 5 million of interest expense is disallowed.

240. In introducing any interest limitation rules, or combination of rules, a country may need to take into account other legal or constitutional obligations. For example, countries which are EU Member States should consider the requirements of EU law.

Example 3: Interest and payments economically equivalent to interest

241. In 2015, A Co and its subsidiary B Co enter into the following arrangements:

1. A Co issues USD 50 million of bonds carrying a fixed interest rate of 5%.
2. A Co enters into an interest rate swap with a third party bank (Bank), under which A Co receives fixed rate payments and pays floating rate payments on a notional principal of USD 50 million.
3. B Co borrows USD 10 million from Bank at a floating interest rate.
4. B Co's borrowing from Bank is covered by a guarantee from A Co. In return, B Co pays a guarantee fee to A Co.
5. B Co also obtains a short term credit facility with Bank whereby it can borrow up to USD 500 000 for small periods at short notice. B Co pays an arrangement fee for this facility.
6. B Co enters into a finance lease for new plant and machinery for use in its business, payments under which include an interest element.
7. A Co enters into an operating lease for new office equipment.
8. B Co enters into a contract to provide 10 million widgets per year to Customer for the next three years. This contract is covered by a performance guarantee from A Co, in return for which B Co pays a guarantee fee to A Co.
9. B Co buys a series of aluminium futures contracts to protect itself against movements in the price of aluminium, a key ingredient in the manufacture of widgets.
10. A Co declares and pays a dividend of USD 1 million to holders of its ordinary shares.

242. The amounts payable by A Co and B Co under 1, 2, 3, 4, 5 and 6 are all interest on a debt, payments economically equivalent to interest, or expenses incurred in connection with the raising of finance. These payments are therefore subject to the fixed ratio rule and the group ratio rule. The amounts payable under 7, 8, 9 and 10 do not fall within these categories (based on this specific fact pattern) and are not subject to these rules.

Example 4: Fixed ratio rule (benchmark net interest/EBITDA ratio of 15%)

Table I.D.3. **Operation of the fixed ratio rule**

	Single entity taxation			Group taxation
	A1 Co USD	A2 Co USD	Total USD	A1 Co + A2 Co USD
Taxable income/(losses) before applying the fixed ratio rule	70m	10m	80m	80m
+ net interest expense	+ 10m	+ 50m	+ 60m	+ 60m
+ depreciation and amortisation	+ 20m	+ 40m	+ 60m	+ 60m
= tax EBITDA	= 100m	= 100m	= 200m	= 200m
x benchmark fixed ratio	x 15%	x 15%	-	x 15%
= maximum allowable deduction	= 15m	= 15m	-	= 30m
Disallowed interest expense	0	35m	35m	30m

243. In Table I.D.3, A1 Co and A2 Co incur a total disallowance of USD 30 million where the fixed ratio rule is applied at the level of the local group (e.g. under a group taxation regime). However, where they are taxed separately under a separate entity taxation regime, they incur a total disallowance of USD 35 million (which arises in A2 Co). This is because A1 Co is not fully utilising its capacity to absorb interest deductions and it is assumed that there are no rules in place to permit the surrender of interest capacity from A1Co to A2Co. The example illustrates the potential advantage of applying the rule at the level of the local group (although this may also be achieved if rules did allow the surrender of interest capacity within the group). However, depending on the individual situation of each group member the application of the rule at the group level may also be disadvantageous as shown in Table I.D.4.

Table I.D.4. **Impact of losses on the operation of the fixed ratio rule**

	Single entity taxation			Group taxation
	A3 Co USD	A4 Co USD	Total USD	A3 Co + A4 Co USD
Taxable income/(losses) before applying the fixed ratio rule	100m	(150m)	(50m)	(50m)
+ net interest expense	+ 20m	+ 20m	+ 40m	+ 40m
+ depreciation and amortisation	+ 30m	+ 30m	+ 60m	+ 60m
= tax EBITDA	= 150m	= (100m)	= 50m	= 50m
x benchmark fixed ratio	x 15%	x 15%	-	x 15%
= maximum allowable deduction	= 22.5m	= 0	-	= 7.5m
Disallowed interest expense	0	20m	20m	32.5m

244. Where one of the group entities is in a loss-making position and the fixed ratio rule is applied at the level of the local group, the total disallowance incurred is greater than if the rule would be applied at the level of each single entity. In Table I.D.4, A3 Co and A4 Co incur a total disallowance of USD 32.5 million where they are taxed under a group taxation regime. However, where they are taxed separately under a separate entity taxation regime, they incur a total disallowance of USD 20 million (which arises in A4 Co). This is because the loss in A4 Co partially reduces A3 Co's capacity to absorb interest deductions.

Example 5: Applying factors to set a benchmark fixed ratio within the corridor

245. As set out in Chapter 6, it is recommended that a country uses the factors in that chapter, along with other relevant factors, to set its benchmark fixed ratio within the recommended corridor of 10% to 30%. This example illustrates some possible ways in which this might be done, based on three countries which intend to introduce a fixed ratio rule: Country A, Country B and Country C. This is not meant to be an exhaustive list of possible approaches.

246. Country A considers each of the factors in Chapter 6:

1. It intends to introduce the fixed ratio rule alongside a group ratio rule.
2. It intends to allow entities to carry back disallowed interest expense for a period of three years.
3. It has no other tax rules which address the risks to be addressed by Action 4.
4. It does not have a high interest rate compared with other countries.
5. There is no legal or constitutional requirement for the same treatment to be applied to different types of entity.
6. It does not intend to apply different fixed ratios depending on the size of an entity's group.

247. In addition, Country A conducts its own analysis and concludes that groups operating in the country typically have low net third party interest/EBITDA ratios. Country A also wishes to apply a strict approach to tackle base erosion and profit shifting involving interest.

248. Country A determines that factors 1 to 5, as well as the additional factors, suggest a lower benchmark fixed ratio, while no factors suggest a higher ratio. Therefore, it concludes that it should set its benchmark fixed ratio towards the lower end of the corridor, within the illustrative range included in Figure I.D.1.

249. Country B considers each of the factors in Chapter 6:

1. It intends to introduce the fixed ratio alongside a group ratio rule.
2. It intends to allow entities to carry forward unused interest capacity without limitation.
3. It has other tax rules which specifically tackle a number of the risks to be addressed by Action 4 but not all of these risks.
4. It has a slightly high interest rate compared with other countries.
5. There is a legal requirement to apply the same fixed ratio to entities in multinational groups, entities in domestic groups and standalone entities.
6. It intends to apply one benchmark fixed ratio to entities in large groups, and a different benchmark fixed ratio to other entities.

250. Country B does not take into account any other factors in addition to the above.

251. Country B determines that two factors (1 and 2) suggest a lower benchmark fixed ratio, while three factors (3 to 5) suggest a higher benchmark fixed ratio. Country B also decides to apply a lower weighting to factors 3 and 4 because (i) although some of the base erosion and profit shifting risks to be addressed by Action 4 are dealt with by other tax rules, some of these risks remain, and (ii) although it has a slightly higher interest rate compared with other countries, this is not significantly higher.

252. Therefore, Country B concludes that it should not set its benchmark fixed ratio for most entities towards the top of the corridor, but rather within the illustrative range indicated in Figure I.D.1. In addition, recognising that large groups tend to have a lower net third party interest/EBITDA ratio than other groups, Country B decides to apply a lower ratio to entities in large groups.

253. Country C considers each of the factors in Chapter 6:

1. It intends to introduce the fixed ratio in isolation, without a group ratio rule.
2. It does not intend to allow entities to carry forward unused interest capacity or carry back disallowed interest expense.
3. It has other tax rules that tackle all of the issues to be addressed under Action 4.
4. It has a high interest rate compared with those of other countries.
5. There is a constitutional requirement to apply the same fixed ratio to entities in multinational groups, entities in domestic groups and standalone entities.
6. It does not intend to apply different fixed ratios depending on the size of an entity's group.

254. In addition, Country C applies a macro-economic policy to encourage third party lending not related to base erosion and profit shifting, to increase investment.

Figure I.D.1. **Applying factors to set a benchmark fixed ratio within the corridor**

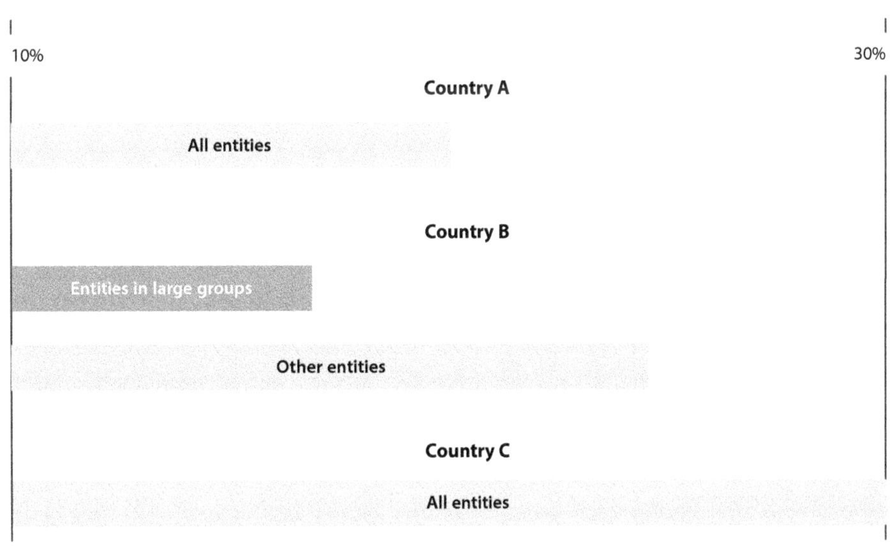

255. Country C determines that factors 1 to 5, as well as the additional factor, suggest a higher benchmark fixed ratio while no factors suggest a lower ratio. Therefore, it concludes that it may set its benchmark fixed ratio at any place in the corridor, from 10% to 30%.

Example 6: Operation of a group ratio rule based on a net third party interest/ EBITDA ratio

256. Examples 6a to 6c below illustrate how, in a simple case, a group ratio rule based on a net third party interest/EBITDA ratio could enable an entity which exceeds the benchmark fixed ratio to deduct more interest up to its group's net third party interest/EBITDA ratio.

257. In these examples, A Co is an entity resident in Country A. Country A applies a fixed ratio rule as described in Chapter 6, with a benchmark fixed ratio of 20%. A Co is part of a multinational group (Group). The net interest expense and EBITDA of A Co and Group are set out in Table I.D.5.

Table I.D.5. **Operation of a group ratio rule based on a net third party interest/EBITDA ratio**

	Net interest expense USD	EBITDA USD
A Co	(10 million)	30 million
Group	(100 million)	400 million

Example 6a – Country A applies a fixed ratio rule in isolation

258. In this example, Country A applies a fixed ratio rule with a benchmark fixed ratio of 20%. Country A does not apply a group ratio rule.

259. A Co's interest capacity is calculated by applying the benchmark fixed ratio of 20% to its EBITDA of USD 30 million. A Co therefore has interest capacity of USD 6 million. Out of its total net interest expense of USD 10 million, USD 6 million may be deducted and USD 4 million is disallowed.

Example 6b – Country A applies a fixed ratio rule alongside a group ratio rule

260. In this example, Country A applies a fixed ratio rule with a benchmark ratio of 20%, and also a group ratio rule based on a net third party interest/EBITDA ratio. Under the group ratio rule, Country A does not apply any uplift to a group's net third party interest expense.

261. Under the fixed ratio rule, A Co's interest capacity is calculated by applying the benchmark fixed ratio of 20% to its EBITDA of USD 30 million. A Co therefore has interest capacity under the fixed ratio rule of USD 6 million.

262. Under the group ratio rule, A Co first calculates its group's net third party interest/ EBITDA ratio, based on the group's net third party interest expense of USD 100 million and group EBITDA of USD 400 million. The group's ratio is therefore 25%. A Co applies the group ratio to its EBITDA of USD 30 million. A Co therefore has interest capacity under the fixed ratio rule of USD 7.5 million.

263. A Co's interest capacity is greater under the group ratio rule and so this rule applies. Out of A Co's total net interest expense of USD 10 million, USD 7.5 million may be deducted and USD 2.5 million is disallowed.

Example 6c – Country A applies a fixed ratio rule alongside a group ratio rule, with a 10% uplift to net third party interest expense

264. In this example, Country A applies a fixed ratio rule with a benchmark ratio of 20%, and also a group ratio rule based on a net third party interest/EBITDA ratio. Under the group ratio rule, Country A applies a 10% uplift to a group's net third party interest expense.

265. Under the fixed ratio rule, A Co's interest capacity is calculated by applying the benchmark fixed ratio of 20% to its EBITDA of USD 30 million. A Co therefore has interest capacity under the fixed ratio rule of USD 6 million.

266. Under the group ratio rule, A Co first calculates its group's net third party interest/ EBITDA ratio. This is based on the group's adjusted net third party interest expense of USD 110 million (after applying an uplift of 10% to the group's actual net third party interest expense of USD 100 million) and group EBITDA of USD 400 million. The group's ratio is therefore 27.5%. A Co applies the group ratio to its EBITDA of USD 30 million. A Co therefore has interest capacity under the fixed ratio rule of USD 8.25 million.

267. A Co's interest capacity is greater under the group ratio rule and so this rule applies. Out of A Co's total net interest expense of USD 10 million, USD 8.25 million may be deducted and USD 1.75 million is disallowed.

Example 7: Definition of a group under a group ratio rule

268. Examples 7a to 7e below show how a group is determined for the purposes of applying a group ratio rule, based on different fact patterns.

Example 7a – Companies held by an individual

269. In Figure I.D.2, an individual owns the majority of the share capital in two companies, A Co and B Co, each of which has a number of subsidiaries. A Co and B Co are the top level company in their respective holding structures (i.e. no company exercises control over them). An individual cannot be the parent of a group. Therefore, for the purposes of applying the group ratio rule, two groups exist. Group A includes A Co and all entities included in A Co's consolidated financial statements, while Group B includes B Co and all entities included in B Co's consolidated financial statements.

270. In applying a group ratio rule, it is also necessary to identify which individuals and entities are related to a group, as this may be relevant in the calculation of the group's net third party interest expense. In this example, Group A is related to the individual, as well as to the entities in Group B. Similarly, Group B is related to the individual and to the entities in Group A.

Example 7b – Companies held by a limited partnership

271. Non-corporate vehicles such as limited partnerships cannot be the parent of a group for the purposes of a group ratio rule. A corporate group held under such a structure may be treated as a group, but this group will not include the limited partnership, any funds set up by the limited partnership to hold investments, or other corporate groups held under the structure. This is illustrated in Figure I.D.3, where Group A, Group B and Group C are treated as separate groups when applying a group ratio rule. However, the limited partnership, the sub-funds and Treasury Company would not form part of any group for these purposes.

Figure I.D.2. **Companies held by an individual**

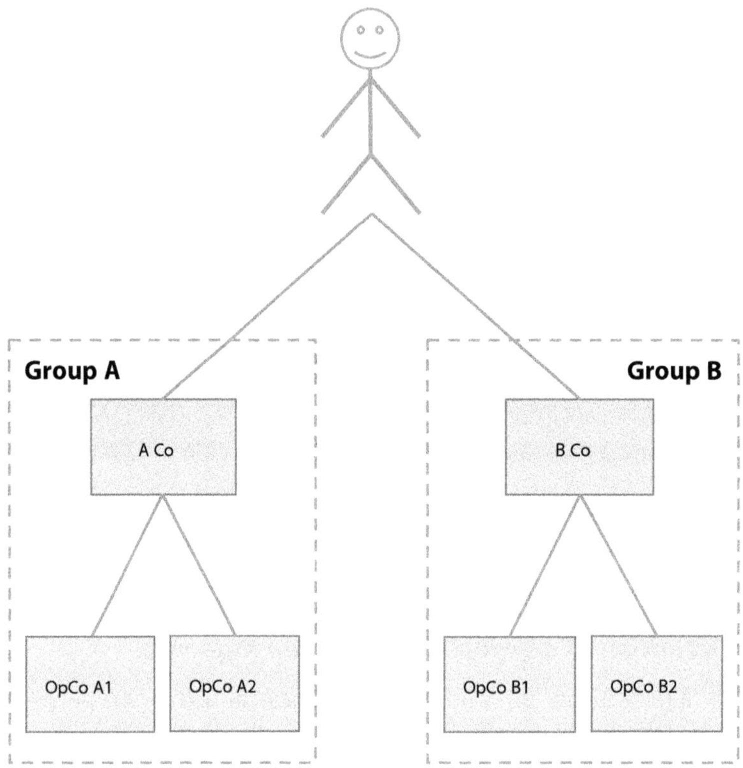

Figure I.D.3. **Companies held by a limited partnership**

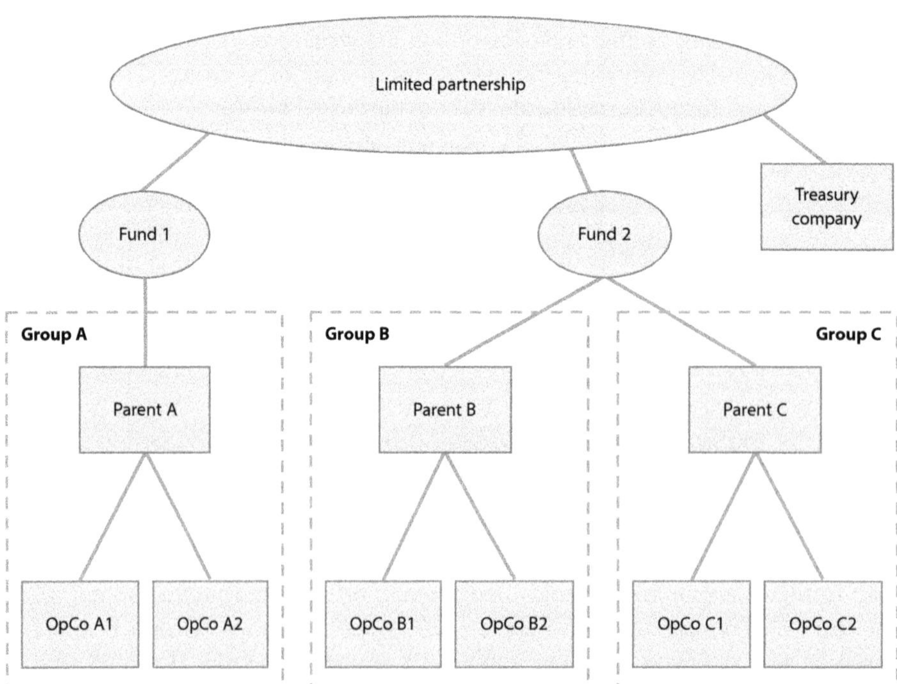

272. Although the limited partnership, the sub-funds and Treasury Company are not part of a group for group ratio rule purposes, they would be treated as related to each of Group A, Group B and Group C. Similarly, entities in each of the three groups would be treated as related to each other (so entities in Group A are related to entities in Group B and Group C, and so on).

Example 7c – Joint venture entity controlled by an investing group

273. Where a joint venture entity is controlled by one of the joint venture partners, the joint venture entity will typically be included in the consolidated financial statements of the controlling group. It will therefore form part of this group for the purposes of applying a group ratio rule. This is shown in Figure I.D.4, where JV Partner A holds a 55% stake in JV Co. In this case, JV Co and its subsidiaries will be part of Group A for the purposes of applying a group ratio rule.

Figure I.D.4. **Joint venture entity controlled by an investing group**

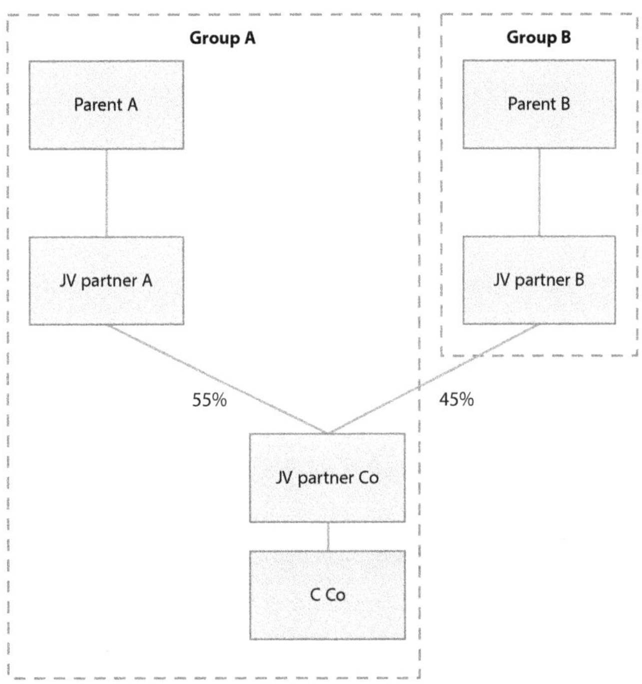

274. JV Partner B and JV Co are not part of the same group. However, JV Partner B holds an investment of greater than 25% in JV Co and so the two entities are related parties (as per the definition of related party in Chapter 9).

Example 7d – Joint venture entity which is not controlled by any investing group

275. Where no investor has overall control of a joint venture entity, each investing group will generally include the joint venture in its consolidated financial statements using equity accounting. The joint venture entity is not consolidated into either investing group and will not form part of these groups for the purposes of a group ratio rule. This is shown in Figure I.D.5, where JV Partner A and JV Partner B each hold 50% stakes in JV Co,

and no other arrangements exist which give control to one of the investors. JV Co and its subsidiary will not be part of either Group A or Group B. Instead, JV Co and its subsidiary will form a separate group (Group C). However, JV Co will be related to both JV Partner A and JV Partner B.

Figure I.D.5. **Joint venture entity which is not controlled by any investing group**

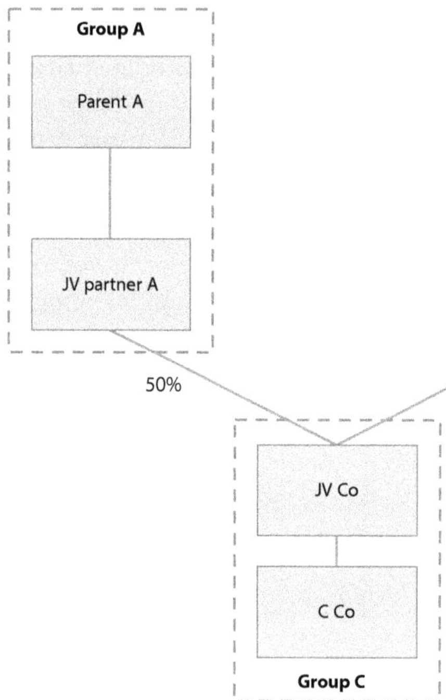

Example 7e – Holding structure headed by an investment entity

276. In Figure I.D.6, Parent A is a company which is an investment entity, and which directly controls three companies. Parent A is the top level company in the structure.

277. Subsidiary A provides services connected with Parent A's investment activities, and is consolidated into Parent A's consolidated financial statements.

278. Parent B and Parent C are held by Parent A for the purposes of capital appreciation and investment income. As such, they are recognised in Parent A's consolidated financial statements as investments and carried at fair value.

279. Parent A and Subsidiary A form a group (Group A) for the purposes of applying the group ratio rule. Parent B and Parent C are not members of Group A. Instead, each of these companies forms a separate group with their respective subsidiaries (Group B and Group C).

Figure I.D.6. **Holding structure headed by an investment entity**

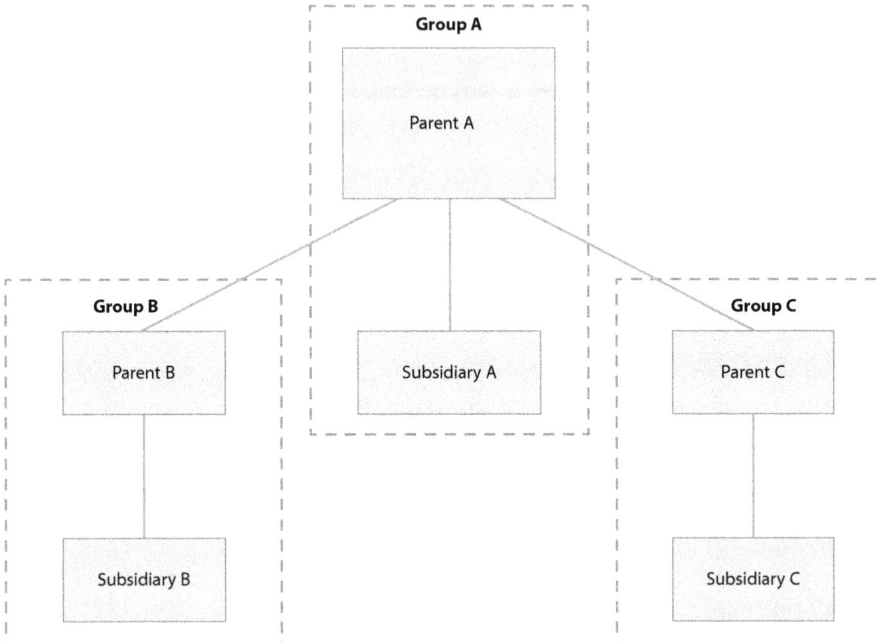

Example 8: Applying a group's ratio to an entity's tax EBITDA or accounting EBITDA

280. As set out in Chapter 7, when applying a group ratio rule an entity's EBITDA may be calculated using tax or accounting principles. Each of these approaches has advantages and disadvantages, which are considered in Examples 8a-8c below, based on the following scenario.

Table I.D.6. **Applying a group's ratio to an entity's tax EBITDA or accounting EBITDA**

	Financial reporting		Tax	
	Net interest expense USD	EBITDA USD	Net interest expense USD	EBITDA USD
Group	(100 million)	1 billion	n/a	n/a
A Co	(20 million)	100 million	(18 million)	80 million

Group net third party interest/EBITDA ratio = (USD 100 million / USD 1 billion) x 100 = 10%

Example 8a – Determining EBITDA using tax principles

281. In this example, A Co's interest capacity is calculated by applying the group's net third party interest/EBITDA ratio of 10%, to A Co's tax EBITDA of USD 80 million. This limit can be applied directly to A Co's net interest expense for tax purposes. Out of A Co's total net interest expense of USD 18 million, USD 8 million is tax deductible and USD 10 million is disallowed.

282. The calculation of EBITDA using tax principles is consistent with that recommended under the fixed ratio rule. It is also straightforward for groups to apply and tax authorities

to audit, and as an approach to tackle base erosion and profit shifting it has the benefit that an entity's interest deductions are linked to its level of taxable income. This means that where an entity's taxable income is higher than its accounting income, its ability to deduct interest expense will be correspondingly greater. Similarly, if an entity undertakes planning to reduce its taxable income, it will be able to deduct less net interest expense.

Example 8b – Determining EBITDA using accounting principles

283. In this example, A Co's interest capacity is calculated by applying the group's net third party interest/EBITDA ratio of 10%, to A Co's accounting EBITDA of USD 100 million. This limit can be applied directly to A Co's net interest expense for tax purposes. Out of A Co's total net interest expense of USD 18 million, USD 10 million is tax deductible and USD 8 million is disallowed.

284. Under this approach interest capacity is calculated using only accounting information. This is straightforward for groups to apply and tax authorities to audit. However, a possible concern remains if there is a significant difference between the calculation of net interest expense under tax and accounting rules. For example, an entity could incur a significant interest disallowance if the definition of interest it applies for tax purposes is wider than that for accounting purposes (because interest capacity has been calculated using the narrower accounting definition).

Example 8c – Adjusting an accounts-based limit on deductions for differences in tax and accounting definitions of interest

285. This example illustrates an approach to reduce the impact of differences between an entity's net interest expense for tax purposes and for accounting purposes. Under this approach, the accounts-based limit on interest deductions calculated in Example 8b is compared with the entities net interest expense for accounting purposes, to determine what percentage falls within the limit. Where this figure is 100% (i.e. all of the entity's accounting net interest expense is within the limit), then all of the entity's net interest expense for tax purposes is deductible, with no disallowance. Where the percentage is less than 100%, the corresponding percentage of the entity's net interest expense for tax purposes is deductible, with the remainder disallowed (i.e. if 90% of the entity's accounting net interest expense falls within the limit, 90% of the entity's tax net interest expense would be deductible).

286. Applying this approach to A Co, the group's net third party interest/EBITDA ratio of 10% is applied to A Co's accounting EBITDA of USD 100 million to produce an accounts-based limit on net interest expense of USD 10 million. This limit is compared with A Co's net interest expense for accounting purpose of USD 20 million, 50% of which falls within the limit. This percentage is then applied to A Co's net interest expense for tax purposes. Therefore, out of A Co's total net interest expense for tax purposes of USD 18 million, USD 9 million is deductible and USD 9 million is disallowed.

287. Compared with the accounts-based approach in Example 8b, this would mean, for example, where an entity's net interest expense for tax purposes exceeds that for accounting purposes, it would receive a correspondingly higher interest capacity. Alternatively, where an entity's net interest expense for tax purposes is lower than that for accounting purposes, its interest capacity would be reduced. In effect, the accounts-based limit on deductions is flexed to take into account differences between net interest expense for tax and accounting purposes.

Example 9: Dealing with loss-making entities within a group

Example 9a – The impact of losses on the operation of a group ratio rule

Table I.D.7. **The impact of losses on the operation of a group ratio rule**

	A Co USD	B Co USD	C Co USD	Group USD
EBITDA	100 million	10 million	(100 million)	10 million
Net interest	(20 million)	(2 million)	10 million	(12 million)
Group net third party interest/ EBITDA ratio	-	-	-	120%
Interest capacity	120 million	12 million	0	-
Deductible interest expense	(20 million)	(2 million)	0	-
Disallowed interest expense	-	-	-	-
Unused interest capacity	100 million	10 million	-	-

288. In Table I.D.7, A Co has EBITDA of USD 100 million and net interest expense of USD 20 million. B Co has EBITDA of USD 10 million and net interest expense of USD 2 million. However, C Co has a negative EBITDA (i.e. losses) of USD 100 million and receives net interest income of USD 10 million. Therefore, looking at the group as a whole, the group has total EBITDA of USD 10 million and a net interest expense of USD 12 million. The group's net third party interest/EBITDA ratio is 120%.

289. This very high group ratio causes two problems. Firstly, in the current year A Co receives interest capacity of USD 120 million, which is higher than the group's actual net third party interest expense. This means that in principle the company could deduct more net interest than the total net third party interest expense of the group. Secondly, even after deducting their current year net interest expense, A Co and B Co still have a high level of unused interest capacity. If a rule allows the carry forward of unused interest capacity, this could be carried into future periods and used to shelter further interest deductions.

290. In a sense, this issue arises because C Co (which has a negative EBITDA of USD 100 million) is not required to recognise negative interest capacity of USD 120 million. If this was the case, then the interest capacity of the group as a whole would equal the group's net third party interest expense of USD 12 million. However, the recognition of negative interest capacity in loss-making entities is not recommended as part of the best practice approach.

Example 9b – Applying an upper limit on interest capacity

291. In Table I.D.8, the group is in the same position as in Example 9a. However, the interest capacity of A Co is now subject to limitation equal to the group's actual net third party interest expense. Therefore, A Co's interest capacity is limited to USD 12 million (i.e. the group's total net third party interest expense). A Co is able to deduct net interest expense of USD 12 million, and may carry forward disallowed interest expense of USD 8 million into future periods, if this is permitted under a rule.

Table I.D.8. **Applying an upper limit on interest capacity**

	A Co USD	B Co USD	C Co USD	Group USD
EBITDA	100 million	10 million	(100 million)	10 million
Net interest	(20 million)	(2 million)	10 million	(12 million)
Group net third party interest/ EBITDA ratio	-	-	-	120%
Interest capacity	12 million	12 million	0	-
Deductible interest expense	(12 million)	(2 million)	0	-
Disallowed interest expense	(8 million)	-	-	-
Unused interest capacity	-	10 million	-	-

292. As before, B Co receives interest capacity of USD 12 million and is able to deduct its full net interest expense of USD 2 million. It is also able to carry forward unused interest capacity of USD 10 million, if this is permitted by a country's rule. As discussed in in Chapter 8, it is suggested that countries consider limiting the scope of any carry forward, and in particular those of unused interest capacity, by time and/or value.

293. Note that if the group's EBITDA had not been reduced by losses in C Co, the group's net third party interest/EBITDA ratio would have been approximately 10.9% (i.e. USD 12 million/ USD 110 million). In this case, A Co would have been able to deduct approximately USD 10.9 million of net interest expense. Therefore, the upper limit on interest capacity has not restricted net interest deductions in A Co to below the level that would have been permitted had the losses in C Co not arisen.

Example 9c – Groups with negative group EBITDA

Table I.D.9. **Groups with negative group EBITDA**

	A Co USD	B Co USD	C Co USD	Group USD
EBITDA	100 million	10 million	(120 million)	(10 million)
Net interest	(20 million)	(2 million)	10 million	(12 million)
Group net third party interest/ EBITDA ratio	-	-	-	n/a
Interest capacity	12 million	2 million	0	-
Deductible interest expense	(12 million)	(2 million)	0	-
Disallowed interest expense	(8 million)	-	-	-
Unused interest capacity	-	-	-	-

294. In Table I.D.9, Co has losses of USD 120 million. The group has an overall loss (negative group EBITDA) of USD 10 million, which means it is not possible to calculate a meaningful group ratio. A Co and B Co therefore receive interest capacity equal to the lower of their net interest expense and the group's net third party interest expense.

295. A Co has net interest expense of USD 20 million, which exceeds the group's net third party interest expense of USD 12 million. A Co's interest capacity is therefore USD 12 million. A Co is able to deduct net interest expense of USD 12 million, and may carry forward disallowed interest expense of USD 8 million into future periods, if this is permitted.

296. B Co has net interest expense of USD 2 million, which is lower than the group's net third party interest expense of USD 12 million. B Co's interest capacity is therefore USD 2 million. B Co may deduct its entire interest expense of USD 2 million. There is no unused interest capacity.

Example 9d – Excluding loss-making entities from the calculation of group EBITDA for a profitable group

Table I.D.10. **Excluding loss-making entities from the calculation of group EBITDA for a profitable group**

	A Co USD	B Co USD	C Co USD	Group USD
EBITDA	100 million	10 million	(100 million)	110 million
Net interest	(20 million)	(2 million)	10 million	(12 million)
Group net third party interest/ EBITDA ratio	-	-	-	10.9%
Interest capacity	10.9 million	1.1 million	0	-
Deductible interest expense	(10.9 million)	(1.1 million)	0	-
Disallowed interest expense	(9.1 million)	(0.9 million)	-	-
Unused interest capacity	-	-	-	-

297. This example is based on the same fact pattern as Example 9a. In this case, the negative EBITDA in C Co has been disregarded in calculating the group's EBITDA. Therefore, the group now has EBITDA of USD 110 million, rather than USD 10 million. This means that the group's interest/EBITDA ratio is now reduced to 10.9%.

298. The effect of this is that A Co has interest capacity of USD 10.9 million and B Co has interest capacity of USD 1.1 million. These total USD 12 million, which is equal to the group's net third party interest expense. By disregarding C Co's losses, the group ratio rule now operates to ensure that the group is able to deduct an amount equal to its actual net third party interest expense. However, it may be very difficult for the tax authorities in the countries of A Co and B Co to accurately establish the existence and value of the negative EBITDA in C Co. Therefore, it may not be feasible for a country to apply this approach in practice.

Example 9e – Excluding loss-making entities from the calculation of group EBITDA for a loss-making group

299. This example is based on the same fact pattern as in Example 9c. However, in this case the negative EBITDA in C Co is disregarded in calculating the group's EBITDA. Therefore, rather than being unable to calculate a meaningful group net third party interest/ EBITDA ratio, the group now has a net third party interest/EBITDA ratio of 10.9%.

Table I.D.11. **Excluding loss-making entities from the calculation of group EBITDA for a loss-making group**

	A Co USD	B Co USD	C Co USD	Group USD
EBITDA	100 million	10 million	(120 million)	110 million
Net interest	(20 million)	(2 million)	10 million	(12 million)
Group net third party interest/ EBITDA ratio	-	-	-	10.9%
Interest capacity	10.9 million	1.1 million	0	-
Deductible interest expense	(10.9 million)	(1.1 million)	0	-
Disallowed interest expense	(9.1 million)	(0.9 million)	-	-
Unused interest capacity	-	-	-	-

300. A Co now has interest capacity of USD 10.9 million and B Co has interest capacity of USD 1.1 million. In total, these come to USD 12 million, which is equal to the group's net third party interest expense. By disregarding C Co's losses, the group is able to deduct an amount equal to its actual net third party interest expense. However, in practice it may be very difficult for the tax authorities in the countries of A Co and B Co to accurately establish the existence and value of the negative EBITDA in C Co.

Example 10: Fixed ratio rule using EBITDA based on a three year average

301. Table I.D.12 illustrates how the negative impact of a temporary fall in profits under a fixed ratio rule may be mitigated through the use of a three year moving average of the EBITDA of an entity.

Table I.D.12. **Fixed ratio rule using EBITDA based on a three year average**

	Year (current tax year = t)					
	t-2 USD	**t-1 USD**	**t USD**	**t+1 USD**	**t+2 USD**	**t+3 USD**
	Using current year tax EBITDA					
Taxable income before applying the fixed ratio rule	380m	350m	100m	300m	320m	300m
+ net interest expense	+ 100m	+ 100m	+ 100m	+ 100m	+ 100m	+ 100m
+ depreciation and amortisation	+ 50m	+ 50m	+ 50m	+ 50m	+ 50m	+ 50m
= tax EBITDA	= 530m	= 500m	= 250m	= 450m	= 470m	= 450m
x benchmark fixed ratio	x 30%	x 30%	x 30%	x 30%	x 30%	x 30%
= maximum allowable deduction	= 159m	= 150m	= 75m	= 135m	= 141m	= 135m
Disallowed interest expense	0	0	25m	0	0	0
	Using three year average tax EBITDA					
Average tax EBITDA of current year + 2 previous years			427m	400m	390m	457m
x benchmark fixed ratio			x 30%	x 30%	x 30%	x 30%
= maximum allowable deduction			= 128m	= 120m	= 117m	= 137m
Disallowed interest expense	0	0	0	0	0	0

302. In the upper part of the table the excessive interest is calculated by using the current year tax EBITDA. In year t the entity suffers a temporary fall in profits and as a result USD 25 million of interest expense is non-deductible. The entity may be able to carry forward this disallowed interest expense for use in future periods, if this is permitted. The lower part of the table illustrates the effect of using the moving average tax EBITDA of the last three years to calculate the maximum allowable interest deduction. As a result of using the three year average the temporary fall in profits is spread over a three year period. The impact of this is that the entity is able to deduct all of its interest expense in year t, and has a lower maximum allowable deduction in years t+1 and t+2 compared to the base case.

Note

1. All monetary amounts in this annex are denominated in United States dollars (USD). These are illustrative examples only, and are not intended to reflect real cases or the position in a particular country.

Part II

Elements of the design and operation of the group ratio rule

Part II contains the outcomes of further work on specific elements of the group ratio rule, conducted following the release of the 2015 Report and completed in 2016. This does not change anything recommended in Part I, but includes additional detail to assist countries in implementing the rule. Part II focuses on three topics:

- the calculation of net third party interest expense
- the calculation of group EBITDA
- approaches to deal with the impact of entities with negative EBITDA on the operation of the rule.

Introduction and overview to Part II

Introduction

303. Part I of this report includes a common approach to tackling BEPS involving interest and payments economically equivalent to interest. At the heart of the common approach is a fixed ratio rule which restricts an entity's net interest deductions to a fixed percentage of its earnings before interest, taxes, depreciation and amortisation (EBITDA) calculated using tax principles.

304. Part I recommends that countries consider introducing a group ratio rule which would allow an entity in a highly leveraged group to deduct net interest expense in excess of the amount permitted under the fixed ratio rule, based on a relevant financial ratio of its worldwide group. Such a group ratio rule should never operate to impose a stricter limit than the fixed ratio rule. Chapter 7 contains a description of such a group ratio rule which permits an entity to deduct net interest expense up to the net third party interest expense/EBITDA ratio of its group where this is higher than the benchmark fixed ratio under the fixed ratio rule. A country may require the rule to be applied to each entity separately, or a country may apply the rule to the overall position of all group entities in the country or those entities that are part of a tax group in that country (i.e. the local group). Chapter 7 also highlights that further work would be conducted, to be completed in 2016, on key elements of the design and operation of the group ratio rule described in that chapter.

305. Part II of this report contains the outcomes of this further work, which focused on approaches:

- to calculate a group's net third party interest expense
- to calculate group EBITDA
- to address the impact of entities with negative EBITDA on the operation of the rule.

306. If a country introduces a group ratio rule, the tax authority in that country is responsible for administering the rule in accordance with its country's tax rules, including auditing the application of the rule by entities in the country. Where the tax authority reaches a conclusion as to the outcome of the rule in that country for a particular entity, this should not in any way impact the operation of group ratio rules in other countries where entities in the same group are located.

307. Part II considers specific elements of the design and operation of the group ratio rule described in Chapter 7. It does not change anything specifically recommended in Part I and does not deal with any other elements of the common approach. As specified in Chapter 11, the design and content of the common approach will be reviewed by countries involved in the BEPS Project by no later than the end of 2020, which will include consideration of the experience of countries, the impact on the behaviour of groups and any additional available data.

Overview

308. A group's net third party interest expense is the numerator in calculating the group ratio and sets a theoretical limit on a group's total net interest deductions under the group ratio rule. As described in Chapter 7, a group's net third party interest expense should be based on figures taken from its consolidated financial statements. However, there are likely to be differences between the items treated as interest in a group's financial statements and those subject to limitation under the common approach. While using interest income and expense figures from a group's accounts without adjustment may be straightforward, this could result in an entity having an excessive interest restriction or excessive interest capacity. It could also result in different outcomes for comparable groups depending on the accounting standards and policies applied. Therefore, the preferred approach is for groups to calculate net third party expense using the definition of interest and payments economically equivalent to interest in Chapter 2. Countries may require this to be done by making adjustments to the interest figures in a group's accounts or by producing a separate computation. However, as the outcome under each approach should be the same, a country should consider allowing an entity to use either approach when preparing this calculation.

309. There are benefits from a group ratio rule that is applied consistently between countries, in terms of providing protection against BEPS and reducing compliance costs. However, there are also scenarios where a country may take into account specific domestic tax policy goals, so long as this does not reduce the effectiveness of the rule in tackling BEPS. In this case a country should weigh these goals against the benefits of a consistent rule before introducing any provisions which mean that its rule might differ from those in other countries. In all cases, a country should ensure that the group ratio rule applied provides effective protection against BEPS involving interest, in line with the principles set out in Part I. Examples of adjustments countries may require or permit in calculating a group's net third party interest expense include:

- applying an uplift of up to 10%
- including a group's share of the net interest expense of an associate or joint venture entity
- excluding some or all payments to related parties
- excluding specific categories of payments that would not be deductible if paid by an entity in that country
- removing the obligation to separately identify interest embedded within fair value adjustments.

310. Group EBITDA is the denominator in the group ratio calculation, which allocates interest capacity between entities in a group. Group EBITDA is calculated by adjusting a group's profit before tax to remove interest income and expense, depreciation and amortisation, subject to the following recommendations.

- The adjustment to remove interest income and expense should be equal to a group's net third party interest expense, with three exceptions:
    - It is suggested that the treatment of capitalised interest should reflect the accounting treatment. This would mean capitalised interest is not included in the figure for interest income and expense removed from profit before tax when calculating group EBITDA, but it would be taken into account over time in the adjustment to remove depreciation and amortisation.
    - The figure for interest income and expense removed from profit before tax when calculating group EBITDA should not include adjustments that were

made to net third party interest expense in order to reflect a country's domestic tax policy (unless the adjustment was to ensure that all interest expense funding a group's earnings is taken into account).

- Items of interest income and expense in a group's consolidated income statement may be removed from profit before tax when calculating group EBITDA, even where these concern payments that are not subject to limitation under the common approach (such as interest on defined benefit pension plans or the interest element of payments under operating leases).

- Depreciation and amortisation removed from profit before tax when calculating group EBITDA should include other items which allocate a group's fixed asset costs between periods, such as charges on the write-off or impairment of assets, and gains or losses on the disposal of assets outside the group (to the extent sale proceeds do not exceed original cost).
- Dividend income and a group's share of the results of associates and joint venture entities should be included in group EBITDA. The results of associates and joint venture entities may be adjusted to remove interest income and expense, depreciation and amortisation.
- A group's consolidated financial statements may include items which do not reflect the level of ongoing economic activity, but which increase earnings volatility. These include fair value gains and losses on assets and liabilities, which may be readily identified from a group's financial statements. To reduce the impact of volatility without significantly increasing complexity, a country may exclude these items from group EBITDA. On the other hand, non-recurring gains and losses are likely to be more difficult to identify and value on an objective basis. To keep a rule reasonable simple, these items should be included in group EBITDA without adjustment, or a country should limit adjustments to specific identifiable items which are clearly defined in the country's rules

311. The group ratio rule must be able to deal with the impact of entities with negative EBITDA within a group. Where a group has positive group EBITDA, losses within the group could inflate the group ratio to very high levels. Countries may deal with this through one or more of (i) excluding entities with negative EBITDA from the calculation of group EBITDA, (ii) limiting an entity's tax capacity to the net third party interest expense of its group, (iii) capping the group ratio at a fixed percentage which it is suggested should not exceed 100%, and/or (iv) restricting the carry forward of unused interest capacity under the group ratio rule combined with targeted rules. Where a group has negative group EBITDA, the group ratio rule cannot be applied. To avoid a cliff-edge effect when a group moves from having low group EBITDA to negative group EBITDA, a country may allow a profitable entity in a group to deduct net interest expense up to the lower of (i) the entity's actual net interest expense, (ii) the net third party interest expense of the group, and/or (iii) a fixed percentage of EBITDA which it is suggested should not exceed 100%.

312. The option for a group ratio rule described in this report represents an approach that should be suitable for most countries. However, countries may apply a different approach to suit their domestic circumstances. Therefore, a country may apply a group ratio rule based on another relevant financial ratio of an entity's worldwide group, such as a different net interest/earnings ratio or an equity/total assets ratio similar to that currently applied in Finland and Germany. These may be applied in place of, or alongside, the group ratio rule set out in this report.

Chapter 12

Calculating net third party interest expense

313. A group's net third party interest expense should include all of the group's interest income and expense for the period, as well as other items of income or expense that are economically equivalent to interest as defined in Chapter 2. Chapter 7 provides that this calculation should be based on a group's consolidated financial statements, prepared using International Financial Reporting Standards (IFRS), Japanese GAAP or US GAAP, or other accounting standards as permitted by the relevant country (e.g. taking into account the geographical region and main sources of foreign investment). It is recommended that these should be audited by an independent regulated accountant, although unaudited financial statements may be permitted. Chapter 7 includes three possible ways in which these may be used to determine a group's net third party interest expense.

- Using interest income and expense figures taken from the consolidated income statement without adjustment (Approach 1).
- Using interest income and expense figures taken from the consolidated income statement, but adjusting these figures to reflect items included in the definition of interest and payments economically equivalent to interest in Chapter 2 (Approach 2).
- Identifying the group's items of income or expense which fall within the definition of interest and payments economically equivalent to interest in Chapter 2, and measuring these items based on how they are treated in the group's consolidated financial statements (Approach 3).

314. Chapter 7 concludes that each of these approaches are acceptable in determining net third party interest expense, but further consideration is required of the feasibility of each approach.

Approach 1

315. The most straightforward approach to calculate a group's net third party interest expense would be to use unadjusted figures from the face of a group's consolidated income statement. Consolidated financial statements may include a single figure for net interest expense or separate figures for interest income and interest expense which would be netted off. Interest income and expense, and amounts economically equivalent to interest, may also be included with other items within broader categories of income and expense, in particular by groups which prepare financial statements using IFRS. In addition to being straightforward, this approach would also enable a group to prepare a single calculation of net third party interest expense which could be used in all countries where it has operations. This would reduce the extent to which a group's compliance costs are increased by the need to prepare different calculations under different countries' rules.

316. There are two significant downsides to Approach 1 as a way of determining a group's net third party interest expense. The first is that the net payments subject to limitation under the common approach are based on a definition of interest and payments economically equivalent to interest contained in Chapter 2. This does not refer to the accounting treatment of payments, and so differences may exist between the items that are treated as interest in a group's consolidated financial statements and the net payments that will be subject to restriction under the group ratio rule. For example, International Financial Reporting Standard IFRS16 (*Leases*) can require lessee groups to treat part of the rental payments under an operating lease as interest expense. However, Chapter 2 specifically excludes income and expenses under operating leases from the scope of the common approach. Applying Approach 1 could therefore result in an entity having an excessive interest restriction under the group ratio rule (e.g. where payments that fall within the Chapter 2 definition of interest are not treated as interest in a group's consolidated financial statements) or having excessive interest capacity (e.g. where payments that are not subject to limitation are treated as interest in a group's consolidated financial statements).

317. The second downside to this approach is that there can be substantial differences in the items which different groups treat as interest income or expense in their consolidated financial statements and the level of information they disclose. Some of these arise due to differences between accounting standards, while others are the result of groups adopting different accounting policies permitted under the same accounting standard. These differences mean that using figures taken directly from the consolidated income statement without adjustment could result in comparable groups having a different net third party interest expense. This could lead to an overstatement or understatement of net third party interest expense for some groups. Where accounting standards permit flexibility in how a particular item of finance income or expense may be treated (e.g. where it may be included within revenue or cost of sales, or separately disclosed as interest income or expense), comparable groups would have different levels of net third party interest expense depending upon the approach adopted. Where an item of expense is economically equivalent to interest, but a group does not currently account for it as interest in its consolidated financial statements, it would be necessary for the group to change its accounting policies to ensure that the expense is taken into account in calculating the group ratio. In some circumstances, such a change in accounting treatment may not be permitted under the relevant accounting standard. Requiring the use of audited financial statements would help ensure that consolidated financial statements are in line with the relevant accounting standard, but may not prevent accounting policy choices being driven by the possible tax impact on the group, which should be avoided where possible.

318. It is important that the calculation of a group's net third party interest expense takes into account all of a group's items of income and expense that are potentially subject to limitation under the common approach. It is also important that groups should be able to prepare consolidated financial statements applying the relevant accounting standards and adopting suitable accounting policies without concern that this could adversely impact their ability to deduct net interest expense under the group ratio rule. It is inevitable that there will be some variance between calculations of net third party interest expense based on consolidated financial statements prepared under different accounting standards but, given the importance of having an objective measure of net third party interest expense which is broadly consistent between groups, Approach 1 has important shortcomings.

Approach 2 and Approach 3

319. Approach 2 and Approach 3 reduce the downsides for groups and countries posed by Approach 1 by applying the definition of interest and payments economically equivalent to interest taken from Chapter 2. This may include certain items which are not treated as interest in a group's consolidated financial statements, and exclude certain items which a group does account for as interest. In practice, Approach 2 and Approach 3 are variants on the same approach and should give rise to the same figure for a group's net third party interest expense figure.

Approach 2

320. Approach 2 uses the interest income and expense figures in a group's consolidated income statement as the starting point for calculating net third party interest expense. However, unlike under Approach 1, these figures are then adjusted to include or exclude items in accordance with whether they fall within the definition of interest and payments economically equivalent to interest in Chapter 2.

321. The adjustments that will be required are likely to vary from group to group, depending upon the types of funding arrangements the group is party to, the accounting standards applied in preparing consolidated financial statements, and the accounting policies adopted. In each case, entities should adjust the interest income and expense figures in the consolidated income statement, as required, to ensure that the following items are included in net third party interest expense:

- capitalised interest
- interest included within other categories of income or expense in the consolidated income statement
- interest income on financial instruments carried at fair value.

322. Adjustments should also be made, as required, to ensure that the following items are excluded from net third party interest expense:

- fair value gains or losses on financial instruments, to the extent these are not economically equivalent to interest
- gains and losses on the sale or redemption of financial instruments, to the extent these are not economically equivalent to interest
- foreign exchange gains or losses, to the extent these are not economically equivalent to interest
- net interest on a group's defined benefit pension liability and similar post-retirement benefits.
- accrued interest on accounting provisions
- non-interest income and expense, to the extent this is not economically equivalent to interest.

323. Where an adjustment is required, this may be made based on information contained in the group's consolidated financial statements, including notes to the financial statements, or in underlying accounting records. Where an adjustment is not required (e.g. because the relevant item is already included in or excluded from interest income and expense in the consolidated financial statements as required) an entity may simply confirm this is the case and provide the relevant supporting evidence.

Approach 3

324. As mentioned above, Approach 3 to calculating a group's net third party interest expense is a variant on Approach 2 and so should give the same result. However, rather than making adjustments to the interest figures in a group's consolidated financial statements, Approach 3 requires an entity to identify all of the group's items of income or expense which fall within the definition of interest and payments economically equivalent to interest in Chapter 2, and then measure these items based on how they are treated in the consolidated financial statements for the group. In some cases these values may be taken directly from the group's consolidated financial statements but in others it may be necessary for an entity to refer to underlying accounting records.

Comparison of the three approaches

325. Approach 1 to calculating a group's net third party interest expense has the benefit of simplicity by allowing all entities in a group to use the interest income and expense figures from the group's consolidated financial statements without adjustment. However, this simplicity also gives rise to concerns that there could be mismatches between the items included in a group's net third party interest expense and the net payments subject to limitation under the common approach, and that there could be substantial differences between the net third party interest expense of comparable groups. This could lead to adverse tax consequences for some groups, encourage groups to adopt accounting policies to avoid these tax consequences and reduce the effectiveness of the group ratio rule as a tool to combat BEPS.

326. Approach 2 and Approach 3 reduce these concerns. Either of these approaches should result in a figure for a group's net third party interest expense which captures the items covered by the definition of interest and payments economically equivalent to interest in Chapter 2. By applying a common definition for the items to be included, they also reduce the risk of differences in net third party interest expense arising between groups as a result of different accounting standards and policies (although these differences are unlikely ever to be eliminated entirely). Therefore, while the benefits of Approach 1 mean that it remains an option available to countries, Approach 2 and Approach 3 are considered to be preferred options.

327. Calculations of net third party interest expense under Approach 2 and Approach 3 would be presented differently. However, the information that an entity would be required to obtain in order to prepare these calculations should be the same, and they should give rise to the same outcome. In some cases, in order to verify specific items within a calculation, a tax authority may request information from a tax authority in another country, but this should be consistent under each of these approaches. A country may have reasons for preferring one of these approaches over the other, but there does not appear to be any particular factors which are sufficiently significant for one to be recommended in preference to the other. However, while a country may have a preference for one of these approaches over the other, it is suggested that countries should also consider options to reduce the compliance burden on groups, in particular in light of the fact that both Approach 2 and Approach 3 are expected to give the same outcome. For example, in order to reduce compliance costs and ensure that a group is only required to prepare one calculation of net third party expense which may be used in all countries where it has operations, countries may consider allowing an entity to apply either Approach 2 or Approach 3 to perform the calculation.

Adjustments to a group's net third party interest expense

328. Whichever approach is adopted by a particular country for the calculation of net third party interest expense, in order to reduce the risk that a group is not able to deduct an amount equivalent to its actual net interest expense, and to ensure that BEPS is appropriately and adequately addressed, the country may require or allow an entity to adjust the figure for net third party interest expense to reflect specific policy goals, including those set out below.

329. The fact that countries may make different policy choices on these issues is not inconsistent with the common approach, so long as the adjustments required or permitted by a country do not reduce the effectiveness of the common approach in tackling BEPS involving interest. The aim of the group ratio rule is to enable countries to take into account the position of entities in highly leveraged groups, and allow an entity to claim net interest deductions in excess of the limit under the fixed ratio rule in particular circumstances. It is therefore appropriate for certain tax policies to be taken into account in setting a limit on net interest deductions under the rule. However, it is also recognised that a benefit of the common approach is to allow multinational groups to apply consistent rules in different countries where they operate, reducing overall compliance costs. Therefore, in deciding whether to require or permit an entity to make adjustments to the common figure for net third party interest expense described above, a country should balance its domestic policy goals against the benefits of a consistent approach to limiting net interest deductions across different countries.

To recognise practical issues that may prevent a group aligning net interest expense and EBITDA

330. The common approach encourages groups to align the location of net interest expense and economic activity, measured using EBITDA. However, Chapter 7 recognises that in some cases there will be practical or legal constraints that make this difficult or impossible. To reduce the likelihood that this could prevent a group from deducting an amount equivalent to its third party interest expense, countries may allow an entity to apply an uplift to its group's net third party interest expense of up to 10%.

331. On the other hand, in cases where a group is able to more closely align the location of its net interest expense and EBITDA, such an uplift could enable entities in the group to claim net interest deductions in excess of the group's net third party interest expense. Therefore a country may also choose to allow entities to apply a smaller uplift or no uplift. The operation of an uplift to net third party interest expense is illustrated by Example 1a in Annex II.A.

To prevent interest capacity being increased by certain non-deductible payments

332. The approaches to determine a group's net third party interest expense set out above are based on consolidated financial reporting figures, rather than tax figures. A group may make payments which are interest or economically equivalent to interest, which are deductible for tax purposes in the group entity which makes the payments, but which would not be tax deductible if paid by a different group entity in another country. For example, dividends paid on fixed rate preference shares may be economically equivalent to interest, but countries differ in whether they allow a tax deduction for these payments.

333. If these payments are included in a group's net third party interest expense, they will increase the group's net third party interest expense/EBITDA ratio and the interest capacity of group entities in all countries where a group ratio rule is applied. If a particular country allows a tax deduction for these payments then including them in net third party interest expense would seem to be clearly the correct result. If a different country does not allow a tax deduction for these payments, it may also allow them to be included in net third party interest expense. This would keep the group ratio rule as simple as possible for entities to apply and for the tax administration to administer, but it would mean that net third party interest expense would include payments that are not within the scope of the rule in that country.

334. There may be cases however where a country has decided that for policy reasons these payments should not be tax deductible and also that they should not be taken into account in calculating the limit on net interest deductions that an entity in that country may claim. In this case, the country may choose to require an entity to exclude particular categories of payment from net third party interest expense in applying the group ratio rule. This is illustrated by Example 1b in Annex II.A. To reduce the complexity of the rule for entities to apply and for tax authorities to audit, where a country requires these adjustments to be made, they should be limited to narrow and clearly identifiable categories of payment which, in the assessment of the country, pose a material BEPS risk.

To address risks posed by interest paid to related parties outside the group

335. Chapter 7 explains that entities may use interest paid to related parties outside a group to increase the group's net third party interest expense and inflate the interest capacity of all entities in the group. In order to ensure the integrity of the group ratio rule and protect countries against BEPS involving interest, countries should introduce measures to prevent this happening. Chapter 7 gives countries flexibility in how this is done, and different approaches may be adopted. One possible approach would be for a country to exclude some or all net interest expense paid to related parties from the definition of net third party interest expense. If this approach is adopted by a country, entities in a group which is funded using only related party debt would be able to apply the fixed ratio rule to deduct net interest expense up to the benchmark fixed ratio, but would not be able to rely on the group ratio rule to deduct net interest expense above this amount. This approach is illustrated by Example 1c in Annex II.A.

336. The term "related parties" for these purposes is defined in Chapter 9. Broadly, two persons (including two entities or an entity and an individual) are related if they are not in the same group, but they meet any of the following conditions.

- The first person has an investment that provides that person with effective control of the second person or there is a third person that holds investments which provide that person with effective control over both persons.
- The first person has a 25% or greater investment in the second person or there is a third person that holds a 25% or greater investment in both.
- They can be regarded as associated enterprises under Article 9.

337. A person will be treated as holding a percentage investment in another person if that person holds, directly or indirectly through an investment in other persons, a percentage of the voting rights of that person or of the value of any equity interests of that person. A person who acts together with another person in respect of the ownership or control of any voting rights or equity interests will be treated as owning or controlling all of those voting rights and equity instruments.

338. In deciding whether to apply such an approach, a country should consider the possible impact on entities which are funded using related party debt for non-tax reasons. For example, where a joint venture entity (JVE) is held equally by two investor groups it will typically not be included in either group for the purposes of applying the group ratio rule. Therefore, where the JVE is funded using third party debt raised by the investor groups and on-lent to the JVE (e.g. to take advantage of a better credit rating or access to lenders), the JVE could be prevented from applying the group ratio rule if the interest on this related party debt is excluded from net third party interest expense. There may be a risk that this could incentivise groups to adopt less efficient structures whereby the JVE raises third party debt directly in order to avoid an interest disallowance, even if this means having to borrow at a higher rate of interest. A country could reduce this by providing exclusions, for example where there is a direct and clear link between third party debt raised by an investor group and a loan to the JVE, and there are no loans from the JVE back to the investor group. Alternatively, a country could rely on a different approach to address the potential risks posed by interest paid to related parties, such as the use of targeted rules to disallow particular payments based on the nature or circumstances of the payment or the profile of the recipient.

To take into account a group's share of the net third party interest expense of an associate or JVE

339. As discussed in Chapter 13, in calculating a group's net third party interest expense/ EBITDA ratio, group EBITDA includes the group's share of the earnings of any associates or JVEs included in its consolidated financial statements under equity accounting principles. However, because a group's consolidated income statement does not specifically include a share of an associate or JVE's net interest expense, where the associate or JVE raises debt directly from third party lenders, the interest expense on this debt will not be included in the group's net third party interest expense determined under the approaches described above. This means that in these cases the group's ratio would take into account its share of the associate or JVE's earnings, but not the interest expense funding those earnings. This puts entities in the group at a disadvantage compared with a scenario where the third party debt is raised by a group member and so the interest on the debt is included in net third party interest expense.

340. To address this concern, countries should consider allowing an entity to adjust net third party interest expense to include the group's share of the net third party interest income or expense of an associate or JVE. This is illustrated by Examples 1d and 1e in Annex II.A. However, obtaining information on an associate or JVE's third party interest position would make a rule more complex to apply, and in many cases the impact on a group's ratio may not be material. Therefore it is suggested that, even where a country permits such an adjustment, entities should have the option not to make an adjustment. Where a country does permit such an adjustment, it may verify the net third party interest expense of an associate or JVE in another country using evidence provided by the entity, or it may use exchange of information provisions in tax treaties and other instruments to obtain the information from the relevant foreign tax authority. It should also consider including safeguards, such as:

- requiring consistent adjustments to be made for all material holdings (i.e. to require adjustments to include a group's share of net third party interest income as well as expense)

- limiting a group's net third party interest expense/EBITDA ratio to the ratio the group would have had if both the net third party interest expense and EBITDA of the associate or JVE were excluded.

To simplify the calculation of net third party interest expense

341. Approach 2 and Approach 3 to determine a group's net third party interest expense use the definition of interest and payments economically equivalent to interest in Chapter 2 to ensure that the items included in net third party interest expense correspond to the payments taken into account when limiting net interest deductions under the common approach. Where a group holds financial assets or liabilities at fair value, this definition would not include fair value gains or losses which are not economically equivalent to interest but may be included within a group's finance income and expense for financial reporting purposes. However, it would include the interest income or expense on these assets and liabilities, even though this may not be required to be separately disclosed in a group's consolidated financial statements.

342. In order to ensure an accurate determination of a group's net third party interest expense, a country may require entities to identify the interest income or expense on financial assets and liabilities which are held at fair value, and include this within net third party interest expense. This is the approach taken in the descriptions of Approach 2 and Approach 3, above. However, as groups may not otherwise be required to separately identify these amounts, this could increase the compliance burden of applying the group ratio rule in practice. Therefore, a country may choose to exclude these interest amounts from net third party interest expense, or permit an entity to exclude these amounts so long as this is done in a consistent manner. This would simplify the calculation of net third party interest expense for groups but, because interest income and expense on financial assets and liabilities held at fair value would no longer be included and in some cases these amounts could be sizeable, it does introduce a risk that net third party interest expense could be overstated or understated.

Chapter 13

Calculating group EBITDA

343. The group ratio rule operates by comparing a group's net third party interest expense with its earnings, measured using EBITDA. This gives a ratio which can be applied to an entity's EBITDA to calculate the entity's interest capacity under the rule.

344. In simple terms, a group's EBITDA is equal to its profit before tax after making adjustments to remove interest income and expense, depreciation and amortisation. However, there are a number of specific elements with respect to this definition which need to be considered. These are:

- items to be included in the adjustment for interest income and expense
- items to be included in the adjustment for depreciation and amortisation
- the treatment of dividend income and a group's share of the earnings of an associate or JVE
- the treatment of fair value gains and losses
- the treatment of non-recurring items.

Items to be included in the adjustment for interest income and expense

345. The calculation of group EBITDA includes an adjustment to remove a group's interest income and interest expense. This is done in order to ensure that a group's earnings are measured without taking into account how the group is funded. In other words, two comparable groups should have the same EBITDA irrespective of whether they are funded using equity, debt or any combination of the two.

346. The approach set out below should result in a measure of interest income and expense which is substantially the same in all countries applying the group ratio rule. However, there are two particular areas where flexibility is provided to countries. Firstly, with respect to the treatment of capitalised interest it is suggested that countries should consider simply excluding capitalised interest from the adjustment for interest income and expense, as a more straightforward approach than the ongoing adjustments to depreciation and amortisation described in Chapter 7. Secondly, in order to give an accurate determination of group EBITDA, the figure for interest income and expense that is removed from earnings in calculating group EBITDA may also include items which are treated as interest in a group's consolidated financial statements but which are not subject to limitation under the common approach. This could include, for example, items such as interest on defined benefit pension liabilities and similar post-retirement benefits, and any part of payments under an operating lease which are accounted for as interest.

Capitalised interest

347. Where a group has incurred an interest expense related to the construction or development of a fixed asset, accounting standards may require or permit this expense to be capitalised and added to the cost of the fixed asset in the group's balance sheet. This interest expense is not charged directly to the consolidated income statement. Instead, as the fixed asset is depreciated over time, the annual depreciation charge includes amortisation of the capitalised interest. In effect, the capitalised interest is taken through the consolidated income statement over the life of the fixed asset.

348. Chapter 7 suggests that capitalised interest may be included in the group's interest income and expense figure which is removed from earnings in calculating group EBITDA. As the group's figures for depreciation and amortisation also include amortisation of its capitalised interest expense, this would need to be stripped out in order to avoid double counting (i.e. to avoid capitalised interest being included in both the adjustment for interest income and expense and the adjustment for depreciation and amortisation). In practice, a requirement to adjust depreciation and amortisation could be difficult for entities to apply and tax authorities to audit. Groups may not currently record the amortisation of capitalised interest and this would need to be introduced. Adjustments to depreciation and amortisation would also need to be made each year over the life of the relevant fixed assets, adding to the complexity.

349. An alternative approach would be to exclude capitalised interest from the adjustment for interest income and expense in calculating group EBITDA. This should be much more straightforward for entities to apply and for tax authorities to audit, as it would involve simply following the accounting treatment of the capitalised interest, disregarding any adjustment to include capitalised interest in the calculation of net third party interest expense. There would be no need to make any ongoing adjustments in future years.

350. Countries are free to apply the approach in Chapter 7 and require entities to include capitalised interest in the adjustment for interest income and expense in the year when the interest is incurred, and make ongoing adjustments to strip capitalised interest out of depreciation and amortisation. However, in light of complexity of this approach, countries should consider instead requiring an entity to reflect the accounting treatment of capitalised interest when calculating group EBITDA.

Adjustments to net third party interest expense to reflect a country's tax policy goals

351. As set out in Chapter 12, a country may require or permit an entity to make adjustments to its group's net third party interest expense, to achieve specific policy goals, including:

i. to apply an uplift of up to 10%

ii. to exclude payments which would not be tax deductible if paid by an entity in the country

iii. to exclude net related party interest

iv. to include a group's share of the net third party interest expense of an associate or JVE.

352. The first three of these possible adjustments are not concerned with determining the actual level of interest expense funding a group's activities, but reflect other tax policy goals that a country may have. Therefore, while these adjustments may be made in calculating a group's net third party interest expense, if they were also made to the interest income

and expense that is removed in calculating group EBITDA, this would give a misleading picture of a group's actual results. It would also undermine a country's tax policy goals in allowing or requiring adjustment to net third party interest expense. This is illustrated by Examples 2a, 2b and 2c in Annex II.A.

353. On the other hand, the fourth possible adjustment listed above is directly concerned with ensuring that a group's net third party interest expense accurately reflects the actual net interest cost incurred in funding the earnings in the group's consolidated income statement. Therefore, as set out in Chapter 12, a group's net third party interest expense may also include the group's share of the net third party expense of an associate or JVE. Where this is done, the group's share of the associate or JVE's net third party interest expense should also be included in the adjustment for interest income or expense in calculating group EBITDA. This is to ensure that group EBITDA includes all of a group's earnings before taking account of the net interest expense funding those earnings.

354. Therefore, in light of these considerations:

- where an adjustment to net third party interest expense is required or permitted to bring it into line with the actual net interest expense funding a group's earnings, the adjustment should also be reflected in the figure for interest income and expense removed in calculating group EBITDA
- where an adjustment to net third party interest expense is required or permitted to achieve any other tax policy goal, the figure for interest income and expense removed in calculating group EBITDA should not reflect these adjustments.

Net interest items that are not subject to restriction under the common approach

355. Part I provides that certain payments which may be treated as interest for financial reporting purposes should not be included in the net interest expense which is subject to restriction under the fixed ratio rule and group ratio rule. These payments include net interest on a group's defined benefit pension liability and similar post-retirement benefits, and the interest element of payments under operating leases. As this net interest expense is not subject to limitation, it is not included in a group's net third party interest expense under Approach 2 or Approach 3. However, in order to ensure an accurate measure of earnings, a country should consider including this net interest expense in the figure for interest income and expense that is removed from earnings when calculating group EBITDA.

Items to be included in the adjustment for depreciation and amortisation

356. Under accounting rules, groups capitalise tangible and (where permitted) intangible fixed assets at cost, and depreciate or amortise this cost through the consolidated income statement over the life of the relevant asset. Depreciation and amortisation are a mechanism to allocate the cost of a group's fixed assets to different periods. In calculating group EBITDA, an adjustment is made to remove these costs from a group's earnings.

357. A group's consolidated income statement may also include other items to allocate a group's fixed assets costs to different periods, which arise in specific circumstances. These items might include charges on the impairment or write-off of a fixed asset, and gains or losses on the disposal of a fixed asset outside the group (to the extent sale proceeds do not exceed the original cost of the asset to the group). It is suggested these items should be treated consistently with the group's charges for depreciation and amortisation. They should therefore be included within the figure for depreciation and amortisation that is removed from earnings in calculating group EBITDA.

The treatment of dividend income and a group's share of the earnings of an associate or JVE

358. For the purposes of applying the group ratio rule, a group includes a parent company and all entities that are fully consolidated on a line-by-line basis in the parent's consolidated financial statements. There are two broad scenarios where a group's consolidated financial statements will include income derived from economic activity carried on by entities which are not part of the group:

- the group receives dividend income
- the group recognises a share of the earnings of an associate or JVE under equity accounting principles.

The treatment of dividend income

359. Where an entity is part of a group, its individual items of income and expense are included in the group's consolidated financial statements on a line-by-line basis. Payments between group entities, including intragroup dividends, are removed on consolidation. In practice, dividend income is only included in a group's consolidated income statement if it is received from an entity which is neither (a) part of the consolidated group, nor (b) included in the consolidated financial statements under equity accounting principles. This will arise where a group does not have significant influence over the entity. In general terms this will be where the group's interest in the entity is less than 20%, although this may vary depending on the specific facts.

360. The BEPS Action Plan provides that one of the key BEPS risks to be addressed by Action 4 is the use of interest expense to fund tax-exempt or deferred income. Part I therefore recommends that in calculating EBITDA at the level of an entity (i.e. entity EBITDA), countries do not include non-taxable income such as dividend income that benefits from a participation exemption. Where dividend income is subject to tax, but this tax is wholly or partly sheltered by underlying tax credits, the level of dividend income included in entity EBITDA should be reduced accordingly. This is to prevent an entity benefiting from a higher level of interest capacity as a result of receiving non-taxable income.

361. Entity EBITDA should not include any non-taxable dividend income. On the other hand, when calculating group EBITDA, all of a group's income in its consolidated income statement should be included, including income which is not subject to tax. This is to ensure that the group ratio rule effectively apportions a group's net third party interest expense across all of its sources of income. To the extent a group's income is subject to tax, the entity receiving the taxable income will be able to claim net interest deductions corresponding to the proportion of the group's net interest expense funding this income. In order to achieve the specific goals identified in the BEPS Action Plan, where part of a group's income is not subject to tax, the corresponding portion of the group's net interest expense that is funding that income should be disallowed.

362. Examples 3a to 3d in Annex II.A illustrate the importance of this approach in ensuring an appropriate outcome for groups and countries. Example 3a shows that where dividend income in a group's consolidated income statement is received by entities which are subject to tax on the income (e.g. because the entity's holding is below any threshold required to benefit from a participation exemption or claim underlying tax credits) then in principle all of the group's net third party interest expense used to fund this income should be deductible in the appropriate entity. However, to the extent that the dividend income is not subject to

tax, Example 3b shows how the part of the group's net third party interest expense which is funding the group's tax-exempt dividend income will be disallowed. This approach therefore gives the correct result for a group whether dividend income is taxable or non-taxable in the entity which receives the income, and also where dividend income is taxed in part. For example, if a country exempts 95% of an entity's dividend income and taxes the remaining 5%, then the part of the group's net third party interest expense which is funding this taxable element should be deductible. This result is also consistent with the outcome should a group receive any other type of income which is included in group EBITDA but which is not subject to tax and so is not included in the entity EBITDA of the relevant entity.

363. In order to test the benefits of this approach, Examples 3c and 3d in Annex II.A illustrate the impact if dividend income is not included in group EBITDA. As seen in Example 3c, this would enable a group to raise third party debt to fund equity investments and claim a deduction for all of its net third party interest expense while receiving dividend income tax-free. This result would be contrary to one of the goals of the BEPS Action Plan, and would reduce the effectiveness of the group ratio rule in tackling BEPS involving interest. Where not all of a group's dividend income is tax-exempt, Example 3d shows how this approach could also result in a group being able to deduct net interest expense in excess of the group's net third party interest expense, which is not the aim of the rule.

364. Another approach would be to include dividend income in the calculation of group EBITDA where the group entity receiving the income is subject to tax on the income. Dividend income which is not subject to tax would be excluded from group EBITDA. This would address the risk that a group would be able to claim net interest deductions in excess of its net third party interest expense. However, it would not deal with the concern that a group could deduct net interest expense which is being used to fund tax-exempt income. This would also increase the complexity of the rule for groups to apply and for tax authorities to audit. From the perspective of a group, this additional complexity may not be too great as it is likely that in most groups only a limited number of entities will receive dividends from outside the group and the tax treatment of these dividends should be known to the group's finance function. On the other hand, the difficulties for tax authorities are likely to be more significant. In many cases, the total amount of dividend income received may be taken from a group's consolidated financial statements, but it would then be necessary to identify in which entity and country the dividends are received and to understand the tax treatment of dividend income in that country or submit a request for information from the relevant foreign tax authority. Particular difficulties would arise where dividends are received in a country which taxes dividends with credit for underlying tax, as information on the level of tax credits that may be claimed would also be required.

365. In light of the considerations set out above and the statement in the BEPS Action Plan that recommendations under Action 4 should address BEPS risk where a group uses interest expense to fund tax-exempt or deferred income, all dividend income in a group's consolidated income statement should be included in group EBITDA without adjustment.

The treatment of a group's share of the profit or loss of an associate or JVE under equity accounting principles

366. Equity accounting principles apply where a group has a significant influence over an entity but this is not sufficient to establish control. This will typically be the case where a group has an interest in an entity of between 20% and 50%, although this can vary depending on the facts of a particular case. This may include JVEs (where the group together with other investors has joint control over the entity) and associates (where the group does not have joint control over the entity with any other investor). Associates may also be referred to as affiliates.

367. An associate or JVE is not part of a group for the purposes of applying the group ratio rule. A group's share of the associate or JVE's earnings does not arise directly in any member of the group, but is included in a single line in the group's consolidated income statement. Instead, the group member holding the investment in the associate or JVE will receive a return in the form of dividends or capital gains.

368. As mentioned above, group EBITDA should include all of a group's sources of income, regardless of whether or not the income is subject to tax in the entity receiving it. Therefore a group's share of the earnings of an associate or JVE, as contained in its consolidated income statement, should be included in group EBITDA without adjustment. Example 4a in Annex II.A shows that, where dividends received from an associate or JVE correspond with the group's share of the entity's profits, and the relevant group member is taxable on the dividend income, then in principle the group should be able to deduct all of its net third party interest expense funding this income. However, to the extent the group is not taxed on this income (because the dividends benefit from a participation exemption or are sheltered by underlying tax credits) or taxation is deferred (because dividends are not declared), then Examples 4b and 4c illustrate how the part of the group's net third party interest expense which is funding this exempt or deferred income will not be deductible. This approach gives the correct outcome for a group irrespective of whether dividends received by the group are taxable in the entity receiving them. In practice, the recognition of a group's share of the results of an associate or JVE may not correspond with the timing of the receipt of dividends from that entity. The impact of this timing difference may be reduced by the use of provisions for the carry forward or carry back of disallowed interest expense and/or unused interest capacity.

369. Countries should therefore include a group's share of the earnings of an equity accounted entity within group EBITDA. A country may also require or permit the group's share of the associate or JVE's earnings to be adjusted to remove interest income and expense, depreciation and amortisation (i.e. so group EBITDA includes the group's share of the associate or JVE's EBITDA). In particular, where an entity is permitted to adjust group net third party interest expense to include the group's share of the net third party interest income or expense of an associate or JVE, it would be consistent for the entity also to make adjustments to the group's share of the associate or JVE's earnings. In many cases, however, this could lead to a level of complexity that is unnecessary where the amounts concerned are not material and so a country may choose not to require such an adjustment in cases where the impact on group EBITDA would be small (e.g. less than 5%).

The treatment of fair value gains and losses

370. Accounting standards require or permit groups to carry certain classes of asset or liability at fair value, with the balance sheet value of the asset/liability adjusted to reflect movements in fair value during the period. This may be required because of the nature of a particular asset/liability, the activities on the entity holding the asset/liability, or the reasons for which the asset/liability is held. Where fair value gains and losses are recognised in the income statement, they will increase or reduce the group's earnings for the relevant period.

371. From the perspective of the group ratio rule, including fair value gains and losses in group EBITDA gives rise to two risks:

- fair value gains and losses may distort group EBITDA as a measure of a group's ongoing economic activity
- fair value gains and losses have the potential to increase volatility in earnings.

372. These risks are exacerbated by the fact that fair value gains and losses may arise on assets and liabilities held in a particular part of a group, but including them in group EBITDA could impact the ability of all entities in the group to deduct interest expense under the group ratio rule. For example, a large fair value gain on an investment asset held by one entity in a group will reduce the group's net third party interest expense/EBITDA ratio and so potentially reduce the interest capacity of entities across the entire group.

373. For the purposes of improving simplicity and consistency in the operation of the group ratio rule between countries, a country may include fair value gains and losses within group EBITDA without adjustment. In this case, the impact of earnings volatility on the ability of entities to deduct net interest expense under the group ratio rule, may be addressed through the use of averaging and/or provisions for the carry forward or carry back of disallowed interest expense and unused interest capacity, as described in Chapter 8. However, countries should also consider applying exceptions to this general approach and requiring or permitting fair value gains and losses on specific categories of asset or liability to be removed from group EBITDA on a consistent basis (i.e. so both fair value gains and fair value losses are removed where they arise on a particular class of asset or liability). This exception may be applied narrowly by a country (e.g. to exclude gains and losses only on a group's debt financing and instruments directly connected to a group's debt financing) or more broadly (e.g. to exclude fair value gains and losses on assets and liabilities including financial instruments, derivatives and/or capital assets held for investment purposes). The case where a country allows an entity to exclude fair value movements on instruments connected with a group's debt financing from group EBITDA is illustrated by Example 5 in Annex II.A.

The treatment of non-recurring items

374. Non-recurring items include any income, expenses, gains or losses which relate to one-off events, rather than to a group's normal activities. Non-recurring items present similar risks to the operation of the group ratio rule as fair value gains and losses, in that they may distort group EBITDA as a measure of economic activity and increase volatility in earnings. However, compared with fair value gains and losses, it may be more difficult to define precisely what a non-recurring item is and in what circumstances such an item should be excluded from group EBITDA.

375. As set out above, losses arising as a result of the impairment or write-off of fixed assets, and gains and losses on the disposal of fixed assets outside the group should be included in the adjustment for depreciation and amortisation and removed from group EBITDA. The argument for removing other non-recurring items from group EBITDA is less strong. In particular, while it may be clear when certain events such as an acquisition or merger take place, other restructurings and reorganisations are likely to be less apparent. In addition, the allocation of income, expenses, gains and losses to these events may be subjective and not specifically subject to statutory audit. This may make it difficult for an entity to identify non-recurring items, in particular where they arise from events in other parts of a group, leading to lengthy discussions between entities and tax authorities and possibly resulting in comparable groups being treated differently.

376. In light of these factors, with the exception of those which are included within the adjustments for interest income and expense or depreciation and amortisation, non-recurring items should in general be included in group EBITDA without adjustment. This is a simple approach, which can be applied easily and consistently in all countries, with the impact of earnings volatility addressed through the use of averaging and/or provisions for the carry

forward or carry back of disallowed interest expense and unused interest capacity. As with respect to fair value gains and losses, a country may apply exceptions to this general approach and require or permit specific categories of non-recurring income and expense to be removed from group EBITDA. However, because of the greater difficulty an entity is likely to have in identifying and obtaining information on non-recurring items in other parts of its group, this should be limited to specific identifiable items which are clearly defined in the country's rules. Any adjustments which are permitted or required should be applied consistently, so if a certain category of income or gains is removed from group EBITDA, the corresponding category of expenses or losses should also be removed.

Chapter 14

Addressing the impact of entities with negative EBITDA on the operation of the group ratio rule

377. As explained in Chapter 7, the presence of loss-making entities within a group (i.e. those with negative EBITDA) will have an impact on the operation of the group ratio rule for other entities in the group. The extent of this impact will depend upon the size of these losses compared with the positive EBITDA of other entities in the group. In designing a group ratio rule, a country therefore needs to consider the treatment of entities in two scenarios:

- where a group has positive group EBITDA, but includes loss-making entities (i.e. the positive EBITDA of profitable entities exceeds the negative EBITDA of loss-making entities)
- where a group has zero or negative group EBITDA (i.e. the negative EBITDA of loss-making entities equals or exceeds the positive EBITDA of profitable entities).

The treatment of entities where a group has positive group EBITDA

378. So long as a group has a positive group EBITDA, the group ratio rule can be applied to calculate the net third party interest expense/EBITDA ratio of the group. However, where the group includes entities with negative EBITDA, the inclusion of these losses will reduce group EBITDA and increase the group's ratio. The effect of this is that the aggregate interest capacity of all group entities could exceed the actual net third party interest expense of the group. This arises because, although the calculation of group EBITDA includes the results of entities with positive and negative EBITDA within the group, the group ratio is only used to calculate interest capacity for entities with positive EBITDA (i.e. entities with negative EBITDA do not have "negative interest capacity"). This is illustrated by Example 6a in Annex II.A. Countries may adopt different approaches to deal with this risk, and are encouraged to consider the following as options:

- excluding entities with negative EBITDA from the calculation of group EBITDA
- restricting the interest capacity of entities with positive EBITDA
- restricting the carry forward of unused interest capacity under the group ratio rule.

Excluding entities with negative EBITDA from the calculation of group EBITDA

379. Excluding entities with negative EBITDA from the calculation of group EBITDA would mean that the denominator in a group's net third party interest expense/EBITDA ratio only includes the results of entities in the group with positive EBITDA. This would enable these entities, taken together, to deduct net interest expense equal to the group's actual net third party interest expense. This is illustrated by Example 6b in Annex II.A.

Net interest expense in excess of this amount is disallowed, but may be carried forward for use in future periods where this is permitted.

380. There are downsides to this approach. Where an entity with negative EBITDA is located in the country where the group ratio rule is being applied, it should be relatively easy for entities in the country to make the necessary adjustments to the calculation of group EBITDA and for these to be audited by the tax authority. However, where the entity with negative EBITDA is in a different country, this would be more difficult. In effect, this approach could oblige a multinational group to have systems in place to calculate entity EBITDA each year for every entity in the worldwide group, including those in countries which do not apply the group ratio rule, in order to ensure that any with negative EBITDA can be identified. This could impose a significant additional burden on groups. From the perspective of a tax authority, it would also be very difficult for tax auditors to confirm whether a group has any such entities and to ensure that losses have been correctly removed from group EBITDA. This information is not typically contained in a group's consolidated financial statements, and so tax auditors would need to rely on information provided by the entity applying the rule or obtained from foreign tax authorities. In addition, although this approach should be effective in addressing the impact of entities with negative EBITDA on the operation of the group ratio rule, it would not deal with the impact of entities with a very low positive EBITDA, which could also potentially inflate a group's ratio to very high levels. A country should carefully consider these issues before adopting this approach.

Restricting the interest capacity of entities with positive EBITDA

381. Irrespective of whether a country includes the results of entities with negative EBITDA in the calculation of group EBITDA, it should consider placing an upper limit on the amount of net interest expense that an entity can deduct under the group ratio rule using one or both of the following options:

- capping a group's net third party interest expense/EBITDA ratio to a set percentage which is higher than the benchmark fixed ratio but it is suggested should not exceed 100%
- limiting an entity's interest capacity to an amount equal to the group's net third party interest expense (after applying an uplift of up to 10%, where permitted).

382. The group ratio rule allows an entity in a highly leveraged group to claim net interest deductions based on the net third party interest expense/EBITDA ratio of its worldwide group. However, where a group includes entities with negative EBITDA, the group's ratio may be inflated to levels that may not be sustainable on an ongoing basis. It is therefore suggested that a country should consider imposing a cap on a group's ratio so that an entity's interest capacity cannot exceed a set percentage of EBITDA.

383. In order for the group ratio rule to operate as intended, this cap should be set at a level which is higher than the benchmark ratio under the fixed ratio rule but it is suggested should not exceed 100%. In setting a cap, a country may choose to take into account available data on the proportion of groups which would in principle be able to deduct all of their net third party interest expense if the cap was set at different levels, including data contained in Annex I.B to Part I. Other considerations may also be relevant and may be taken into account in setting a cap. Where the presence of loss-making entities means that a group's net third party interest expense/EBITDA ratio is very high, group entities with positive EBITDA would be able to apply the group ratio rule subject to this cap, while any net interest expense in excess of the cap would be carried forward, if permitted under a

country's rules. Entities with negative EBITDA in the group would also carry forward their disallowed interest expense, if permitted. This is illustrated by Example 6c in Annex II.A.

384. A country should also consider restricting an entity's interest capacity under the group ratio rule, so that it cannot exceed the total net third party interest expense of the group as a whole. This is illustrated by Example 6d in Annex II.A. One of the key risks of BEPS involving interest is where entities in a group claim net interest deductions in excess of the group's actual net third party interest expense. In a group where there are no entities with negative EBITDA, the group ratio rule should not in general result in an entity being able to deduct net interest expense in excess of the net third party interest expense of its group. Limiting an entity's interest capacity under the group ratio rule to the net third party interest expense of its group is consistent with this. In certain circumstances this would still allow more than one entity in a group to claim net interest deductions up to the full amount of the group's net third party interest expense. However, in some groups one entity could carry on all of the group's economic activity (e.g. where a group comprises a holding company and a single operating entity). In order to ensure that such an entity does not incur an undue restriction on its net interest deductions, it is not suggested that a country impose a monetary limit below this level.

385. An illustration of these restrictions operating together is included as Example 6e in Annex II.A. Where a country imposes either or both of these restrictions, they should be applied to all entities making use of the group ratio rule and not only to those in groups which include entities with negative EBITDA. This simplifies the operation of the group ratio rule by imposing clear limits on an entity's interest capacity without the need to determine whether or not a group contains any entities with negative EBITDA. This should protect countries from the worst impact of entities with losses or very low profits in a group with positive group EBITDA, while not being overly complicated or excessively restricting net interest deductions for entities with positive EBITDA.

Restricting the carry forward of unused interest capacity under the group ratio rule

386. Alongside the above approaches, or as an alternative to restricting net interest deductions under the group ratio rule, a country may also consider reducing the impact of entities with negative EBITDA by restricting the carry forward of unused interest capacity. This may be done by allowing the carry forward of unused interest capacity only where this arises under the fixed ratio rule, or by limiting the carry forward of unused interest expense under the group ratio rule. For example, a country could allow an entity to use the group ratio rule to calculate its interest capacity for the current period. However, if not all of this interest capacity is utilised, the amount of unused interest capacity that can be carried forward could be limited as if the group ratio had been subject to a cap. This cap should be set at a level which is higher than the benchmark fixed ratio but it is suggested should not exceed 100%. This is illustrated in Example 6f in Annex II.A. This would be reasonably simple to apply and administer. It would also allow entities to benefit from the carry forward of unused interest capacity up to the cap, but removes the risk of a very high group ratio giving rise to large amounts of unused interest capacity that could be carried forward and used in future periods.

387. Where this approach is applied without limiting the net interest deductions permitted under the group ratio rule, an entity may still be able to claim high levels of net interest deductions in the current year, in excess of the net third party interest expense of the group and representing a percentage of EBITDA which would not be sustainable in normal circumstances on an ongoing basis. This could include net interest expense arising in

the current period, or disallowed interest expense carried forward from earlier periods. Therefore, if a country takes this approach, cases where entities in a group enter into arrangements to take advantage of this should be addressed through targeted rules.

The treatment of entities where a group has zero or negative group EBITDA

388. In some cases, losses in group entities will be so significant that the group as a whole has a zero or negative group EBITDA. In this scenario, the group ratio rule cannot be applied as it is not possible to calculate a meaningful net third party interest expense/EBITDA ratio. However, there may still be profitable entities within the group making a positive contribution to group EBITDA.

389. In applying the common approach, a country may decide that this is the correct outcome. An entity with positive EBITDA in a loss-making group may still apply the fixed ratio rule and deduct net interest expense up to the benchmark fixed ratio. The downside to this approach is that it creates a cliff-edge effect where a group moves from having a very low group EBITDA to having a zero or negative group EBITDA. Where an entity with positive EBITDA is in a group with a low group EBITDA it would be able to deduct net interest expense up to the group ratio, subject to a possible cap on the group ratio and/or an upper limit equal to the group's net third party interest expense, where these are applied. However, if losses elsewhere in the group meant that the group moved to having zero or negative group EBITDA, the same entity would be unable to apply the group ratio rule and would have to rely on the fixed ratio rule to obtain relief. This could lead to lengthy discussions between an entity and a tax authority in cases where group EBITDA is close to zero, as the impact of having group EBITDA of zero rather than just above zero could be significant. It could also have a distortive impact on a group's behaviour as it seeks to avoid a zero or negative group EBITDA, placing additional pressure on statutory auditors. If a country wishes to address this issue, it may do so in a number of different ways. Possible options include excluding entities with negative EBITDA from the calculation of group EBITDA and/or introducing a concession to allow entities with positive EBITDA to deduct net interest expense in excess of the amount that would be permitted under the fixed ratio rule, subject to restrictions.

390. Where a country excludes the earnings of entities with negative EBITDA from group EBITDA, this would enable a group's net third party interest expense/EBITDA to be calculated and the group's net third party interest expense to be allocated among profitable entities in the group. This approach would remove the cliff-edge effect where a group moves from positive group EBITDA to zero or negative EBITDA, and would ensure that a group with negative group EBITDA would still be able to deduct an amount equivalent to its actual net interest expense. However, as noted earlier, there are a number of practical issues that would need to be taken into account by a country in adopting such an approach.

391. A country should also consider allowing an entity with positive EBITDA in a group with negative group EBITDA to utilise interest capacity up to the lower of the entity's actual net interest expense, and either or both of (i) the group's net third party interest expense and (ii) a set percentage of entity EBITDA. In this case, it is suggested that these restrictions should correspond with those applied to entities in groups with positive group EBITDA and the set percentage of entity EBITDA should be the same as the cap on the group ratio described above (i.e. it should be higher than the benchmark fixed ratio under the fixed ratio rule, but it is suggested should not exceed 100%). This approach is illustrated by Example 6g in Annex II.A.

392. In terms of the ability of an entity with positive EBITDA to deduct net interest expense in the current period, the outcome would be consistent with that from applying a limit on interest capacity and/or a cap on the group ratio to an entity in a group with positive group EBITDA. This removes the cliff-edge effect described above, where an entity in a group with negative group EBITDA is required to apply the fixed ratio rule, and would reduce pressure on groups and tax authorities. On the other hand, where a group has negative group EBITDA, an entity which has deducted all of its net interest expense in the current period would not have any unused interest capacity available to be carried forward. This would prevent entities in loss-making groups accumulating potentially large carry forwards of unused interest capacity which could be monetised in future periods by increasing the level of net interest expense or reducing the level of taxable income in an entity.

Annex II.A

Examples to Part II

Example 1 – Adjustments to a group's net third party interest expense

Example 1a – Applying an uplift to net third party interest expense

Table II.A.1. **Applying an uplift to net third party interest expense**

	A Co USD	B Co USD	Group USD
EBITDA	60 million	200 million	260 million
Net interest	(10 million)	(55 million)	(65 million)
Group net third party interest expense/ EBITDA ratio	-	-	25%
Interest capacity	15 million	50 million	-
Deductible interest expense	(10 million)	(50 million)	-
Disallowed interest expense	-	(5 million)	-
Unused interest capacity	5 million	-	-

393. In Table II.A.1, a group consists of two entities: A Co and B Co. A Co has EBITDA of USD 60 million and net interest expense of USD 10 million. B Co has EBITDA of USD 200 million and net interest expense of USD 55 million. The group has total EBITDA of USD 260 million and net interest expense of USD 65 million. The group's total net third party interest expense/EBITDA ratio is 25%.

394. A Co has interest capacity of USD 15 million. It can deduct all of its net interest expense of USD 10 million and has unused interest capacity of USD 5 million. B Co has interest capacity of USD 50 million. It can deduct net interest expense of USD 50 million, and incurs an interest disallowance of USD 5 million. This disallowance arises because the net interest expense in the two entities is not precisely aligned with where EBITDA is earned. If the two entities are in the same country, a rule could allow the interest disallowance in B Co to be set against the unused interest capacity in A Co. However, this would not be possible if the entities are in different countries.

395. Table II.A.2 concerns the same group, but in this case the countries where the entities are located allow an uplift to net third party interest expense of 10%. Therefore, the group now has net third party interest expense of USD 71.5 million (i.e. USD 65 million x 110%) and a net third party interest expense/EBITDA ratio of 27.5%.

Table II.A.2. **Applying an uplift to net third party interest expense of 10%**

	A Co USD	B Co USD	Group USD
EBITDA	60 million	200 million	260 million
Net interest	(10 million)	(55 million)	(65 million)
Net third party interest expense (after uplift)	-	-	(71.5 million)
Group net third party interest expense/ EBITDA ratio	-	-	27.5%
Interest capacity	16.5 million	55 million	-
Deductible interest expense	(10 million)	(55 million)	-
Disallowed interest expense	-	-	-
Unused interest capacity	6.5 million	-	-

396. B Co is now able to deduct all of its net interest expense of USD 55 million with no interest disallowance. The application of the uplift to net third party interest expense has reduced the impact on the group of net interest expense not being fully aligned with the location of EBITDA.

397. On the other hand, unused interest capacity in A Co has increased from USD 5 million to USD 6.5 million. To the extent this unused interest capacity can be carried forward, this may create a greater incentive in the future for A Co to take on more debt to the point where its net interest expense/EBITDA ratio is higher than that of the group as a whole.

Example 1b – Excluding non-deductible payments from net third party interest expense

Table II.A.3. **Excluding non-deductible payments from net third party interest expense**

	A Co USD	B Co USD	Group USD
EBITDA	100 million	100 million	200 million
Fixed rate preference dividends	(25 million)	(15 million)	(40 million)
Other net interest expense	(20 million)	(30 million)	(50 million)
Net interest expense (consolidated financial statements)			(90 million)
Group net third party interest	(90 million)	(50 million)	
Group net third party interest expense/ EBITDA ratio	45%	25%	-
Interest capacity	45 million	25 million	-
Deductible interest expense	(45 million)	(25 million)	-
Disallowed interest expense	-	(5 million)	-
Unused interest capacity	-	-	-

398. In Table II.A.3, a group consists of two entities: A Co and B Co. A Co has EBITDA of USD 100 million and a net interest expense of USD 20 million. A Co also pays dividends on fixed rate preference shares of USD 25 million. B Co has EBITDA of USD 100 million and net interest expense of USD 30 million. B Co also pays dividends on fixed rate preference shares of USD 15 million. The group has total EBITDA of USD 200 million. In the group's consolidated financial statements, fixed rate preference share dividends are treated as an interest expense and so the group has a total net interest expense of USD 90 million.

399. A Co is resident in Country A, which allows a tax deduction for dividends on fixed rate preference shares as interest. Based on the total net third party interest expense in the group's consolidated financial statements of USD 90 million, the group has a net third party interest expense/EBITDA ratio of 45%. A Co therefore has interest capacity of USD 45 million. This means that all of A Co's net interest expense and fixed rate preference share dividends are deductible with no disallowance.

400. B Co is resident in Country B, which does not allow a tax deduction for dividends on fixed rate preference shares. Country B takes the view that, as these payments are not tax deductible if paid by a resident entity, they also should not be able to be used by group to increase the level of a resident entity's interest capacity. Therefore, in applying the group ratio rule, B Co must deduct the group's fixed rate preference share dividends from net third party interest expense. The group now has net third party interest expense of USD 50 million and a net third party interest expense/EBITDA ratio of 25%. Out of B Co's total net interest expense of USD 30 million, USD 25 million is deductible and USD 5 million is disallowed.

Example 1c – Excluding net related party interest expense from net third party interest expense

Table II.A.4. **Applying the group ratio rule to a group with no net related party interest expense**

	A Co USD	B Co USD	Group USD
EBITDA	100 million	100 million	200 million
Net interest expense paid to related parties	-	-	-
Other net interest expense	(25 million)	(25 million)	(50 million)
Net interest expense (consolidated financial statements)	-	-	(50 million)
Group net third party interest expense/ EBITDA ratio			25%
Interest capacity	25 million	25 million	-
Deductible interest expense	(25 million)	(25 million)	-
Disallowed interest expense	-	-	-
Unused interest capacity	-	-	-

401. In Table II.A.4, a group consists of two entities: A Co and B Co. A Co and B Co each have EBITDA of USD 100 million and net interest expense paid to third parties of USD 25 million. The group has total EBITDA of USD 200 million and total net third party interest expense of USD 50 million, with a net third party interest expense/EBITDA ratio of 25%. Under the group ratio rule, A Co and B Co would each be able to deduct all of their net interest expense of USD 25 million with no disallowance.

402. In Table II.A.5, the group has been acquired by investors who have replaced part of the group's equity with shareholder debt. A Co and B Co now each have an additional net interest expense payable to related parties of USD 50 million. The group's consolidated financial statements now show a total net interest expense of USD 150 million.

Table II.A.5. **Applying the group ratio rule to a group with net related party interest expense**

	A Co USD	B Co USD	Group USD
EBITDA	100 million	100 million	200 million
Net interest expense paid to related parties	(50 million)	(50 million)	(100 million)
Other net interest expense	(25 million)	(25 million)	(50 million)
Net interest expense (consolidated financial statements)	-	-	(150 million)
Group net third party interest expense/ EBITDA ratio	75%	25%	-
Interest capacity	75 million	25 million	-
Deductible interest expense	(75 million)	(25 million)	-
Disallowed interest expense	-	(50 million)	-
Unused interest capacity	-	-	-

403. A Co is resident in Country A. Under the group ratio rule in Country A, A Co calculates the group net third party interest expense/EBITDA ratio using a figure for net third party interest expense which includes net interest expense to related parties. This gives a group ratio of 75%. A Co has net interest expense of USD 75 million, and in principle is able to deduct all of this net interest expense without limitation. As set out in Chapter 7, Country A should introduce rules to prevent related party debt being used to increase net third party interest expense, which may apply in this case.

404. B Co is resident in Country B. Under the group ratio rule in Country B, B Co calculates the group net third party interest expense/EBITDA ratio using a figure for net third party interest expense which excludes net interest expense to related parties. This gives a group ratio of 25%. Out of its total net interest expense of USD 75 million, B Co is able to deduct USD 25 million and incurs an interest disallowance of USD 50 million.

405. Table II.A.6 shows a different group including three entities: A Co, B Co and C Co. A Co and B Co each have EBITDA of USD 100 million and net interest expense paid to third parties of USD 50 million). C Co has EBITDA of USD 200 million and net interest expense paid to related parties of USD 200 million.

406. A Co is resident in Country A, which includes related party interest in the definition of net third party interest expense. Therefore under the group ratio rule in Country A, because of the high level of related party interest in C Co, the group's net third party interest expense/EBITDA ratio is 300 million/400 million or 75%. A Co therefore has interest capacity of USD 75 million. It is able to deduct all of its net interest expense of USD 50 million with unused interest capacity of USD 25 million.

407. B Co is resident in Country B, which does not include related party interest in the calculation of net third party interest expense. Under the group ratio rule in Country B, the group's net third party interest expense/EBITDA ratio is 100 million/400 million or 25%.

B Co therefore has interest capacity of USD 25 million. It is able to deduct net interest expense of USD 25 million and incurs an interest disallowance of USD 25 million.

Table II.A.6. **Net related party interest expense in other parts of the group**

	A Co USD	B Co USD	C Co USD	Group USD
EBITDA	100 million	100 million	200 million	400 million
Net interest expense paid to related parties	-	-	(200 million)	(200 million)
Other net interest expense	(50 million)	(50 million)	-	(100 million)
Net interest expense (consolidated financial statements)	-	-	-	(300 million)
Group net third party interest expense/ EBITDA ratio	75%	25%	25%	-
Interest capacity	75 million	25 million	50 million	-
Deductible interest expense	(50 million)	(25 million)	(50 million)	-
Disallowed interest expense	-	(25 million)	(150 million)	-
Unused interest capacity	25 million	-	-	-

408. C Co is resident in Country C, which does not include related party interest in the definition of net third party interest expense. Under the group ratio rule in Country B, the group's net third party interest expense/EBITDA ratio is 100 million/400 million or 25%. C Co therefore has interest capacity of USD 50 million. Out of C Co's total net related party interest expense of USD 200 million, USD 50 million is deductible and USD 150 million is disallowed.

Example 1d – The impact of third party debt raised directly by an equity accounted entity

Table II.A.7. **Applying the group ratio rule where third party debt is raised by members of the group**

	A Co USD	B Co USD	Consolidation adjustments	Group USD
Share of profit of JVE	-	-	50 million	50 million
Dividend income	50 million	-	(50 million)	-
Taxable EBITDA	50 million	100 million	-	150 million
EBITDA	100 million	100 million	-	200 million
Net interest expense	(25 million)	(25 million)	-	(50 million)
Group net third party interest expense/ EBITDA ratio			-	25%
Taxable entity EBITDA	50 million	100 million	-	
Interest capacity	12.5 million	25 million	-	-
Deductible interest expense	(12.5 million)	(25 million)	-	-
Disallowed interest expense	(12.5 million)	-	-	-
Unused interest capacity	-	-	-	-

409. In Table II.A.7, a group consists of two entities: A Co (resident in Country A) and B Co (resident in Country B). A Co has a 50% holding in a JVE which distributes all of its net profit as a dividend. Country A applies a participation exemption on dividends with no requirement for underlying tax to be paid, and so the dividends received by A Co are tax-exempt. A Co also has other EBITDA of USD 50 million, all of which is subject to tax. B Co has EBITDA of USD 100 million which is fully taxable. Both A Co and B Co have net third party interest expense of USD 25 million.

410. Under equity accounting rules, the group recognises a 50% share of the profits of JVE in its consolidated income statement, but does not recognise the dividend income received by A Co (as to include both a share of the JVE's profits and dividends received from the entity would be double counting). Country A and Country B both include the group's share of the JVE's profit within group EBITDA. Therefore the group has net third party interest expense of USD 50 million and group EBITDA of USD 200 million, giving a group net third party interest expense/EBITDA ratio of 25%.

411. Under the group ratio rule, A Co applies the group's ratio of 25% to its taxable EBITDA of USD 50 million (not including its tax-exempt dividend income) to give interest capacity of USD 12.5 million. A Co may therefore deduct net interest expense of USD 12.5 million and incurs an interest disallowance of USD 12.5 million. This corresponds with the proportion of A Co's EBITDA which is subject to tax.

412. B Co applies the group's net third party interest expense/EBITDA ratio of 25% to its taxable EBITDA of USD 100 million to give interest capacity of USD 25 million. B Co is able to deduct all of its net interest expense with no unused interest capacity.

413. In Table II.A.8, A Co has repaid part of its third party debt, reducing its net third party interest expense to USD 12.5 million. Instead, the JVE has raised third party debt directly. The group's share of the JVE's profit is therefore reduced by USD 12.5 million, which corresponds to the group's share of the JVE's net third party interest expense. Overall, the group is in the same economic position as before – its share of the JVE's profit is reduced by USD 12.5 million, but the group's net interest expense is also reduced by the same amount. However, the group's net third party interest expense is now USD 37.5 million and group

Table II.A.8. **Impact of third party debt raised directly by an equity accounted entity**

	A Co USD	B Co USD	Consolidation adjustments	Group USD
Share of profit of JVE	-	-	37.5 million	37.5 million
Dividend income	37.5 million	-	(37.5 million)	-
Taxable EBITDA	50 million	100 million	-	150 million
EBITDA	87.5 million	100 million	-	187.5 million
Net interest expense	(12.5 million)	(25 million)	-	(37.5 million)
Group net third party interest expense/ EBITDA ratio			-	20%
Taxable entity EBITDA	50 million	100 million	-	
Interest capacity	10 million	20 million	-	-
Deductible interest expense	(10 million)	(20 million)	-	-
Disallowed interest expense	(2.5 million)	(5 million)	-	-
Unused interest capacity	-	-	-	-

EBITDA is USD 187.5 million, giving a group net third party interest expense/EBITDA ratio of 20%.

414. Under the group ratio rule, A Co would apply the group ratio of 20% to its taxable EBITDA of USD 50 million to give interest capacity of USD 10 million. Of its total net interest expense of USD 12.5 million, USD 10 million would be deductible and USD 2.5 million would be disallowed. B Co would also apply the group ratio of 20% to its taxable EBITDA of USD 100 million to give interest capacity of USD 20 million. Therefore, out of its total net interest expense of 25 million, USD 20 million would be deductible and USD 5 million would be disallowed.

415. This may be an appropriate result for the group, as it now has a reduced net third party interest expense and so its group ratio has reduced. However, given the economic effect of raising third party debt at the level of A Co and at the level of the JVE are comparable, a country may for policy reasons allow adjustments to be made to reduce this impact, as in Example 1e.

Example 1e – Attributing the group's share of the third party debt of an equity accounted entity

416. This example is based on the same facts as in Table II.A.8 in Example 1d. However, in this case Country A and Country B allow A Co and B Co to attribute part of the JVE's net third party interest expense to the group. Therefore, in Table II.A.9, the group is now treated as having net third party interest expense of USD 50 million and group EBITDA of USD 200 million, giving a net third party interest expense/EBITDA ratio of 25%. For the purposes of calculating this ratio, this has put the group in a position comparable to that in Table II.A.7 in Example 1d, where the third party debt funding the JVE was raised by A Co rather than directly in the JVE.

Table II.A.9. **Attributing the group's share of the third party debt of an equity accounted entity**

	A Co USD	B Co USD	Consolidation adjustments	Group USD
Share of profit of JVE	-	-	37.5 million	37.5 million
Dividend income	37.5 million	-	(37.5 million)	-
Taxable EBITDA	50 million	100 million	-	150 million
EBITDA	87.5 million	100 million	-	187.5 million
EBITDA adjusted for share of net third party interest expense of JV	-	-	-	200 million
Net interest expense	(12.5 million)	(25 million)	-	(37.5 million)
Net interest expense adjusted for share of net third party interest expense of JV			-	(50 million)
Group net third party interest expense/ EBITDA ratio			-	25%
Taxable entity EBITDA	50 million	100 million	-	
Interest capacity	12.5 million	25 million	-	-
Deductible interest expense	(12.5 million)	(25 million)	-	-
Disallowed interest expense	-	-	-	-
Unused interest capacity	-	-	-	-

417. Under the group ratio rule, A Co would apply the group ratio of 25% to its taxable EBITDA of USD 50 million to give interest capacity of USD 12.5 million. A Co would therefore be able to deduct all of its net interest expense with no disallowance. B Co would also apply the group ratio of 25% to its taxable EBITDA of USD 100 million to give interest capacity of USD 25 million. Again, B Co would be able to deduct all of its net interest expense with no disallowance.

418. This is a more complex approach, allowing entities in a group to take into account third party interest expense arising in an entity outside of the group. However, given the importance of joint venture arrangements in certain countries and sectors, this may be something a country could consider in introducing a group ratio rule.

Example 2 – Items to be included in the adjustment for interest income and expense when calculating group EBITDA

Example 2a – Excluding an uplift to net third party interest expense from the adjustment for interest income and expense when calculating group EBITDA

419. This example is based on the same fact pattern as in Example 1a, but focuses on the treatment of B Co in Country B. Country B has adopted a policy that in calculating a group's net third party interest expense/EBITDA ratio, the group's net third party interest expense may be subject to an uplift of 10%. Therefore, while the group has an actual net third party interest expense of USD 65 million, for the purposes of calculating the group's ratio, this is increased to USD 71.5 million.

420. In Table II.A.10, in Scenario 1, group EBITDA of USD 260 million is calculated on the basis that the adjustment for interest income and expense does not include the uplift of 10%. This was the approach taken in Example 1a. This gives rise to a group net third party

Table II.A.10. **Excluding an uplift to net third party interest expense from the adjustment of interest income and expense when calculating group EBITDA**

	A Co USD	B Co USD	Group USD
Net profit (before adding back net interest expense)	50 million	145 million	195 million
EBITDA	60 million	200 million	-
Net interest	(10 million)	(55 million)	(65 million)
Net third party interest expense (after uplift)	-	-	(71.5 million)

	Scenario 1 B Co USD	Scenario 2 B Co USD
Group net profit (before adding back net interest expense)	195 million	195 million
Group Net interest	(65 million)	(71.5 million)
Group EBITDA	260 million	266.5 million
Group net third party interest expense/EBITDA ratio	27.5%	26.8%
Interest capacity	55 million	53.7 million
Deductible interest expense	(55 million)	(53.7 million)
Disallowed interest expense	-	(1.3 million)
Unused interest capacity	-	-

interest expense/EBITDA ratio of 27.5%. As shown in Example 1a, this increases B Co's interest capacity by 10%, from USD 50 million to USD 55 million. B Co is therefore able to deduct all of its net interest expense with no interest disallowance.

421. In Scenario 2, group EBITDA has been re-calculated on the basis that the adjustment for interest income and expense includes the uplift of 10%. Therefore, group EBITDA is increased by USD 6.5 million to USD 266.5 million. This gives rise to a net third party interest expense/EBITDA ratio of 26.8%, which is lower than that in Scenario 1. B Co now has interest capacity of USD 53.7 million and incurs an interest disallowance of USD 1.3 million.

422. It is suggested that the approach in Scenario 2 does not achieve the intended policy goal of Country B. Although Country B has adopted a policy that a group's net third party interest expense should be subject to an uplift of 10%, the increase in the group's net third party interest expense/EBITDA ratio is just 7.2%. This is because the 10% uplift has also been applied to the adjustment for interest income and expense in calculating group EBITDA. Therefore, where a country allows an uplift of up to 10% to be applied to a group's net third party interest expense, this uplift should not be applied to the adjustment for interest income and expense in calculating group EBITDA.

Example 2b – Including non-deductible payments in the adjustment for interest income and expense when calculating group EBITDA

Table II.A.11. **Including non-deductible payments in the adjustment for interest income and expense when calculating group EBITDA**

	A Co USD	B Co USD	Group USD
EBITDA	100 million	100 million	200 million
Fixed rate preference dividends	(25 million)	(15 million)	(40 million)
Other net interest expense	(20 million)	(30 million)	(50 million)
Net interest expense (consolidated financial statements)			(90 million)
Group net third party interest	(90 million)	(50 million)	
	Scenario 1 B Co USD	**Scenario 2 B Co USD**	
Group EBITDA	200 million	160 million	
Group net third party interest expense/ EBITDA ratio	25%	31.25%	-
Interest capacity	25 million	31.25 million	-
Deductible interest expense	(25 million)	(30 million)	-
Disallowed interest expense	(5 million)	-	-
Unused interest capacity	-	1.25 million	-

423. This example is based on the same fact pattern as in Example 1b, but focuses on the treatment of B Co in Country B. Country B has adopted a policy that dividends paid on fixed rate preference shares, which are not tax deductible in the country, should not be used to increase an entity's interest capacity under the group ratio rule. In applying the group ratio rule,

B Co is required to exclude fixed rate preference dividends from the group's net third party interest expense. Therefore, the group has net third party interest expense of USD 50 million.

424. In Table II.A.11, in Scenario 1, group EBITDA of USD 200 million is calculated on the basis that the adjustment for interest income and expense still includes the fixed rate preference dividends paid by the group. This was the approach taken in Example 1b. This gives rise to a group net third party interest expense/EBITDA ratio of 25%. Out of its total net interest expense of USD 30 million, USD 25 million is tax deductible and USD 5 million is disallowed. This approach reflects the fact that in economic terms, the group has incurred net interest payments of USD 90 million (including fixed rate preference dividends that are economically equivalent to interest). However, USD 40 million of this is paid in a form that would not be tax deductible in Country B.

425. In Scenario 2, group EBITDA has been re-calculated on the basis that the adjustment for interest income and expense does not include fixed rate preference dividends paid by the group. Therefore, group EBITDA is reduced by USD 40 million to USD 160 million. This gives rise to an increased net third party interest expense/EBITDA ratio of 31.25%. B Co may now deduct all of its net interest expense and also has unused interest capacity of USD 1.25 million.

426. It is suggested that the approach in Scenario 2 does not achieve the intended policy goal of Country B, as the calculation of group EBITDA does not recognise the full extent to which the group is debt funded in economic terms, albeit that part of this is in a form that Country B does not treat as debt for tax purposes. Therefore, payments which are interest or economically equivalent to interest should still be included in the adjustment for interest income and expense in calculating group EBITDA, even if for policy reasons a country chooses to exclude them from net third party interest expense.

Example 2c – Including net interest paid to related parties in the adjustment for interest income and expense when calculating group EBITDA

427. This example is based on the same fact pattern as in Example 1c, but focuses on the treatment of B Co in Country B. Country B has adopted a policy that net interest expense paid to related parties should not be used to increase an entity's interest capacity under the group ratio rule. In applying the group ratio rule, B Co is required to exclude net interest paid to related parties from the group's net third party interest expense. Therefore, the group has net third party interest expense of USD 50 million.

428. In Table II.A.12, in Scenario 1, group EBITDA of USD 200 million is calculated on the basis that the adjustment for interest income and expense still includes the net related party interest paid by the group. This was the approach taken in Example 1c. This gives rise to a group net third party interest expense/EBITDA ratio of 25%. Out of its total net interest expense of USD 75 million, USD 25 million is tax deductible and USD 50 million is disallowed. This approach reflects the fact that in economic terms, the group has incurred net interest payments of USD 150 million (including net payments to related parties). However, USD 100 million of this is related party interest which Country B believes should not be taken into account to increase the interest capacity of entities.

429. In Scenario 2, group EBITDA has been re-calculated on the basis that the adjustment for interest income and expense does not include net related party interest paid by the group. Therefore, group EBITDA is reduced by USD 100 million to USD 100 million. This gives rise to an increased net third party interest expense/EBITDA ratio of 50%. B Co may now deduct net interest expense of USD 50 million with a reduced disallowance of USD 25 million.

Table II.A.12. **Including net interest paid to related parties in the adjustment for interest income and expense when calculating group EBITDA**

	A Co USD	B Co USD	Group USD
EBITDA	100 million	100 million	200 million
Net interest expense paid to related parties	(50 million)	(50 million)	(100 million)
Other net interest expense	(25 million)	(25 million)	(50 million)
Net interest expense (consolidated financial statements)			(150 million)
Group net third party interest	(150 million)	(50 million)	
	Scenario 1 B Co USD	**Scenario 2 B Co USD**	
Group EBITDA	200 million	100 million	
Group net third party interest expense/ EBITDA ratio	25%	50%	-
Interest capacity	25 million	50 million	-
Deductible interest expense	(25 million)	(50 million)	-
Disallowed interest expense	(50 million)	(25 million)	-
Unused interest capacity	-	-	-

430. It is suggested that the approach in Scenario 2 does not achieve the intended policy goal of Country B, as the calculation of group EBITDA does not recognise the full extent to which the group is debt funded, albeit that part of this is with related party debt. Therefore, net interest paid to related parties should still be included in the adjustment for interest income and expense in calculating group EBITDA, even if for policy reasons a country chooses to exclude these payments from net third party interest expense.

Example 3 – The treatment of dividend income when calculating group EBITDA

Example 3a – Including dividend income in group EBITDA (taxable dividends)

431. In Table II.A.13, a group consists of two entities: A Co (resident in Country A) and B Co (resident in Country B). A Co receives dividend income of USD 50 million from entities outside the group. This dividend income does not qualify for the participation exemption in Country A and is subject to tax. The A Co also has other EBITDA of USD 50 million, all of which is subject to tax. B Co has EBITDA of USD 100 million which is fully taxable. Both A Co and B Co have net third party interest expense of USD 25 million. Country A and Country B both include dividend income within group EBITDA. Therefore the group has net third party interest expense of USD 50 million and group EBITDA of USD 200 million, giving a group net third party interest expense/EBITDA ratio of 25%.

432. Under the group ratio rule, A Co and B Co would both apply the group's net third party interest expense/EBITDA ratio of 25% to their taxable EBITDA of USD 100 million. This would give both A Co and B Co interest capacity of USD 25 million. The two entities are able to deduct all of their net interest expense with no disallowance and no unused interest capacity.

Table II.A.13. **Including dividend income in group EBITDA (taxable dividends)**

	A Co USD	B Co USD	Group USD
Dividend income	50 million	-	50 million
Other taxable EBITDA	50 million	100 million	150 million
EBITDA	100 million	100 million	200 million
Net interest expense	(25 million)	(25 million)	(50 million)
Group net third party interest expense/ EBITDA ratio			25%
Taxable entity EBITDA	100 million	100 million	
Interest capacity	25 million	25 million	-
Deductible interest expense	(25 million)	(25 million)	-
Disallowed interest expense	-	-	-
Unused interest capacity	-	-	-

Example 3b – Including dividend income in group EBITDA (tax-exempt dividends)

433. In Table II.A.14, a group consists of two entities: A Co (resident in Country A) and B Co (resident in Country B). A Co receives dividend income of USD 50 million from entities outside the group. This dividend income qualifies for the participation exemption in Country A and is exempt from tax. A Co also has other EBITDA of USD 50 million, all of which is subject to tax. B Co has EBITDA of USD 100 million which is fully taxable. Both A Co and B Co have net third party interest expense of USD 25 million. Country A and Country B both include dividend income within group EBITDA. Therefore the group has net third party interest expense of USD 50 million and group EBITDA of USD 200 million, giving a group net third party interest expense/EBITDA ratio of 25%.

434. Under the group ratio rule, A Co applies the group ratio of 25% to its taxable EBITDA of USD 50 million to give interest capacity of USD 12.5 million. A Co may therefore deduct net interest expense of USD 12.5 million and incurs an interest disallowance of

Table II.A.14. **Including dividend income in group EBITDA (tax-exempt dividends)**

	A Co USD	B Co USD	Group USD
Dividend income	50 million	-	50 million
Taxable EBITDA	50 million	100 million	150 million
EBITDA	100 million	100 million	200 million
Net interest expense	(25 million)	(25 million)	(50 million)
Group net third party interest expense/ EBITDA ratio			25%
Taxable entity EBITDA	50 million	100 million	
Interest capacity	12.5 million	25 million	-
Deductible interest expense	(12.5 million)	(25 million)	-
Disallowed interest expense	(12.5 million)	-	-
Unused interest capacity	-	-	-

USD 12.5 million. As 50% of A Co's net income is subject to tax, it is appropriate that 50% of its net interest expense should be deductible. The net interest expense which is disallowed corresponds to the proportion of the expense that in economic terms is funding tax-exempt dividend income.

435. B Co applies the group's net third party interest expense/EBITDA ratio of 25% to its taxable EBITDA of USD 100 million to give interest capacity of USD 25 million. As in Example 3a, B Co is able to deduct all of its net interest expense with no unused interest capacity.

436. Taking the results of Example 3a and Example 3b together, these show that the inclusion of dividend income in group EBITDA should ensure the correct result in cases where dividend income is taxable and also in cases where dividend income is tax-exempt. In cases where some or all of a group's dividend income is tax-exempt, an appropriate response is for a proportionate share of the group's net third party interest expense to be restricted, in line with the goals set out in the BEPS Action Plan.

Example 3c – Removing dividend income from group EBITDA (tax-exempt dividends)

437. This example is based on the same facts as in Example 3b. However, in Table II.A.15 Country A and Country B both require groups to remove dividends received from outside the group in calculating group EBITDA. Therefore, for the purposes of applying the group ratio rule, the group now has net third party interest expense of USD 50 million and group EBITDA of USD 150 million, giving a group net third party interest expense/EBITDA ratio of 33.3%.

438. Under the group ratio rule, A Co applies the group ratio of 33.3% to its taxable EBITDA of USD 50 million to give interest capacity of USD 16.7 million. A Co may deduct net interest expense of USD 16.7 million and incurs a disallowance of USD 8.3 million. This means that, although only 50% of A Co's net income is subject to tax, it can deduct 67% of its net interest expense. Compared with the position in Example 3b, USD 4.2 million of A Co's net interest expense, which in economic terms is funding its tax-exempt dividend income, may be used to shelter the tax on its other taxable income.

Table II.A.15. **Removing dividend income from group EBITDA (tax-exempt dividends)**

	A Co USD	B Co USD	Group USD
Dividend income	50 million	-	50 million
Taxable EBITDA	50 million	100 million	150 million
Remove dividends from group EBITDA	(50 million)		(50 million)
EBITDA	50 million	100 million	150 million
Net interest expense	(25 million)	(25 million)	(50 million)
Group net third party interest expense/ EBITDA ratio			33.3%
Taxable entity EBITDA	50 million	100 million	
Interest capacity	16.7 million	33.3 million	-
Deductible interest expense	(16.7 million)	(25 million)	-
Disallowed interest expense	(8.3 million)	-	-
Unused interest capacity	-	8.3 million	-

439. B Co applies the group's net third party interest expense/EBITDA ratio of 33.3% to its taxable EBITDA of USD 100 million to give interest capacity of USD 33.3 million. B Co is able to deduct all of its net interest expense and has unused interest capacity of USD 8.3 million. Compared with the position in Example 3b (in which B Co could deduct all its net interest expense but did not have unused interest capacity), B Co may now be incentivised to increase its level of net interest deductions to utilise this interest capacity and reduce the amount of income subject to tax in Country B.

Example 3d – Removing dividend income from group EBITDA (taxable dividends)

440. This example is based on the same facts as in Example 3a. However, in Table II.A.16 Country A and Country B both require groups to remove dividends received from outside the group in calculating group EBITDA. Therefore, for the purposes of applying the group ratio rule, the group now has net third party interest expense of USD 50 million and group EBITDA of USD 150 million, giving a group net third party interest expense/EBITDA ratio of 33.3%.

Table II.A.16. **Removing dividend income from group EBITDA (taxable dividends)**

	A Co USD	B Co USD	Group USD
Dividend income	50 million	-	50 million
Other taxable EBITDA	50 million	100 million	150 million
Remove dividends from group EBITDA	(50 million)		(50 million)
EBITDA	50 million	100 million	150 million
Net interest expense	(25 million)	(25 million)	(50 million)
Group net third party interest expense/ EBITDA ratio			33.3%
Taxable entity EBITDA	100 million	100 million	
Interest capacity	33.3 million	33.3 million	-
Deductible interest expense	(25 million)	(25 million)	-
Disallowed interest expense	-	-	-
Unused interest capacity	8.3 million	8.3 million	-

441. Under the group ratio rule, A Co and B Co both apply the group's net third party interest expense/EBITDA ratio of 33.3% to their taxable EBITDA of USD 100 million. This would give both entities an interest capacity of USD 33.3 million. Taken together, the companies have total interest capacity of USD 66.6 million, which is higher than the actual net third party interest expense of the group. A Co and B Co are both able to deduct all of their net interest expense, but each now has unused interest capacity of USD 8.3 million.

442. Therefore, where a group has taxable dividend income, excluding dividend income from group EBITDA could result in group entities being able to claim net interest deductions in excess of the actual net third party interest expense of the entire group.

Example 4 – The treatment of a group's share of the profit or loss of an associate or JVE when calculating group EBITDA

Example 4a – Including the share of profit of an equity accounted entity within group EBITDA (taxable dividends)

443. In Table II.A.17, a group consists of two entities: A Co (resident in Country A) and B Co (resident in Country B). A Co has a 50% holding in a JVE which distributes all of its net profit as a dividend. Country A does not apply a participation exemption and taxes dividend income with credit for underlying tax. However, as a result of a tax preference in the country where it operates, the JVE does not pay any tax. Therefore A Co is fully taxable on its dividend income. A Co also has other EBITDA of USD 50 million, all of which is subject to tax. B Co has EBITDA of USD 100 million which is fully taxable. Both A Co and B Co have net third party interest expense of USD 25 million.

Table II.A.17. **Including the share of profit of an equity accounted entity within group EBITDA (taxable dividends)**

	A Co USD	B Co USD	Consolidation adjustments	Group USD
Share of profit of JVE	-	-	50 million	50 million
Dividend income	50 million	-	(50 million)	-
Other taxable EBITDA	50 million	100 million	-	150 million
EBITDA	100 million	100 million		200 million
Net interest expense	(25 million)	(25 million)	-	(50 million)
Group net third party interest expense/ EBITDA ratio			-	25%
Taxable entity EBITDA	100 million	100 million	-	
Interest capacity	25 million	25 million	-	-
Deductible interest expense	(25 million)	(25 million)	-	-
Disallowed interest expense	-	-	-	-
Unused interest capacity	-	-	-	-

444. Under equity accounting rules, the group recognises a 50% share of the profits of JVE in its consolidated income statement, but does not recognise the dividend income received by A Co (as to include both a share of the JVE's profits and dividends received from the entity would be double counting). Country A and Country B both include the group's share of the JVE's profit within group EBITDA. Therefore the group has net third party interest expense of USD 50 million and group EBITDA of USD 200 million, giving a group net third party interest expense/EBITDA ratio of 25%.

445. Under the group ratio rule, A Co and B Co both apply the group's net third party interest expense/EBITDA ratio of 25% to their taxable EBITDA of USD 100 million. This would give both A Co and B Co interest capacity of USD 25 million. They are able to deduct all of their net interest expense with no disallowance and no unused interest capacity.

Example 4b – Including the share of profit of an equity accounted entity within group EBITDA (deferred dividends)

446. Table II.A.18 is based on the same fact pattern as in Example 4a, with the exception that in this case the JVE has not paid any dividends and so A Co does not receive any taxable dividend income. For the purposes of this example, it is assumed CFC rules do not apply. If A Co is subject to tax on an attribution of profits under CFC rules then the result should be the same as in Example 4a.

Table II.A.18. **Including the share of profit of an equity accounted entity within group EBITDA (deferred dividends)**

	A Co USD	B Co USD	Consolidation adjustments	Group USD
Share of profit of JVE	-	-	50 million	50 million
Dividend income	-	-	-	-
Taxable EBITDA	50 million	100 million	-	150 million
EBITDA	50 million	100 million	-	200 million
Net interest expense	(25 million)	(25 million)	-	(50 million)
Group net third party interest expense/ EBITDA ratio			-	25%
Taxable entity EBITDA	50 million	100 million	-	
Interest capacity	12.5 million	25 million	-	-
Deductible interest expense	(12.5 million)	(25 million)	-	-
Disallowed interest expense	(12.5 million)	-	-	-
Unused interest capacity	-	-	-	-

447. Under the group ratio rule, A Co applies the group ratio of 25% to its taxable EBITDA of USD 50 million to give interest capacity of USD 12.5 million. A Co may therefore deduct net interest expense of USD 12.5 million and incurs an interest disallowance of USD 12.5 million. If Country A allows the carry forward of disallowed interest expense, then this disallowed expense may be deducted in the future when A Co receives dividends from the JVE which are subject to tax.

448. B Co applies the group's net third party interest expense/EBITDA ratio of 25% to its taxable EBITDA of USD 100 million to give interest capacity of USD 25 million. B Co is able to deduct all of its net interest expense with no unused interest capacity.

Example 4c – Including the share of profit of an equity accounted entity within group EBITDA (tax-exempt dividends)

449. Table II.A.19 is based on the same fact pattern as in Example 4a, with the exception that in this case Country A applies a participation exemption on dividends with no requirement for underlying tax to be paid, and so the dividends received by A Co are tax-exempt. The group is in the same position as set out in Table II.A.7 under Example 1d.

450. Under the group ratio rule, A Co applies the group's ratio of 25% to its taxable EBITDA of USD 50 million (not including its tax-exempt dividend income) to give interest capacity of USD 12.5 million. A Co may therefore deduct net interest expense of USD 12.5 million and incurs an interest disallowance of USD 12.5 million. This corresponds with the proportion of A Co's EBITDA which is subject to tax.

Table II.A.19. **Including the share of profit of an equity accounted entity within group EBITDA (tax-exempt dividends)**

	A Co USD	B Co USD	Consolidation adjustments	Group USD
Share of profit of JVE	-	-	50 million	50 million
Dividend income	50 million	-	(50 million)	-
Taxable EBITDA	50 million	100 million	-	150 million
EBITDA	100 million	100 million	-	200 million
Net interest expense	(25 million)	(25 million)	-	(50 million)
Group net third party interest expense/ EBITDA ratio			-	25%
Taxable entity EBITDA	50 million	100 million	-	
Interest capacity	12.5 million	25 million	-	-
Deductible interest expense	(12.5 million)	(25 million)	-	-
Disallowed interest expense	(12.5 million)	-	-	-
Unused interest capacity	-	-	-	-

451. B Co applies the group's net third party interest expense/EBITDA ratio of 25% to its taxable EBITDA of USD 100 million to give interest capacity of USD 25 million. B Co is able to deduct all of its net interest expense with no unused interest capacity.

452. Taking the results of Examples 4a, 4b and 4c together, these show that the inclusion of the group's share of the JVE's profits in group EBITDA should ensure the correct result in cases where dividend income is taxable and also in cases where dividend income is deferred or tax-exempt. In cases where some or all of a group's dividend income is deferred or tax-exempt, an appropriate response is for a proportionate share of the group's net third party interest expense to be restricted, in line with the goals set out in the BEPS Action Plan.

Example 5 – The treatment of fair value adjustments when calculating group EBITDA

453. Table II.A.20 shows the position of a group which consists of two entities: A Co (resident in Country A) and B Co (resident in Country B). A Co raises third party borrowing to fund the acquisition of assets which give rise to a fixed income stream. Under the loan, A Co incurs interest expense based on a floating interest rate. Interest rates in Country A are currently volatile and, as the loan is funding a fixed level of income, A Co enters into an interest rate swap with a third party bank, to swap this floating interest expense into a fixed interest expense. The swap is not a designated hedge of the loan for financial reporting purposes, and fair value movements on the swap are taken through A Co's income statement. Country A and Country B include fair value movements on financial instruments within group EBITDA in applying the group ratio rule.

454. In period 1, A Co has taxable EBITDA of USD 100 million and a fair value gain on the swap of USD 40 million. A Co incurs an interest expense of USD 15 million on the floating rate loan and has a notional interest expense of USD 10 million on the swap, giving a total net interest expense of USD 25 million. B Co has taxable EBITDA of 100 million and a net interest expense of USD 25 million.

Table II.A.20. **Including fair value adjustments when calculating group EBITDA**

	Period 1			Period 2		
	A Co USD	B Co USD	Group USD	A Co USD	B Co USD	Group USD
Fair value gain/(loss) on swap	40 million	-	40 million	(40 million)	-	(40 million)
Taxable EBITDA	100 million	100 million	200 million	100 million	100 million	200 million
EBITDA	140 million	100 million	240 million	60 million	100 million	160 million
Interest expense on loans	(15 million)	(25 million)	(40 million)	(35 million)	(25 million)	(60 million)
Notional interest on swap	(10 million)	-	(10 million)	10 million	-	10 million
Net third party interest expense	(25 million)	(25 million)	(50 million)	(25 million)	(25 million)	(50 million)
Group net third party interest expense/EBITDA ratio	-	-	20.8%	-	-	31.25%
Taxable entity EBITDA	100 million	100 million	-	100 million	100 million	-
Interest capacity	20.8 million	20.8 million	-	31.25 million	31.25 million	-
Deductible interest expense	(20.8 million)	(20.8 million)	-	(25 million)	(25 million)	-
Disallowed interest expense	(4.2 million)	(4.2 million)	-	-	-	-
Unused interest capacity	-	-	-	6.25 million	6.25 million	-

455. In period 2, A Co has taxable EBITDA of USD 100 million and a fair value loss on the swap of USD 40 million. A Co incurs an interest expense of USD 35 million on the floating rate loan and has notional interest income of USD 10 million on the swap, giving a total net interest expense of USD 25 million. B Co has taxable EBITDA of 100 million and a net interest expense of USD 25 million.

456. Because Country A and Country B include the fair value movements on the swap within group EBITDA, the group has a net third party interest expense/EBITDA ratio of 20.8% in period 1 and 31.25% in period 2. This means that in period 1, A Co and B Co each incur an interest disallowance of USD 4.2 million, and in period 2 they have unused interest capacity of USD 6.25 million. To the extent Country A and Country B allow the carry forward and/or carry back of disallowed interest expense and/or unused interest capacity, the impact of these fluctuations may be reduced. However, this may not always provide groups with full relief, and even where all net interest expense can be claimed over the life of a loan, there could still be a serious cash flow impact for groups. Because fair value gains and losses on the swap should net to nil over the life of the instrument, a country may decide to address this volatility by excluding fair value gains and losses from group EBITDA, where these arise on financial instruments which are directly linked to the group's debt funding. The impact of this is illustrated below.

457. Table II.A.21 is based on the same facts as before, but in this case Country A and Country B exclude the fair value gains and losses on the swap from group EBITDA. The impact of this is that the group has a net third party interest expense/EBITDA ratio of 25% in both period 1 and period 2. Therefore, A Co and B Co are able to deduct all of their net interest expense with no disallowance and no unused interest capacity.

Table II.A.21. **Excluding fair value adjustments when calculating group EBITDA**

	Period 1			Period 2		
	A Co USD	B Co USD	Group USD	A Co USD	B Co USD	Group USD
Fair value gain/(loss) on swap	40 million	-	40 million	(40 million)	-	(40 million)
Taxable EBITDA	100 million	100 million	200 million	100 million	100 million	200 million
Remove fair value movements on swap	(40 million)		(40 million)	40 million		40 million
EBITDA	100 million	100 million	200 million	100 million	100 million	200 million
Interest expense on loans	(15 million)	(25 million)	(40 million)	(35 million)	(25 million)	(60 million)
Notional interest on swap	(10 million)	-	(10 million)	10 million	-	10 million
Net third party interest expense	(25 million)	(25 million)	(50 million)	(25 million)	(25 million)	(50 million)
Group net third party interest expense/ EBITDA ratio	-	-	25%	-	-	25%
Taxable entity EBITDA	100 million	100 million	-	100 million	100 million	-
Interest capacity	25 million	25 million	-	25 million	25 million	-
Deductible interest expense	(25 million)	(25 million)	-	(25 million)	(25 million)	-
Disallowed interest expense	-	-	-	-	-	-
Unused interest capacity	-	-	-	-	-	-

Example 6 – Addressing the impact of entities with negative EBITDA on the operation of the group ratio rule

Example 6a – The impact of entities with negative EBITDA on the operation of a group ratio rule

458. In Table II.A.22, a group consists of three entities: A Co, B Co and C Co. A Co has EBITDA of USD 100 million and net third party interest expense of USD 40 million. B Co has EBITDA of USD 10 million and net third party interest expense of USD 6 million. C Co has a negative EBITDA (i.e. losses) of USD 100 million and receives net third party interest income of USD 10 million. Therefore, the group has total EBITDA of USD 10 million and a net third party interest expense of USD 36 million. The group's net third party interest expense/EBITDA ratio is 360%.

Table II.A.22. **The impact of entities with negative EBITDA on the operation of a group ratio rule**

	A Co USD	B Co USD	C Co USD	Group USD
EBITDA	100 million	10 million	(100 million)	10 million
Net interest	(40 million)	(6 million)	10 million	(36 million)
Group net third party interest expense/ EBITDA ratio	-	-	-	360%
Interest capacity	360 million	36 million	0	-
Deductible interest expense	(40 million)	(6 million)	0	-
Disallowed interest expense	-	-	-	-
Unused interest capacity	320 million	30 million	-	-

459. This very high group ratio causes two problems. Firstly, in the current year A Co receives interest capacity of USD 360 million, which is higher than the group's actual net third party interest expense. This means that in principle the company could deduct more net interest than the total net third party interest expense of the group. Secondly, even after deducting their current year net interest expense, A Co and B Co still have a high level of unused interest capacity. If a country allows the carry forward of unused interest capacity, this could be carried into future periods and used to shelter further interest deductions.

460. In a sense, this issue arises because C Co (which has a negative EBITDA of USD 100 million) is not required to recognise negative interest capacity of USD 360 million. If this was the case, then the interest capacity of the group as a whole would equal the group's net third party interest expense of USD 36 million. However, the recognition of negative interest capacity in loss-making entities is not recommended as part of the best practice approach.

Example 6b – Excluding entities with negative EBITDA from the calculation of group EBITDA for a profitable group

461. This example is based on the same fact pattern as Example 6a. In Table II.A.23, the negative EBITDA in C Co has been disregarded in calculating group EBITDA. Therefore, the group now has EBITDA of USD 110 million, rather than USD 10 million. This means that the group's net third party interest expense/EBITDA ratio is now reduced to 32.7%.

Table II.A.23. **Excluding entities with negative EBITDA from the calculation of group EBTIDA for a profitable group**

	A Co USD	B Co USD	C Co USD	Group USD
EBITDA	100 million	10 million	(100 million)	110 million
Net interest	(40 million)	(6 million)	10 million	(36 million)
Group net third party interest expense/ EBITDA ratio	-	-	-	32.7%
Interest capacity	32.7 million	3.3 million	0	-
Deductible interest expense	(32.7 million)	(3.3 million)	0	-
Disallowed interest expense	(7.3 million)	(2.7 million)	-	-
Unused interest capacity	-	-	-	-

462. The effect of this is that A Co has interest capacity of USD 32.7 million and B Co has interest capacity of USD 3.2 million. Taken together, the interest capacity of A Co and B Co are USD 36 million, which is equal to the group's net third party interest expense. By disregarding C Co's negative EBITDA, the group ratio rule now operates to ensure that the group is able to deduct an amount equal to its actual net third party interest expense. However, it may be very difficult for the tax authorities in the countries of A Co and B Co to accurately establish the existence and value of the negative EBITDA in C Co. Therefore, it may not be feasible for a country to apply this approach in practice.

Example 6c – Applying a cap to the group ratio

463. In this example, the group is in the same position as in Example 6a. However, the group's net third party interest expense/EBITDA ratio is now subject to a cap of 50%. Therefore, compared with Example 6a, in Table II.A.24 B Co's interest capacity is now limited to USD 5 million (i.e. 50% of B Co's entity EBITDA of USD 10 million). B Co is able to deduct net interest expense of USD 5 million, and may carry forward disallowed interest expense of USD 1 million into future periods, if this is permitted.

Table II.A.24. **Applying a cap to the group ratio**

	A Co USD	B Co USD	C Co USD	Group USD
EBITDA	100 million	10 million	(100 million)	10 million
Net interest	(40 million)	(6 million)	10 million	(36 million)
Group net third party interest expense/ EBITDA ratio	-	-	-	50% (capped)
Interest capacity	50 million	5 million	0	-
Deductible interest expense	(40 million)	(5 million)	0	-
Disallowed interest expense	-	(1 million)	-	-
Unused interest capacity	10 million	-	-	-

464. A Co receives interest capacity of USD 50 million. This is less than in Example 6a, where the un-capped group ratio of 360% applies. However, it still significantly exceeds the group's net third party interest expense of USD 36 million. A Co is able to deduct its full net interest expense of USD 40 million and is able to carry forward unused interest capacity of USD 10 million, if this is permitted.

Example 6d – Applying an upper limit on interest capacity

465. In the table above, the group is in the same position as in Example 6a. However, the interest capacity of A Co is now subject to a limit equal to the group's actual net third party interest expense. Therefore, in Table II.A.25 A Co's interest capacity is limited to USD 36 million (i.e. the group's total net third party interest expense). A Co is able to deduct net interest expense of USD 36 million, and may carry forward disallowed interest expense of USD 4 million into future periods, if this is permitted.

466. As before, B Co receives interest capacity of USD 36 million and is able to deduct its full net interest expense of USD 6 million. It is also able to carry forward unused interest capacity of USD 30 million, if this is permitted. However, given B Co's interest capacity exceeds 100% of its EBITDA, this may be considered excessive.

467. Note that if the group's EBITDA had not been reduced by negative EBITDA in C Co, the group's net third party interest expense/EBITDA ratio would have been approximately 32.7% (i.e. USD 36 million/USD 110 million). In this case, A Co would have been able to deduct approximately USD 32.7 million of net interest expense. Therefore, the upper limit on interest capacity has not restricted net interest deductions in A Co to below the level that would have been permitted had the losses in C Co not arisen.

Table II.A.25. **Applying an upper limit on interest capacity**

	A Co USD	B Co USD	C Co USD	Group USD
EBITDA	100 million	10 million	(100 million)	10 million
Net interest	(40 million)	(6 million)	10 million	(36 million)
Group net third party interest expense/ EBITDA ratio	-	-	-	360%
Interest capacity	36 million	36 million	0	-
Deductible interest expense	(36 million)	(6 million)	0	-
Disallowed interest expense	(4 million)	-	-	-
Unused interest capacity	-	30 million	-	-

Example 6e – Applying a cap to the group ratio and an upper limit on interest capacity

468. In Table II.A.26, the group is in the same position as in Example 6a. However, the group ratio is now subject to a cap of 50% and there is an upper limit on interest capacity equal to the group's actual net third party interest expense.

469. Therefore, as in Example 6d, A Co's interest capacity is limited to USD 36 million (i.e. the group's total net third party interest expense). A Co is able to deduct net interest expense of USD 36 million, and may carry forward disallowed interest expense of USD 4 million into future periods, if this is permitted. As in Example 6c, B Co receives interest capacity of USD 5 million and is able to deduct net interest expense of USD 5 million. It is also able to carry forward disallowed interest expense of USD 1 million, if this is permitted.

Table II.A.26. **Applying a cap to the group ratio and an upper limit on interest capacity**

	A Co USD	B Co USD	C Co USD	Group USD
EBITDA	100 million	10 million	(100 million)	10 million
Net interest	(40 million)	(6 million)	10 million	(36 million)
Group net third party interest expense/ EBITDA ratio	-	-	-	50% (capped)
Interest capacity	36 million	5 million	0	-
Deductible interest expense	(36 million)	(5 million)	0	-
Disallowed interest expense	(4 million)	(1 million)	-	-
Unused interest capacity	-	-	-	-

Example 6f – Restricting the carry forward of unused interest capacity under the group ratio rule

470. In Table II.A.27, the group is in the same position as in Example 6a. The group ratio is not capped, but in the event that an entity has unused interest capacity, it can only carry this forward to the extent it would have arisen if the group ratio had been capped at 50%.

Table II.A.27. **Restricting the carry forward of unused interest capacity under the group ratio rule**

	A Co USD	B Co USD	C Co USD	Group USD
EBITDA	100 million	10 million	(100 million)	10 million
Net interest	(40 million)	(6 million)	10 million	(36 million)
Group net third party interest expense/ EBITDA ratio	-	-	-	360%
Interest capacity (current year)	360 million	36 million	0	-
Deductible interest expense	(40 million)	(6 million)	0	-
Disallowed interest expense	-	-	-	-
Unused interest capacity (limited based on an assumption the group ratio was capped at 50%)	10 million	-	-	-

471. A Co has current year interest capacity of USD 360 million and is able to deduct all of its net interest expense of USD 40 million, which represents 40% of its EBITDA. A Co also calculates the amount of unused interest capacity it can carry forward as if the group ratio had been capped at 50%. If the cap of 50% had applied, A Co would have had interest capacity of USD 50 million. Therefore, A Co is able to carry forward unused interest capacity of USD 10 million (i.e. the difference between USD 50 million and USD 40 million).

472. B Co has current year interest capacity of USD 36 million and is able to deduct all of its net interest expense of USD 6 million, which represents 60% of its EBITDA. B Co also calculates the amount of unused interest capacity it can carry forward as if the group ratio had been capped at 50%. If the cap of 50% had applied, B Co would have had interest capacity of USD 5 million. This does not restrict B Co's net interest deductions in the current period but, as it has already deducted more that this amount, B Co is unable to carry forward any unused interest capacity.

473. This approach does not restrict the ability of entities to deduct their interest expense in the current year, but it does reduce the risk of a very high group ratio giving rise to large amounts of unused interest capacity to carry forward into future periods. A country may consider introducing targeted rules to address the risk that the group enters into arrangements to take advantage of the very high levels of current year interest capacity in A Co and B Co.

Example 6g – Groups with negative group EBITDA

474. In this example, C Co has negative EBITDA of USD 120 million. In Table II.A.28. the group therefore has an overall negative group EBITDA of USD 10 million. This means it is not possible to calculate a meaningful group net third party interest expense/EBITDA ratio. However, the countries where A Co and B Co are resident allow these entities to claim interest capacity equal to the lower of their net interest expense, 50% of entity EBITDA and the group's net third party interest expense.

Table II.A.28. **Groups with negative group EBITDA**

	A Co USD	B Co USD	C Co USD	Group USD
EBITDA	100 million	10 million	(120 million)	(10 million)
Net interest	(40 million)	(6 million)	10 million	(36 million)
Group net third party interest expense/ EBITDA ratio	-	-	-	n/a
Interest capacity	36 million	5 million	0	-
Deductible interest expense	(36 million)	(5 million)	0	-
Disallowed interest expense	(4 million)	(1 million)	-	-
Unused interest capacity	-	-	-	-

475. A Co has net interest expense of USD 40 million, which is less than 50% of A Co's EBITDA, but exceeds the group's net third party interest expense of USD 36 million. A Co's interest capacity is therefore limited to USD 36 million. A Co is able to deduct net interest expense of USD 36 million, and may carry forward disallowed interest expense of USD 4 million into future periods, if this is permitted.

476. B Co has net interest expense of USD 6 million, which is less than the group's net third party interest expense of USD 36 million but exceeds 50% of B Co's EBITDA of USD 10 million. B Co's interest capacity is therefore limited to USD 5 million. B Co may deduct net interest expense of USD 5 million and may carry forward disallowed interest expense of USD 1 million, if this is permitted.

477. This is the same outcome for both A Co and B Co as in Example 6e. Therefore, the fact that the group now has negative group EBITDA has not reduced the ability of entities in the group to deduct net interest expense in the current period.

Part III

Approaches to address BEPS involving interest in the banking and insurance sectors

Part I of this report identifies key features of the banking and insurance industries which indicate that the common approach set out in chapters 1-11 may not be suitable for addressing BEPS risks involving interest posed by entities in these sectors. Part III contains the outcomes of further work, conducted following the release of the 2015 Report and completed in 2016, which explores elements of banking and insurance business which can impose constraints on a group's ability to use interest for BEPS purposes, and the limits on these constraints. It also considers risks which countries involved in work on Action 4 have identified as posed by banking and insurance groups, and how these risks may be addressed.

Introduction and overview to Part III

Introduction

478. The common approach contained in the Part I is suitable for addressing BEPS involving interest in the majority of groups. However, there are a number of factors identified in Chapter 10 which mean that a different approach may be appropriate when dealing with entities in the banking and insurance sectors.

- Banks and insurance companies rely on interest income to ensure their profitability and liquidity and for banks interest is also usually the biggest single item of operating expense.
- Banking and insurance groups are subject to strict regulatory capital rules which limit their ability to place excessive levels of debt in certain entities.
- Banks and insurance companies are key providers of debt finance, either as lenders or investors in corporate bonds, and so typically have net interest income rather than net interest expense.

479. In light of this, Chapter 10 concludes that, while countries should have an approach to deal with BEPS involving interest where it arises, a country may exclude entities in banking and insurance groups, and regulated banks and insurance companies in non-financial groups, from the scope of the fixed ratio rule and group ratio rule. Chapter 10 also highlights that further work would be conducted, to be completed in 2016, to identify appropriate approaches to address BEPS risks in these entities, taking into account the risks posed, the role interest plays in banking and insurance businesses, and restrictions already imposed by capital regulation. In particular it was noted that any approaches adopted should not conflict with or reduce the effectiveness of regulatory capital rules intended to reduce the risk of a future financial crisis. Part III contains the outcomes of this further work, which focused on the BEPS risks involving interest that countries see posed by banking and insurance groups and how these risks may be addressed.

Overview

480. Banking and insurance groups are at the heart of the global economy, representing 41 of the world's 100 biggest groups in 2016.[1] It is therefore vital that countries have responses in place to deal with BEPS risks that banks and insurance companies pose, but these responses must take into account the unique characteristics of these sectors and in particular the evolving regulatory landscape. Part III explores key elements of banking and insurance businesses that can impose constraints on the ability of groups to engage in BEPS involving interest, together with limits on these constraints. This includes consideration of the interest profile of banking and insurance groups, and of different entities in these groups; the impact of regulatory capital rules on the ability of banks and insurance companies to have excessive

interest deductions or to use interest to fund non-taxable income; and the impact of group regulation on other entities in banking and insurance groups.

481. In most cases it is expected that regulatory capital rules will be effective in protecting countries from excessive interest deductions in a solo-regulated bank or insurance company. Group regulation also reduces the risk of excessive deductions in other group entities, but this varies. Generally, regulatory rules that apply at the level of a country group are likely to be the most effective in reducing BEPS risk. Regulatory rules and commercial considerations also impose limits or downsides that reduce the benefits to groups from using interest to fund non-taxable income, in particular from equity investments. Overall, significant regulatory and commercial factors reduce the risks of BEPS involving interest posed by banking and insurance groups, but differences exist between countries and sectors. Therefore, it is not possible to conclude there is no material risk of BEPS involving interest in the banking and insurance sectors, but this risk varies between countries and may also vary between sectors within a country.

482. These findings are consistent with the experience of countries engaged in work on Action 4. Countries have identified that the main general BEPS risks involving interest in the banking and insurance sectors they encounter relate to (i) excessive interest deductions in entities that are part of a group with a bank or insurance company, and (ii) banks or insurance companies, and entities in a group with a bank or insurance company, using interest to fund non-taxable income. Some countries also see excessive interest deductions in banks or insurance companies as a concern in specific circumstances but this is not viewed as a general risk.

483. It is recommended that each country should identify the specific risks it faces, taking into account the characteristics of banking and insurance groups and the requirements of regulators. This should distinguish between risks posed by banks and those posed by insurance companies, and between risks posed by entities in a group with a bank and those posed by entities in a group with an insurance company.

484. Where no material risks are identified, for example where potential risks are already addressed by existing regulatory capital rules and/or tax rules, it is not expected that the country should introduce new rules to deal with a risk that does not exist or is already addressed. In this case, a country may reasonably exempt banking and/or insurance groups from the fixed ratio rule and group ratio rule without the need for additional tax rules. Where BEPS risks involving interest are identified, a country should introduce rules which are appropriate to address these risks, taking into account the regulatory regime and tax system in that country.

485. Because banks and insurance companies typically have net interest income, the fixed ratio rule in the Action 4 Report is unlikely to provide protection against BEPS risks that have been identified in a bank or insurance company, or in another group entity where the rule is applied to a local group including banks and insurance companies. However, where a group also includes entities engaged in non-banking/insurance activities, the fixed ratio rule may be applied to a local group excluding banks, insurance companies and entities directly connected with banking or insurance. Risks concerning interest funding non-taxable income in a bank, insurance company or an entity directly connected with banking or insurance business may be addressed by disallowing interest expense funding this income or by reducing the income that benefits from a tax exemption or other beneficial tax treatment. Countries should also have measures in place to deal with specific risks they face. Annex III.B includes an outline of rules to address BEPS risks involving interest in the banking and insurance sectors currently applied by countries.

486. In all cases, it is vital that rules to protect countries from BEPS should not weaken the effectiveness of capital regulation in providing protection against default, insolvency and a future financial crisis. Therefore, when introducing rules to deal with BEPS risks posed by banking and insurance groups, a country should ensure that the interaction of tax and regulatory rules and the possible impact on groups is fully understood.

Note

1. Forbes "World's Biggest Public Companies List 2016", including companies categorised as Diversified Insurance, Life & Health Insurance, Major Banks, Property & Casualty Insurance and Regional Banks.

Chapter 15

BEPS risks involving interest posed by entities in the banking and insurance sectors

487. Banks and insurance companies are at the heart of the modern financial system and the global economy. In 2016, 41 of the world's 100 biggest groups and 215 of the world's 1 000 biggest groups were banking or insurance groups.[1] To the extent groups in these sectors pose a risk of BEPS involving interest, it is important that countries have approaches in place to deal with this. Banking and insurance groups are fundamentally different in terms of their businesses, their structures and how they are funded, and these differences need to be recognised. However, in terms of identifying suitable approaches to tackle BEPS involving interest, banks and insurance companies have three key features in common. It is not suggested that these features increase the BEPS risks posed by banks and insurance companies, but where a risk of BEPS involving interest is identified, they should be taken into account in identifying an appropriate response.

- Although banks and insurance companies are engaged in very different businesses, in both cases third party interest income is vitally important to ensure a group's profitability and liquidity. For most banks, interest income and expense are largely operating items and play a role which is broadly comparable with revenue and cost of sales for entities in non-financial sectors. For insurance companies, interest income is a major form of investment income used to meet insurance liabilities as they fall due. In both cases, the nature of interest is fundamentally different to that for most other businesses, where interest income is linked to the treasury function of managing a group's net debt.
- Banks and insurance companies are subject to regulatory capital rules and commercial constraints (e.g. from credit rating agencies) which require them to hold minimum amounts of equity and restrict their ability to place an excessive level of debt in particular entities or to use debt to fund equity investments in subsidiaries. It is essential that the nature, extent and impact of these requirements are understood in order to assess if and how they reduce the opportunities for certain entities to engage in particular types of BEPS activity.
- Banks and insurance companies are key providers of debt finance to groups in other sectors, either as lenders or as investors in corporate bonds. As such, entities engaged in banking or insurance business will typically have net interest income rather than net interest expense. The fixed ratio rule and group ratio rule apply a limit to the net interest deductions that an entity may claim, but have no impact on the ability of an entity with net interest income to deduct all of its interest expense, even if part of this is related to BEPS.

The interest profile of banking and insurance groups

488. Modern banks are engaged in providing a broad range of financial services to individuals and businesses. However, for most banks the use of deposits and short term debt to make loans remains a core activity. In undertaking this activity a bank generates profit by charging more interest on the loans it makes than it pays on its deposits and its debt, and managing its exposure to default and other risks. Interest is therefore a key source of a bank's profitability, which may be compared with revenue and cost of sales for entities in other sectors. This means that a bank will typically be very highly leveraged and interest expense is usually the biggest single expense item on a bank's income statement. However, once a bank's interest income is taken into account, in the significant majority of cases a bank will have net interest income overall. A possible exception may apply in the case of groups with significant investment banking or similar activities, including securities trading (on behalf of the bank and/or its clients), deal arrangement, underwriting security issuances and the provision of advisory services and research. These activities may be funded using debt but give rise to non-interest income, which in some cases could result in a bank having net interest expense. Whether there is net interest income or net interest expense at the level of a group will depend upon the mix of investment banking and other banking activities. However, in the significant majority of cases it would be expected that a banking group will have net interest income.

489. Insurance business follows a very different model to banking, and concerns the taking of insurance premiums to underwrite risk, and paying out claims and other benefits to customers. Insurance companies invest premiums in stable income-producing assets, often long-term debt instruments, in order to generate income and ensure sufficient liquidity to pay claims as they fall due. To the extent that premiums and investment income exceed claims and expenses, an insurance company will earn a profit. The generation of interest income is therefore a key part of an insurance company's business and overall profitability. Most of an insurance company's investments are funded using premiums rather than debt, and so insurance companies and groups typically have very low levels of leverage compared with banks. However, taking into account the income from investments, they are generally net interest income recipients by a significant margin.

490. Although banks and insurance companies, and banking and insurance groups as a whole, will typically have net interest income, other entities in a banking or insurance group may have significant levels of net interest expense on loans used to support regulated activities.

- Regulators may prefer or require regulatory capital to be issued out of a "single point of entry" which is often, although not always, a holding company at the top of the group. These may include interest-bearing instruments, where these may be treated as regulatory capital for the purposes of a group's capital adequacy ratios. There are also important practical benefits for a group from issuing regulatory capital instruments out of a single entity, which enables the group to maximise the flexibility and efficiency of its capital. Following an issuance, capital may be retained by the issuing entity in order to ensure flexibility in the event that additional capital is required by a particular part of the group; it may be on-lent within the group as interest-bearing regulatory capital, which may be on the same terms as the third party instrument or on different terms, in which case the interest rate on the third party and intragroup instruments could differ; or it may be injected into a group entity in the form of equity. In each of these cases, the entity issuing interest-bearing regulatory capital may incur a net interest expense, either because it has no interest income or its interest income is lower than its interest expense.

- Regulators may also require foreign-headed groups to establish a local holding company, which must issue regulatory capital instruments to third parties or intragroup to support the activities of banks and insurance companies in that country. In this case the local holding company acts as a single point of entry for the country group, and similarly may find itself in a net interest expense position.
- Entities in banking and insurance groups may also incur net interest expense on ordinary loans used to support banking or insurance activities. These might include money market loans entered into through a group treasury operation, acquisition finance to fund the purchase of regulated businesses, or intragroup or third party loans to fund the activities of group service companies that support regulated businesses.

The impact of regulatory capital rules on leverage in a bank or insurance company for tax purposes

491. Banks and insurance companies are subject to regulatory capital requirements at an entity level (referred to as "solo-regulation") which require them to hold minimum levels of equity to ensure they have sufficient loss-absorbing capital to adequately support the risks they face and deal with financial or economic shocks. Regulatory capital rules thus play a vital role in ensuring that banks and insurance companies are not leveraged too highly taking into account their business, their structure and the markets in which they operate. A high level overview of the impact of regulatory capital rules on the level of equity in a bank or insurance company, as well as other relevant regulatory requirements, is included in Annex III.A. To the extent regulatory capital rules ensure that a bank or insurance company is capitalised with an appropriate level of equity, where the definition of equity for tax and regulatory purposes is consistent, these rules may also provide protection against excessive leverage for tax purposes and in many countries this will be the case. However, there are a number of factors that mean this may not always happen.

492. First, there are benefits from regulators and tax authorities taking a consistent approach in assessing the leverage of entities and groups, improving coherency between the regulatory and tax rules groups are required to comply with in a country and reducing any possible conflict between these rules. However, in practice differences exist in how regulators and tax authorities view the issue of excessive leverage and the risks they aim to address. Regulators are concerned with protecting depositors, policyholders and the wider economy by ensuring that banks and insurance companies are able to survive financial shocks long enough either for them to recover, or for an orderly resolution to take place. On the other hand, tax authorities are concerned with ensuring that an excessive level of interest-bearing debt is not raised by an entity, reducing the level of profits subject to tax. This may lead to differences in how regulators and tax authorities view the leverage of a particular regulated entity. For example, although banking and insurance regulation typically requires a minimum amount of capital to be in the form of ordinary shares and retained earnings, some countries also allow interest-bearing instruments to be treated as regulatory capital for certain purposes and subject to prescribed limits. This may be because, although the instruments are legally in the form of debt, they include certain characteristics which mean they are able to absorb losses. For example, they may be automatically written-down or converted into equity on certain trigger events, or they may be long-dated and subordinated to other forms of debt. However, a country may take the view that these instruments should be viewed as debt for tax purposes, resulting in the interest on them being tax deductible. In this case, a bank or insurance company's leverage for tax purposes may be higher than its leverage for regulatory purposes.

493. Second, regulatory capital rules differ between countries and the type of regulated activity undertaken. This is in particular the case for insurance companies where there

is currently no single common international standard for capital regulation, although as described in Annex III.A there are moves towards greater consistency and co-ordination. While there is broad consistency in how the Basel III framework on the regulation of banks has been introduced in different countries, differences still remain. Therefore, it is not possible to reach a conclusion that regulatory capital rules provide the same level of protection against excessive leverage for tax purposes in all countries and in all cases.

494. Third, as described in Chapter 6, differences in the economic environment or legal frameworks in place in different countries mean that it is not possible to set a single limit on net interest deductions for tax purposes to be applied in all countries. Therefore, in introducing the fixed ratio rule, countries set a benchmark fixed ratio within a corridor of 10%-30%, taking into account relevant factors. Similarly, countries may take different views on what represents an appropriate level of leverage for a bank or insurance company for tax purposes, so long as this is not based on considerations that are inconsistent with the aims of Action 4. In light of this, even where two countries apply the same regulatory capital rules to a particular type of regulated entity, these countries may take different views as to the amount of interest expense that should be deductible for tax purposes.

495. Finally, while regulatory capital rules provide protection against excessive leverage in a bank or insurance company as a whole, in many countries there is no specific regulatory requirement for capital to be allocated to a local branch. Therefore, in principle, a risk remains that a permanent establishment of a bank or insurance company could claim an interest deduction for excessive funding costs without limitation. However, this risk is dealt with by the *2010 Report on the Attribution of Profits to Permanent Establishments* (the 2010 Report), which contains an authorised OECD approach for the attribution of profits to permanent establishments of banks and insurance companies, including the determination of the permanent establishment's "free capital". Free capital is the part of a permanent establishment's capital base which does not give rise to a funding cost in the nature of interest that is tax deductible in the host country. In broad terms, this can be compared with the equity capital of a separate entity. The 2010 Report includes options to determine the free capital in a permanent establishment, using the level of risk-weighted assets attributable to a permanent establishment of a bank or the level of investments assets attributable to a permanent establishment of an insurance company. These may be based on an allocation of the actual free capital of the entity as a whole (taking into account regulatory capital rules in the home country of the entity) or on the level of free capital that would be required by an independent enterprise carrying on the same or similar activities under the same or similar conditions (taking into account regulatory capital rules in the host country of the permanent establishment). Where a country applies the authorised OECD approach, a permanent establishment should in general be attributed an arm's length amount of free capital. The protection provided against excessive leverage for tax purposes should therefore be equivalent to that for banks and insurance companies in general.

The impact of regulatory capital rules on the ability of banks and insurance companies to use interest to fund non-taxable income

496. The BEPS Action Plan identifies cases where groups use interest to fund non-taxable or deferred income as a key risk to be addressed under Action 4. The common approach in Part I of this report reduces this risk by linking an entity's net interest deductions to a percentage of its EBITDA, which is calculated so as to exclude non-taxable income such as dividend income and the profits of a foreign permanent establishment which benefit from a participation exemption. However, while it is possible for a bank or insurance company to

hold equity investments and receive non-taxable income, there are a number of regulatory and commercial considerations which impose costs or other down-sides as a result of it doing so. Therefore in practice groups will typically avoid these structures where possible.

497. First, where a bank or insurance company holds an equity investment in a subsidiary or in a financial undertaking outside the group, regulatory capital rules often require the value of this investment to be deducted from the bank or insurance company's own equity when assessing whether it meets capital adequacy ratios. This is to prevent "double leverage" or "double gearing", where capital which in economic terms is the same equity is taken into account by different entities, to support multiple tranches of risk. In effect, if a bank or insurance company uses borrowings to fund such an equity investment, it would then need to issue more equity in order to maintain its capital ratios. This would increase its cost of capital, as holders of equity typically demand a higher return than holders of debt. It is therefore relatively expensive for a bank or insurance company to over-capitalise a subsidiary. However, there are exceptions to this rule. For example, deductions against capital are typically only required for investments in subsidiaries or financial undertakings, and exceptions may apply where the parent and subsidiary are "solo-consolidated" (e.g. where there are no restrictions on the subsidiary's capital being paid up to support the assets of the parent, and so regulatory capital rules can be applied to the consolidated position of both entities).

498. Second, even where a bank or insurance company is not required to deduct a particular investment from its equity capital, regulators and ratings agencies both encourage groups to avoid using debt to fund equity investments. This is to prevent strain on a parent's cash flows where payments of interest and principal on its debt are in effect subject to the ability of a subsidiary to pay regular dividends. This will be exacerbated if there are restrictions on those dividends, either because the subsidiary may not have sufficient earnings after financing its own debt or because the payment of dividends requires the approval of a local regulator. The approaches used by regulators to monitor this risk vary by country and sector and, while these rules do not prohibit all cases where debt is funding an equity investment, regulators may intervene if the level is excessive or if the debt issued by the parent does not appear to be sustainable.

499. Finally, groups and regulators will typically try to avoid situations where an excessive level of equity capital is "trapped" in a subsidiary. Equity is less flexible than debt and once injected into a foreign subsidiary it can be difficult to redeem the equity and repatriate the capital to the parent. This is particularly the case where the subsidiary is subject to regulatory capital requirements, and so equity capital can only be redeemed in limited circumstances including at the approval of the local regulator. Because of this lack of flexibility, a group's regulator may require a parent to obtain approval before capitalising a foreign subsidiary using equity, to limit the risk of capital being trapped in scenarios where it is needed by rest of the group.

The impact of regulatory capital rules on entities in a group with a bank or insurance company

500. A bank or insurance company will typically be part of a group with other entities. These may include holding companies, entities which support the activities of the bank or insurance company, entities engaged in financial activities which are not subject to regulatory capital requirements, and entities engaged in non-financial activities. This final category will be particularly relevant where a bank or insurance company is part of a non-financial sector group (such as a manufacturing or retail group) but may also arise in some financial sector groups.

501. Banks and insurance companies are subject to regulatory capital requirements at an entity level. Regulators may also require capital ratios to be met at the level of a worldwide group, a regional group (e.g. in the European Union) and/or a country group (e.g. including all group entities in the same country). In these cases, debt issued by a group entity which is not a bank or insurance company to lenders outside the relevant group will be taken into account in testing whether the group meets required capital ratios. Similarly, where a group entity makes an equity investment in a subsidiary or financial undertaking outside the group, this may be deducted from the group's equity capital. These rules operate as limits on the capital structure of the worldwide, regional or country group and have direct implications for each entity in the group.

502. Depending upon how it is applied, group regulation can provide protection against excessive leverage in entities in a group with a bank or insurance company, but this may not always be the case. Where a regulated group includes entities in more than one country, there may still be scope for these entities to have high levels of net interest expense without this preventing the group as a whole from meeting its regulatory capital requirements. For example, where a banking or insurance group includes non-solo regulated entities in two different countries, these entities may be able to use intragroup loans to shift taxable income between the countries without causing the worldwide group to breach required capital ratios. Group regulation therefore provides greater protection against BEPS involving interest where it is applied to a country group, comprising all group entities in a particular country. This is because any intragroup loans from foreign entities will be taken into account when determining whether the country group is adequately capitalised. However, there are cases where a country imposes regulatory capital requirements to a country group, but this does not include all members of the worldwide group that are taxpayers in that country. For example, a regulated country group could comprise a local holding company and all entities in the country held below that holding company, but this may not include entities and permanent establishments in the country that are held directly by a foreign parent rather than by the local holding company. In this case, regulatory capital rules applied to the regulated country group may not provide protection against BEPS involving interest by these entities and permanent establishments. This risk may be increased if these entities and permanent establishments are included in the country group for tax purposes (i.e. so taxable income of entities within the regulated country group can be set against interest deductions in entities and permanent establishments outside the regulated country group).

503. Non-solo regulated entities in a group with a bank or insurance company will be particularly significant where the bank or insurance company is part of a non-financial sector group, such as a manufacturing or retail group. To the extent entities engaged in non-financial sector activities are not included in a regulated group, group regulation may not offer protection against possible BEPS risks involving these entities.

Note

1. Forbes "World's Biggest Public Companies List 2016", including companies categorised as Diversified Insurance, Life & Health Insurance, Major Banks, Property & Casualty Insurance and Regional Banks.

Chapter 16

Approaches to address BEPS involving interest in the banking and insurance sectors

Risks areas identified during the work on Action 4

504. Countries engaged in work on Action 4 identified a number of BEPS risks involving interest in banking and insurance groups. These drew distinctions between the risks posed by banks or insurance companies and those posed by entities in a group with a bank or insurance company. These can be compared against BEPS risks which the Action 4 common approach is intended to deal with.

- Excessive third party or intragroup interest expense was identified as a risk posed by entities in a group with a bank or insurance company, which were able to set these deductions against taxable income in the bank or insurance company. Excessive interest expense in solo-regulated banks or insurance companies was identified by some countries in certain circumstances but was not seen as a general risk.
- The use of third party or intragroup interest to fund non-taxable income was identified as a risk posed by banks or insurance companies, and also by entities in a group with a bank or insurance company. In particular this risk arises where interest is used to fund equity investments giving rise to income which benefits from a tax exemption or is taxed in a preferential manner.
- Because banking and insurance groups typically have net interest income at the level of the worldwide group and also at the level of a country group, entities in a group using intragroup interest expense to claim total net interest deductions in excess of the group's actual net interest expense is not a relevant measure of BEPS activity in the banking and insurance sectors.

505. While the same categories of risk were identified by different countries, the manner and extent to which these risks arise vary and it is considered that countries should introduce rules to deal with the risks they face. There are benefits to groups and countries from a single common approach. However, this must be weighed against the additional compliance and administrative burdens if countries introduce rules to address risks they do not encounter in practice.

506. It is therefore recommended that each country should identify the specific risks it faces, taking into account the characteristics of banking and insurance groups and the requirements of regulators, including those aspects discussed in this report. This should distinguish between risks posed by banks and those posed by insurance companies, and between risks posed by entities in a group with a bank and those posed by entities in a group with an insurance company. It should also identify where risks arise primarily in a

subset of these sectors that are material in that country (e.g. retail banking *vs* investment banking, life and health insurance *vs* property and casualty insurance, etc.).

507. Where no material risks are identified, for example where potential risks are already addressed by existing regulatory capital rules and/or tax rules, a country may reasonably exempt a group from the fixed ratio rule and group ratio rule described in Part I without the need for additional tax rules. Where BEPS risks involving interest are identified, a country should introduce rules which are appropriate to address these risks, taking into account the regulatory regime and tax system in that country. These rules may include, but are not limited to, those described in this report. In determining whether a rule is appropriate to address a given risk, a country may take into account factors such as:

- whether a rule is likely to be effective in dealing with a particular risk
- the costs of applying and administering a rule compared with the risks it is intended to protect against
- the structure of a country's tax system, including whether entities are taxed separately or on a consolidated or group basis
- the impact of a rule on entities which are not engaged in BEPS involving interest
- whether a rule should be restricted to a particular sector or type of entity in order to better target the risks a country faces
- whether an alternative approach may be more appropriate.

508. Rules to address BEPS involving interest will typically encourage entities to reduce their net interest expense or to restructure existing debt into a different form. In general, it is not expected that these rules should conflict with the goals of regulators. However, it is vital that rules to protect countries from BEPS should not weaken the effectiveness of capital regulation in providing protection against default, insolvency and a future financial crisis. Therefore, it is suggested that in identifying an approach to deal with a risk it has identified, a country should ensure that rules are suitably targeted, they avoid a disproportionate impact on banking and insurance groups relative to rules applied in other sectors, and the interaction of tax and regulatory rules and the possible impact on groups is fully understood. In order to achieve this, the views of local banking and insurance regulators may be sought and taken into account.

General interest limitation rules

509. General interest limitation rules limit BEPS risk arising from excessive leverage by limiting the interest deductions that an entity may claim, usually based on a relevant financial ratio. Because these rules do not require consideration of the nature or circumstances of particular transactions, they have the benefit of being reasonably straightforward for groups to apply and for tax authorities to administer, and in most cases should give rise to predictable outcomes.

510. In connection with the work on Action 4, excessive leverage in a bank or insurance company has not been identified as a general risk at this point in time and so it is anticipated that, in the majority of cases, countries will find this risk to be low. Excessive leverage in entities in a group with a bank or insurance company has been identified as a greater risk. However, because of differences in regulatory and tax rules between countries, there may be countries where this risk is also already adequately addressed. Where this is the case, there is no expectation that a country should apply a general interest limitation rule aimed at dealing with a risk that does not exist or is already addressed.

511. If a country does identify a material BEPS risk from excessive leverage in banks or insurance companies, or in entities in a group with a bank or insurance company, this would suggest that existing rules are not providing adequate protection in this area. Unless suitable changes are planned, the country should consider introducing a general interest limitation rule to deal with this.

Applying general interest limitation rules to banking and insurance groups

512. Table III.B.1 in Annex III.B includes a description of general interest limitation rules currently applied to banks and insurance companies in different countries. In some cases these rules are sector-specific, while in other cases they apply to groups in all sectors. As it is not expected that excessive leverage in a bank or insurance company will be a material concern for the majority of countries, at this time there is no need to develop a single common approach.

513. Because general interest limitation rules have a broad scope, where a country does propose to apply such a rule to a bank or insurance company, it should carefully consider the possible implications of the rule in a range of circumstances. For example, because banks and insurance companies typically have net interest income rather than net interest expense, a rule which applies a general limit to an entity's net interest deductions is unlikely to have any impact. Therefore where a country has identified a material risk of excessive leverage in banks or insurance companies, such a rule is unlikely to address this risk in most cases. On the other hand, a rule which applies a general limit to an entity's gross interest deductions could risk having an excessive impact. A general interest limitation rule that does not adequately take this into account could result in an entity being unable to claim relief for what is in practice a normal operating expense. In all cases it is important that the impact of interest limitation rules on banks and insurance companies should be fully understood which may include discussions with local banking and/or insurance regulators prior to implementation. However, where a country is considering introducing general interest limitation rules that will apply to banks or insurance companies, a detailed understanding of the possible interaction of the rule with existing or planned regulatory capital requirements and the potential impact on entities and groups is especially important.

Applying the fixed ratio rule to a bank or insurance company

514. The fixed ratio rule in Chapter 6 sets a limit on an entity's net interest expense based on a percentage of entity EBITDA calculated under tax principles. Because in the significant majority of cases a bank or insurance company will be in the position of having net interest income rather than net interest expense, the fixed ratio rule would have no application. Therefore, Chapter 10 concludes that a country may exclude banks and/or insurance companies from the scope of the rule. However, there may be cases where a country chooses to or is required to apply a rule consistently to all sectors, and so the rule is also applied to banks and insurance companies.

515. Although in most cases a bank or insurance company should be in a net interest income position, there may be particular circumstances where a bank or insurance company has net interest expense. In practice, this may be more likely with respect to a bank rather than an insurance company, as typically insurance companies have a very low leverage, but in principle it could happen to either type of entity. Net interest expense could arise because of economic circumstances, such as where losses on a loan portfolio mean that the expected level of interest income is not received but the entity still incurs interest expense on its debt funding. More commonly, net interest expense may be a result of activities generating non-interest income. For example, banks engaged in investment banking activities may

earn non-interest income of different types, including trading profits, dividend income, commissions and fees. Where the interest expense funding these activities exceeds the bank's interest income, it will have net interest expense.

516. Where a country does apply the fixed ratio rule to banks and insurance companies, the question as to whether or not it could result in a disallowance where an entity has net interest expense depends on a number of factors. Chapter 11 provides that the fixed ratio rule may be applied entity-by-entity or to the net position of the local group. Where a country applies the fixed ratio rule to the position of the local group, which includes a bank or insurance company with net interest expense and also a bank or insurance company with net interest income, the local group may still have net interest income overall and the rule would have no effect. However, if a country applies the fixed ratio rule to each entity separately, or if a local group has net interest expense overall, then there could be a disallowance to the extent net interest expense exceeds the benchmark fixed ratio.

517. In principle, these outcomes would be consistent with the treatment of entities in other sectors. However, because interest income is the main or a main source of operating income for most banks and insurance companies, even a profitable entity is likely to have low or negative EBITDA once all of its interest income and expense is removed. Therefore, even though the fixed ratio rule may be applied to banks and insurance companies in a manner which is consistent with groups in other sectors, the impact on a bank or insurance company with net interest expense could be more significant. For example, because a bank or insurance company is likely to have low or negative EBITDA, where such an entity finds itself in a net interest expense position, the fixed ratio rule is likely to result in a disallowance of most or all of this net expense. In particular for banks, as interest expense is typically a bank's largest single operating expense, this disallowance could seriously hinder an entity's ability to survive financial shocks. Where a country permits disallowed interest expense to be carried forward and used in later periods, entities in other sectors which incur an interest disallowance as a result of low EBITDA in a particular period will generally be able to deduct this interest expense once their earnings recover. However, as most banks and insurance companies will always have a low or negative EBITDA, even when they are highly profitable in terms of their level of net interest income, any disallowance that is incurred under the fixed ratio rule is likely to be permanent.

Applying the fixed ratio rule to entities in a group with a bank or insurance company

518. Countries engaged in work on Action 4 have identified greater concerns regarding excessive interest deductions in entities in a group with a bank or insurance company, rather than in a bank or insurance company itself. As described in Chapter 15, although these entities are not themselves solo-regulated, in many cases they will be included within a consolidated group for regulatory purposes and so are taken into account when determining whether the group as a whole meets its regulatory capital obligations. However, in some countries there is still scope for such entities to incur a high level of net interest deductions relative to their economic activity, while the group overall is still adequately capitalised.

519. For entities in other sectors, the fixed ratio rule provides protection for countries by linking an entity's net interest deductions to its level of tax EBITDA. In principle, the fixed ratio rule could also be applied to entities in a group with a bank or insurance company and this could be done in three ways:

- The fixed ratio rule could be applied to a local group including all entities.
- The fixed ratio rule could be applied to a local group excluding certain entities.
- The fixed ratio rule could be applied on an entity-by-entity basis.

Applying the fixed ratio rule to a local group including all entities

520. Chapter 11 provides that the fixed ratio rule may be applied to the net position of a local group, including all group entities in a country (or those that are part of a tax group in a country). In most cases, the net interest income of a bank or insurance company will exceed the net interest expense of other entities in its group. Therefore, even where entities in a group with a bank or insurance company have net interest expense, if the fixed ratio rule is applied to the net position of a local group including all entities, the local group is likely to have net interest income. The fixed ratio rule would therefore provide no protection against excessive net interest deductions in non-bank or non-insurance entities in a group with a bank or insurance company. On the other hand, because most banking and insurance groups typically have low or negative EBITDA, unless a group includes entities engaged in non-bank or non-insurance business which generate material levels of non-interest income, where a local group does have net interest expense, the fixed ratio rule could operate to deny a deduction for most or all of this net expense.

521. For policy reasons, a country may apply the fixed ratio rule to the net position of a local group including banks and insurance companies (e.g. in order for a rule to apply in the same way as for entities in other sectors). This may also be the most consistent and practical approach where entities in a group are taxed on a consolidated or similar basis which allows for the offset of profits and losses in different entities in a group. However, while this approach may be reasonably straightforward to apply, it is unlikely to provide protection against excessive interest deductions in non-bank or non-insurance entities in a local group with a bank or insurance company and so, where a country has identified such a risk in these entities, targeted rules may also be required.

Applying the fixed ratio rule to a local group excluding certain entities

522. One of the concerns with applying the fixed ratio rule to a local group including banking and insurance companies is that, in effect, an important source of business income (i.e. interest income) is being used to shelter a group's interest expense. Groups in other sectors are not generally able to offset business income against interest expense in applying the fixed ratio rule, and a country may conclude that this is also not appropriate for groups including banks and insurance companies if this prevents the fixed ratio rule from providing protection against BEPS involving interest in other group entities.

523. A country may seek to address this concern by applying the fixed ratio rule to the net position of a local group excluding certain entities. For example, the fixed ratio rule could be applied to a local group including all group entities in the country with the exception of banks and insurance companies. Banks and insurance companies could be excluded from the scope of the fixed ratio rule or could form a second local group to which the fixed ratio rule could be applied separately. Interest expense in a bank or insurance company would typically be offset by interest income and be fully deductible, while net interest expense in other group entities would be deductible up to a fixed percentage of tax EBITDA. However, this approach raises a number of important practical concerns.

- Where a group is wholly or mainly engaged in banking or insurance activities, the entities remaining in the local group once banks and insurance companies have been excluded will primarily be holding companies, service companies and other entities which support the banking or insurance business and have no substantial business activities of their own. In some cases, these entities conduct activities which are intrinsic to the business of banks and insurance companies in their group, but which are required by regulators to be conducted outside of the solo-regulated entities as part of the group's resolution plan. Because these entities typically will not be engaged in an active business, they may have very low levels of tax EBITDA and so any net interest expense is likely to be disallowed.

- Holding companies and other non-solo regulated entities may, for regulatory or operational reasons, issue debt which is used to fund regulated activities in a bank or insurance company. Net interest expense on this debt could be excluded from the scope of the fixed ratio rule, but this could be complex for groups to apply and for tax authorities to audit.
- Treating banks and insurance companies differently to group entities directly connected to their business could have an undesirable behavioural impact on groups, encouraging them to adopt less efficient structures in order to avoid an interest disallowance. For example, to the extent permitted, groups may consolidate service and support activities into solo-regulated entities, and issue debt directly out of banks and insurance companies, even where this is not the most effective structure and may not be favoured by regulators. In some countries this type of consolidation may not be permitted by regulators, putting groups at a disadvantage.
- Under the common approach, countries are encouraged to consider introducing a group ratio rule to allow entities in highly leveraged groups to deduct more net interest expense than permitted under the fixed ratio rule. Where the fixed ratio rule is modified to apply to a local group excluding banks and insurance companies, entities in the local group may incur a disallowance but, as banking and insurance groups typically have net interest income, the group ratio rule as described in Chapter 7 is unlikely to grant any relief. This concern may be reduced if similar modifications are applied to the group ratio rule (e.g. to exclude the net interest income and EBITDA of banks and insurance companies in calculating a group's net third party interest expense/EBITDA ratio). However, this would mean stripping the results of banks and insurance companies out of a group's consolidated financial statements, which could be burdensome for groups and difficult for tax authorities to audit effectively. Also, the group ratio rule relies on an assumption that equity and debt are fungible within a worldwide group. However, this begins to break down when key operating entities are excluded from the group, leaving entities which are secondary to the group's main business, which may have no direct relationship to each other and which may be subject to regulatory rules that restrict them from reallocating equity and debt between countries. In any case there may be limited benefit from applying the group ratio rule if the entities that remain in a local group have low levels of EBITDA (although this may not be a concern if a different form of group ratio rule is applied, as permitted in Chapter 7).

524. The possible impact of applying the fixed ratio rule to a local group including all entities except banks and insurance companies is illustrated in Example 1 in Annex III.C. It appears that, in most cases, this approach will not give rise to an appropriate outcome and is not recommended. However, to a large extent the concerns set out above may be addressed if the local group also excludes holding companies, service companies and other entities that have a direct connection to a group's banking or insurance business. This would recognise that income and expenses that are intrinsically linked to banking or insurance activities may, for regulatory or commercial reasons, arise outside of a solo-regulated entity. It would also provide countries with protection against BEPS involving interest, as net interest income arising from a group's banking or insurance business would not be available to offset interest expense funding other business activities.

525. Where a group is engaged wholly or mainly in banking or insurance, all of the entities in the group may be directly connected to that business. For these groups, where a country does not apply the fixed ratio rule to entities excluded from a local group, this approach would in practice be the same as applying an exemption for the entire group. Therefore a simple exemption from the fixed ratio rule for such groups may be a more practical approach for the country to adopt.

526. Where a group also includes a material level of non-banking or non-insurance activities (e.g. where a manufacturing or retail group owns a bank or insurance company), applying the fixed ratio to the local group excluding banks, insurance companies and entities directly connected to banking or insurance could be an effective way to deal with BEPS risks posed by entities engaged in these other activities. In this case, the fixed ratio rule could be applied to the manufacturing, retail and other entities remaining in the local group in a way that is substantially similar to groups in other sectors. This is illustrated in Example 2a and Example 2b in Annex III.C.

527. A country could also allow a group to apply the group ratio rule based on an assumption that the worldwide group excludes banks, insurance companies and entities directly connected with these activities. This would involve some additional complexity, as a group may not otherwise prepare consolidated financial statements which separate out the results of entities engaged in different businesses, but this may be appropriate in order to strike a balance between providing protection for countries and ensuring a reasonable outcome for groups. Modifications to the application of the group ratio rule should however be optional, as in some cases they may not be required (e.g. where the entities in a local group are able to deduct all of their net interest expense under the group ratio rule even without making adjustments to strip out banking and insurance operations).

528. Applying the fixed ratio rule (and group ratio rule) to a local group excluding certain entities is unlikely to be straightforward in practice. Where a country adopts such an approach it should consider including measures to deal with cases where groups seek to reduce the impact of the rules, for example by shifting interest expense into banking or insurance entities where it can be offset against interest income, or shifting interest income into other group entities to reduce the net interest expense subject to limitation. This would be consistent with statements in Chapter 9 that rules to address BEPS involving interest should be robust against attempts to avoid or reduce their effect.

Applying the fixed ratio rule entity-by-entity

529. Finally, Chapter 11 provides that a country may apply the fixed ratio rule to all groups on an entity-by-entity basis. When applied to entities in banking and insurance groups, this raises similar practical concerns to those mentioned above, in that entities may incur net interest expense on loans funding banking or insurance activities, but they may have relatively low levels of tax EBITDA and so most or all of this net interest expense may be disallowed.

530. A country which applies the fixed ratio rule on an entity-by-entity basis should consider introducing measures to address this impact (e.g. by excluding net interest expense on loans which fund banking or insurance business from the scope of the fixed ratio rule). However, the country may conclude that the need to make such adjustments is less than in the scenario where the fixed ratio rule is applied to a local group excluding banks and insurance companies. This is because, where the fixed ratio rule is applied consistently on an entity-by-entity basis across all sectors, any entity which incurs net interest expense on loans funding income in another entity could incur a disallowance. An entity which

does so in a group that includes a bank or insurance company may not necessarily be in a worse position than an entity in a group in a different sector, although regulatory capital restrictions may limit the ability of banking and insurance groups to restructure loans to avoid this outcome.

Rules to address the use of interest to fund non-taxable income

531. As outlined in Chapter 15, there are regulatory and commercial restrictions that limit the ability of banks and insurance companies, and entities in banking and insurance groups, to use debt to fund equity investments. Despite this, countries involved in the work on Action 4 have identified cases where solo-regulated entities and other entities in banking and insurance groups claim deductions for interest funding investments which give rise to dividend income or capital gains which are either exempt from tax or are taxed in a preferential manner. Countries which have identified such a concern should therefore consider introducing measures to deal with this kind of risk.

532. Where a country applies the fixed ratio rule to entities in a group with a bank or insurance company on an entity-by-entity basis, or to a local group excluding banks and insurance companies, this should provide protection against interest funding non-taxable income comparable with other sectors. However, the fixed ratio rule has no application where an entity or local group has net interest income. Therefore, it will not reduce the risk of interest funding non-taxable income in a bank or insurance company, or in other group entities where the rule is applied to a local group that includes a bank or insurance company.

533. Countries currently apply different approaches to deal with this risk, a number of which are summarised in Table III.B.2 in Annex III.B. These include rules which limit interest deductions where these arise on loans used to fund non-taxable income, and also rules which address the same risk by reducing the extent to which income benefits from a tax exemption or other beneficial tax treatment. Where a country applies CFC rules to tax an entity on undistributed income arising in a controlled foreign company, there is no expectation that the country should also apply rules to disallow interest funding subsequent dividends paid by the CFC out of CFC income or to reduce the extent to which such dividends are exempted from tax.

534. Where a country does not currently apply such an approach but has identified a risk posed by interest being used to fund non-taxable dividend income (or other forms of non-taxable income) by entities in a banking or insurance group, it should adopt the rule which is most suitable based on the structure of its tax system and the risks it has identified. However, there are a number of practical benefits from rules which address the risk by reducing the amount of dividend income that benefits from a participation exemption or preferential tax treatment. Money is fungible and tracing the use of specific funds over time may be difficult or impossible. An approach which applies directly to the treatment of income in the hands of an entity would reduce the need to identify which loans are being used to fund a particular investment. It may also be easier under such an approach for a country to take into account features of its regulatory regime to ensure a consistent outcome under regulatory rules and tax rules. For example, where a bank or insurance company is required by regulatory capital rules to deduct the value of an equity investment from its own equity capital, a tax rule may treat this investment as funded wholly using equity, in which case there would be no requirement to reduce the income that benefits from a participation exemption.

535. In order to ensure fairness and consistency in the operation of interest limitation rules, a country which introduces a rule to target interest funding non-taxable dividend income may want to apply the rule to all entities and not only to those in banking and insurance groups. Where this is the case, and an entity is also subject to the fixed ratio rule, the country should ensure that the rules operate consistently to avoid the risk of an excessive interest restriction.

536. Where a country applies the authorised OECD approach set out in the 2010 Report to attribute free capital to a permanent establishment of a bank or insurance company, this should in general prevent an excessive amount of free capital being allocated to the permanent establishment, which could otherwise result in deductions for excessive interest expense in the residence country. This should therefore provide robust protection against interest being used to fund non-taxable branch profits (e.g. where the residence country applies an exemption) and additional tax rules to deal with this should not be required.

Targeted rules to address specific risks

537. Although regulatory capital requirements reduce the risk of a bank or insurance company, or an entity in a group with a bank or insurance company, being over-leveraged or using interest to fund non-taxable income, they are unlikely to prevent an entity in all cases from entering into arrangements that gives rise to particular BEPS outcomes. Alongside the fixed ratio rule and group ratio rule, countries should apply targeted rules to deal with specific risks that they face, where these are material. For example, Chapter 9 recommends that countries consider introducing rules to address the following risks:

- An entity which would otherwise have net interest income enters into an arrangement which involves the payment of interest to a group entity outside the country or a related party to reduce the level of interest income subject to tax in the country
- An entity makes a payment of interest on an "artificial loan", where no new funding is raised by the entity or its group.
- An entity makes a payment of interest to a third party under a structured arrangement, for instance under a back-to-back arrangement.
- An entity makes a payment of interest to a related party which is excessive or is used to finance the production of tax exempt income
- An entity makes a payment of interest to a related party, which is subject to no or low taxation on the corresponding interest income.

538. Where targeted rules are introduced to address these specific risks, they may be applied to banks or insurance companies in the same way as to other entities, unless applying a particular rule to a bank or insurance company without modification could have an unintended or excessive impact. In this case, to ensure a comparable protection against BEPS in different sectors, a country should consider applying a modified version of the rule to banks and/or insurance companies, taking into account their particular characteristics. Table III.B.3 in Annex III.B includes a non-exhaustive summary of rules applied by countries involved in the work on Action 4, which may be used to inform a country when considering rules to address the risks it faces.

Transitional rules

539. As set out in Chapter 11, a country may exclude interest on existing loans from the scope of rules, either for a fixed period or indefinitely. This may be particularly relevant for third party loans which form part of a group's regulatory capital, as these loans are often long-dated and there may be substantial penalties if they are repaid early. In any case, these "grandfathering" rules should only apply to loans entered into before interest limitation rules are announced, and should cease to apply if a loan is subsequently re-financed or if the terms of the loan are significantly modified, to the extent this results in an increase to the tenor of the loan, the principal of the loan or to the rate of interest that applies.

Annex III.A

An overview of capital regulation in the banking and insurance sectors

540. Regulatory capital rules for banks are aimed at ensuring that banks and banking groups have sufficient high quality capital and liquidity to absorb financial and economic shocks or, if the shock cannot be fully absorbed, to achieve an ordered resolution with minimum impact on the wider financial system and the real economy. Most countries apply rules based on a framework established by the Bank for International Settlements. The previous framework (Basel II) is currently in the process of being extended and strengthened by the latest standard (Basel III) which was introduced as a response to the financial crisis and implementation is being phased in over the period to 2019.

541. One of the main goals of Basel III is to strengthen the capital base of banking groups to protect the solvency of banks, and this has a direct impact on the ability of banks to be over-leveraged. In placing limits on the capital structure of banks, these rules focus on the amount and nature of a bank's capital as a percentage of its risk-weighted assets (RWAs). This reflects the fact that banks undertaking different types of lending carry different amounts of risk. Under the framework, most banks must have Common Equity Tier 1 capital (i.e. ordinary share capital and retained earnings) of at least 4.5% of RWAs and total Tier 1 capital of at least 6% of RWAs. Tier 1 capital may be made up of Common Equity Tier 1 capital and also Additional Tier 1 capital such as preferred shares and certain types of hybrid debt which have the capacity to absorb losses either by being written down or converting into common shares upon a trigger event. A bank must also have total capital of at least 8% of RWAs, including Tier 1 capital and Tier 2 capital, which includes some categories of long-term subordinated debt. In order to avoid restrictions on the ability to pay dividends, banks must in addition maintain a capital conservation buffer comprising Common Equity Tier 1 capital equal to a further 2.5% of RWAs. In cases where a country is concerned that there is a build-up of excessive credit and system-wide risk, it may impose an additional countercyclical buffer of up to 2.5% of RWAs.

542. While these ratios apply to most banks, from 2018 Basel III will also require globally systemically important banks (G-SIBs) to hold additional Common Equity Tier 1 capital of between 1% and 3.5% of RWAs. The level of this G-SIB surcharge for a particular bank reflects its systemic importance, taking into account its size, interconnectedness, substitutability, complexity and global reach. Countries may apply similar surcharges to banks which are considered to be systemically important on a national level. In addition, in 2015 the Financial Stability Board announced that G-SIBs will be required to hold total loss-absorbing capital equal to 16% of RWAs by 2019 and equal to 18% of RWAs by 2022. Total loss-absorbing capital includes both Tier 1 capital and Tier 2 capital, but does not include capital held as part of the capital conservation buffer, countercyclical buffer or G-SIB surcharge.

543. Capital requirements under Basel III apply to internationally active banks. These requirements must be met at the level of the worldwide consolidated group, and also on a consolidated basis by internationally active banks at each tier within a group. In addition, regulators often require capital adequacy ratios to be met by specific solo-regulated entities in their country. This means that banks will often be subject to oversight in more than one country where they have operations. Where two regimes overlap in their coverage, it will be the stricter of the two approaches that in effect takes precedence. Where a group operates in multiple jurisdictions, the aggregated capital requirements of local regulators mean that a group will often hold more capital than would be required by the parent country regulator if it had sole oversight of the group.

544. In order to ensure an orderly resolution of a group in the event of insolvency, a group's parent country regulator will typically prefer regulatory capital instruments to be issued out of an entity at the top of a group, from which capital can be made available to any part of the group. This capital will then flow down a group as required by local regulators, so that at each level of consolidation the group is adequately capitalised. This ensures that the loss-absorbing capacity of capital flows up the group to a single point, from which the group can be resolved with minimum knock-on effects.

545. Alongside these capital adequacy requirements, regulators impose additional requirements on banks which can directly or indirectly act as constraints on a group's ability to engage in BEPS involving interest.

- One cause of the financial crisis was the build-up by banks of excessive on-balance sheet and off-balance sheet leverage while maintaining strong risk-based capital ratios. The Basel III framework addresses this by supplementing risk-based capital requirements with a non-risk based leverage ratio. The leverage ratio is equal to total Tier 1 capital divided by the total exposure to on-balance sheet and off-balance sheet items, and this is tested at the level of a solo-regulated bank and a regulated group. For a transitional period from 1 January 2013, banks are required to report their leverage ratio to national regulators, based on a minimum ratio requirement of 3%. However, a number of countries including Switzerland and the United States have introduced stricter minimum ratios for systemically important groups. During the transitional period, the design and level of the ratio will be assessed with a view to any changes being made and the leverage ratio becoming a minimum capital requirement from 1 January 2018. The leverage ratio imposes an additional layer of restriction on the capital structure of banks and banking groups, which must be met using Tier 1 capital only. While a bank may meet some of its Tier 1 capital requirements using interest-bearing instruments, the majority of this must be in the form of Common Equity Tier 1.
- Regulatory capital rules ensure that a bank has sufficient capital available to absorb losses arising on a diversified portfolio of risk. However, it does not necessarily provide protection in cases where a bank has significant exposure to default from a single counterparty or group of connected counterparties. Therefore, banks and banking groups are subject to large exposure limits whereby they must report any exposure equal to 10% or more of eligible capital (defined as Tier 1 capital under Basel III), and must not have total exposure to a single counterparty (or group of connected counterparties) of more than 25% of eligible capital. This upper limit is reduced to 15% where it concerns a G-SIB's exposure to other G-SIBs. While large exposure limits are intended to protect against contagion where a single default has a ripple effect throughout the financial system, they also provide some

protection against banks making very high levels of loans to push debt into related parties. Banks may avoid breaching large exposure limits by using eligible credit risk mitigation techniques to reduce their exposure to default. They may also seek approval from the regulator to waive large exposure limits with respect to entities in the same group, subject to strict conditions.

- A key element of Basel III is to improve the resilience of banks against liquidity risk. The introduction of a liquidity coverage ratio (LCR) supports this by ensuring a bank has sufficient high quality liquid assets that can be converted easily and readily into cash that can meet liquidity needs for 30 calendar days in a severe stress scenario. This is complemented by a net stable funding ratio (NSFR) requirement that requires banks to fund their activities using stable sources of funding able to support the business for the following year. Together, these requirements apply pressure on a group to hold more short term assets (which tend to yield lower interest income) and more long term liabilities (which tend to bear higher interest costs), reducing the level of a group's net interest income overall. In many cases the need to hold high quality liquid assets will give rise to a "negative cost of carry", where the cost of funding an asset is higher than the income it generates.
- A local regulator needs to ensure that the balance sheet of a group in its country is as stable as possible. Therefore it may also impose restrictions on the ability of subsidiaries or branches to transfer funds to a parent or head office, in particular in stress scenarios. This may reduce the ability or willingness of a group to place excessive funds including debt into a particular country where there are concerns that this may not be available to the parent or head office in the event of a crisis.

546. Although the overall framework for bank capital regulation is agreed on a global basis, there may still be differences in how the framework is implemented by countries. For example, in some cases countries may "gold-plate" their regimes by applying stricter rules either to all banks or to those which are seen as systemically important. It is also important to note that these requirements continue to evolve and have not yet been fully implemented by countries.

547. Within the European Union, the "banking union" is a single banking supervision and resolution system, including all euro area countries and some other EU Member States. It aims to strengthen financial stability in the euro area and the EU as a whole by ensuring banks are robust, situations where taxpayers' money is used to save failing banks are avoided and fragmentation caused by differing rules is reduced. The banking union consists of three main building blocks: the Single Rulebook, the Single Supervisory Mechanism and the Single Resolution Mechanism. The Single Rulebook includes rules on capital requirements, protection for depositors and the management of bank failures. This implements the Basel III framework into EU law, through the Capital Requirements Directive IV (CRD IV) and Capital Requirements Regulation (CRR). The Single Supervisory Mechanism ensures consistent and co-ordinated supervision of banks operating across the EU, including both the supranational European Central Bank and national supervisory authorities in close co-operation. The Single Resolution Mechanism, which became operational in 2016, is designed to manage the resolution of failing banks within the euro area with minimal cost to taxpayers and the real economy. This includes a Single Resolution Fund, to be built up over eight years through contributions from the banking sector, which will be used for resolving failing banks after all other options, including bail-in triggers on interest-bearing regulatory capital, have been exhausted.

548. Unlike for banks, there is currently no single global standard for the capital regulation of insurance groups and so there is much greater variance in the nature and level of protection provided in different countries. Within the European Union, a new regulatory framework (Solvency II) came into force on 1 January 2016 which aims to increase the level of harmonisation of insurance regulation and introduce requirements that are more sensitive to the level of risk undertaken. The framework aims to ensure that an insurance company's obligations arising from all types of risk are sufficiently covered by loss-absorbing capital to protect against insolvency, and its capital is invested in high quality assets to protect against illiquidity. Solvency II is used here as an example of a regulatory capital regime for insurance companies which is applied in 28 countries with additional countries applying regimes which meet a strict "equivalency" standard. EU insurers that reinsure risk into non-EU jurisdictions are expected to demonstrate that regulation in those jurisdictions is equivalent to that under Solvency II.

549. Under Solvency II, an insurance company should hold sufficient capital to cover all of its obligations arising from underwriting risk, market risk, credit risk and operational risk over the next 12 months, with a probability of 99.5% (the Solvency Capital Requirement). This is intended to limit the risk to customers and the wider economy of an insurance company being unable to withstand these risks to a 1-in-200 year event. The Solvency Capital Requirement may take into account risk mitigation techniques that a group can demonstrate it would apply, and can be calculated using a standard formula or a model developed by the group and approved by the regulator.

550. Solvency II also includes a Minimum Capital Requirement, which is based on an insurance company being able to meet its obligations over the next 12 months with a probability of 85%. However, in all cases this should be no lower than 25% and no higher than 45% of the Solvency Capital Requirement. This gives regulators scope to make greater interventions as an insurance company's capital falls below its Solvency Capital Requirement and gets closer to its Minimum Capital Requirement. If capital falls below the Minimum Capital Requirement, an insurance company's liabilities may be transferred to another insurer and its licence withdrawn.

551. In terms of the proportion of an insurance company's capital that must be in the form of equity, 50% of the capital needed to meet the Solvency Capital Requirement and 80% of that needed to meet the Minimum Capital Requirement must be Tier 1 capital. Of this Tier 1 capital, at least 80% must be in the form of ordinary shares and retained earnings. The remaining 20% of Tier 1 capital may be made up of other items which are permanently available and subordinated, including paid-up preference shares and certain long-dated debt instruments with an original term of at least 30 years which meet certain conditions (e.g. they must include clauses for them to be written-down or converted into ordinary shares on a trigger event).

552. The remaining capital needed to meet the Solvency Capital Requirement or the Minimum Capital Requirement may be in the form of either Tier 1 capital or Tier 2 capital. Tier 2 capital includes certain long-dated debt instruments with an original term of at least 10 years, subject to conditions such as terms that provide for the suspension of interest payments and redemption in circumstances such as where the Solvency Capital Requirement is not met. For the Solvency Capital Requirement only, up to 15% of the capital needed may be in the form of Tier 3 capital which includes subordinated debt with a minimum original term of at least 3 years.

553. In addition to these minimum capital requirements, there are two further features of Solvency II which operate to restrict the excessive use of interest-bearing regulatory capital instruments by insurance companies.

- First, any Tier 2 or Tier 3 capital which does not count towards the Solvency Capital Requirement or Minimum Capital Requirement is re-categorised as an ordinary liability. A company would incur a high funding cost but obtain no additional regulatory capital benefit to support new business.
- Second, at all times Tier 1 capital must exceed the total amount of debt treated as Tier 2 or Tier 3 capital. This means that in principle an insurance company could meet its Solvency Capital Requirement and Minimum Capital Requirements using 50% Tier 1 capital and 50% Tier 2 capital (or 35% Tier 2 capital and 15% Tier 3 capital). However, if such a company incurred a loss which reduced its retained earnings, its Tier 1 capital would fall. Because Tier 1 capital must at all times be equal to or exceed the total of Tier 2 and Tier 3 capital, the maximum amount of debt that can be treated as Tier 2 or Tier 3 capital would also fall, and some of this capital would be re-characterised as an ordinary liability. In effect the fall in retained earnings would result in a reduction in capital which is double that which would have occurred had all of the insurance company's capital been in the form of Tier 1. This creates an incentive for an insurance company to include more than the minimum amount of Tier 1 as a proportion of its overall capital base. A similar incentive exists for an insurance company to hold more equity as a proportion of its total Tier 1 capital than the 80% minimum required.

554. Solvency II operates across the European Union, and requirements must be met by each insurance company as well as by the consolidated group (i.e. the worldwide group for EU-headed groups and to the EU-headed sub-group for foreign-headed groups). Where a group has material operations in more than one Member State, national regulators will consult together and agree that one will act as primary regulator for the EU group. This will typically be the regulator in the Member State where the group has its largest operations irrespective of whether there is a higher level holding company in a different Member State. The primary regulator will monitor the overall capitalisation of the EU group (including entities held by members of the EU group) while regulators in each Member State will focus on the structure of entities in that country.

555. A number of countries outside the European Union apply risk-based capital regimes which contain similar elements to Solvency II, although in many cases there are differences in the rules applied and the amounts and types of capital which must be held. For example, some countries do not allow any types of debt to be treated as regulatory capital, and so an insurance company will be required to meet all of its capital adequacy ratios using equity. Solvency II also applies equally to insurance companies engaged in different types of business, including life insurance, general insurance (also referred to as non-life insurance or property and casualty insurance) and reinsurance. However, outside the European Union countries may apply different rules depending on the business carried on.

556. Despite the lack of a single common model for insurance company regulation, steps are being taken towards a more globally consistent approach.

- In addition to the 28 EU Member States that apply Solvency II, two countries (Bermuda and Switzerland) currently have regimes which are judged to be fully equivalent to Solvency II and a further six countries (Australia, Brazil, Canada, Japan, Mexico and the United States) have regimes judged to be provisionally equivalent to Solvency II.

- Where an insurance group has significant activities in multiple jurisdictions, the insurance regulator in each of these countries will participate in a "College of Supervisors". This has responsibility for the efficient, effective and consistent supervision of groups operating across national borders, and provides a platform for gathering and disseminating information, developing a common understanding of the risk profile of a group and establishing plans for the assessment and mitigation of risk at group level.
- The International Association of Insurance Supervisors (IAIS) actively promotes the effective and consistent supervision of the insurance industry across different countries and has established core principles, which are globally accepted requirements for the supervision of the insurance sector. The IAIS is also developing group-wide global capital standards for all internationally active insurance groups as well as high loss absorbency requirements for globally systemically important insurers (G-SIIs).

557. In addition to formal regulatory capital requirements, the demands of credit ratings agencies play a key role in determining the capital structure of insurance groups. The nature of insurance business means that many lines of business cannot be written unless a group is able to secure a high credit rating. This will be put in jeopardy if a group has excessive external leverage, or is structured in such a way that there is a risk that it will be unable to meet ongoing obligations on its debt as they fall due. This acts as a natural limit on the level of debt held by insurance groups, as well as on the ability of insurance companies and holding companies in insurance groups to use debt to fund equity investments with variable or uncertain income flows.

Annex III.B

Selected rules applied by countries to address BEPS involving interest in the banking and insurance sectors

Table III.B.1. **General interest limitation rules based on a financial ratio**

No.	Country	Applies to	Description of rule	Exceptions
1	Australia (thin capitalisation)	Banking sector	Authorised Deposit-Taking Institutions (ADIs) must: • have average equity capital allocated to Australian operations of at least 6% of their Australian risk-weighted assets (the safe harbour capital amount); • meet an arm's length capital test; or • have average equity capital which is equal to or more than the worldwide capital of the ADI and its controlled foreign entities (for outward investing ADIs only). Where none of these tests are met, a proportion of gross interest deductions on third party and related party debt will be denied based on the difference between the safe harbour capital amount and the ADI's actual average equity capital.	The rule does not apply if: • total debt deductions are less than AUD 2 million; • the ADI is an outward investor and 90% of its assets (including associates) are Australian assets; or • the ADI falls into any of several categories of entity set up to manage certain risks.
2	Belgium (thin capitalisation)	All sectors	Interest on "tainted loans" is denied where the tainted loan/debt ratio exceeds 5/1. Tainted loans include intragroup loans and loans from lenders that are not subject to income tax or which benefit from a tax regime substantially more favourable than the general regime in Belgium. Where the rule is applied to companies engaged in centralised treasury management for a group, only net interest paid on loans which exceed the 5/1 ratio is disallowed.	The rule does not apply to: • publicly issued bonds; • loans from Belgian or EEA credit institutions; • borrowings by leasing and factoring companies; or • borrowings by companies involved in PPP projects.
3	Canada (thin capitalisation)	All sectors	Interest on loans from non-resident "specified shareholders" and non-residents that do not deal at arm's length with specified shareholders is subject to limitation based on a debt/equity ratio of 1.5/1. Specified shareholders are those which, alone or together with non-arm's length persons, own 25% of the votes or value of the Canadian corporation.	The rule does not apply to loans from Canadian permanent establishments of non-resident insurance companies and authorised foreign banks.
4	Canada (thin capitalisation)	Non-resident insurers and resident multinational life insurers	Non-resident insurance companies and resident life insurers with insurance business outside Canada can only deduct interest expense with respect to property they designate as used or held in the year in the course of carrying on an insurance business in Canada.	None.

Table III.B.1. **General interest limitation rules based on a financial ratio** *(continued)*

No.	Country	Applies to	Description of rule	Exceptions
5	Canada (thin capitalisation)	Authorised foreign banks	Canadian branches of authorised foreign banks can only deduct interest expense on actual liabilities to other persons or partnerships to the extent these liabilities do not exceed 95% of the business's assets. To the extent actual liabilities are less than 95% of the business's assets, notional interest may be deducted on amounts allocated by the banks to or for the benefit of its Canadian banking business ("branch advances"). Where actual liabilities and branch advances are less than 95% of the business's assets, an amount of interest calculated by applying the Bank of Canada bank rate to this shortfall may also be deducted.	None.
6	Czech Republic (thin capitalisation)	Banking and insurance sectors	Interest on related party debt is subject to limitation based on a debt/equity ratio of 6/1.	None.
7	France (thin capitalisation)	All sectors except banking	The rule applies where • related party debt exceeds 1.5 times net equity; • related party interest exceeds 25% of adjusted tax EBITDA; and • interest expense on loans from related parties exceeds interest income on loans to related parties. For these purposes, related party debt includes third party loans which are guaranteed by a related party. The proportion of an entity's interest expense that meets all of these requirements is disallowed.	This rule does not apply to interest expense relating to the centralised cash management for a group, where the interest is paid to the entity responsible for that centralised cash management.
8	Germany (earnings stripping)	All sectors	Net interest expense is deductible up to 30% of tax EBITDA. The rule may be applied to the position of a consolidated fiscal unit ("Organschaft"). Under this rule, disallowed interest expense may be carried forward indefinitely. The carry forward of unused interest capacity is also possible, but limited to five years.	The rule does not apply if: • Net interest expense is below EUR 3 million; • The business is a standalone entity; or • The business belongs to a fully consolidated group and its equity/total assets ratio at the end of the preceding financial year is equal to or greater than that of the consolidated group, or is below that of the consolidated group by no more than two percentage points (the "equity escape"). A business cannot benefit from the "standalone entity" exemption if more than 10% of its net interest expense is paid to related parties. A business cannot benefit from the equity escape exemption if interest payments on related party loans from shareholders outside the consolidated group are more than 10% of the net interest expense of any domestic or foreign group company.

Table III.B.1. **General interest limitation rules based on a financial ratio** *(continued)*

No.	Country	Applies to	Description of rule	Exceptions
9	Italy (fixed disallowance)	Banks and insurance companies, and holding companies in banking and insurance groups	Banks and insurance companies, and holding companies of banking and insurance groups, can deduct up to 96% of their gross interest expense (including payments economically equivalent to interest). Within a consolidated tax group, interest paid between banks and insurance companies in the group is fully deductible so long as it does not exceed the gross interest expense paid by banks and insurance companies within the consolidated tax group to entities outside the group. This rule will cease to apply to banks and holding companies in banking groups from 2017.	None.
10	Japan (thin capitalisation)	All sectors	Where a resident company has debt to its foreign parent which exceeds three times its equity held by that foreign parent (i.e. based on a debt/equity ratio of 3/1), interest expense corresponding to the excess is denied.	The rule applies only if the company's total debt exceeds three times its total equity capital. To the extent interest paid to the foreign parent is included in the parent's taxable income in Japan, this interest is not subject to limitation. In applying the rule, the 3/1 ratio can be replaced by the debt/equity ratio of a company that conducts similar business under similar circumstances. This rule does not apply where more interest expense would be denied under Japan's earnings stripping rules.
11	Japan (earnings stripping)	All sectors	An entity's net related party interest expense is limited to 50% of EBITDA.	The rule does not apply if: • the entity's net interest expense does not exceed JPY 10 million; • the entity's interest expense paid to related parties is does not exceed 50% of its total interest expense; or • more interest expense would be denied under Japan's thin capitalisation rules. To the extent interest paid to a related party is included in the related party's taxable income in Japan, this interest is not subject to limitation.
12	Mexico (thin capitalisation)	All sectors	Where debt with non-resident related parties exceeds three times the equity of the taxpayer (i.e. a debt/equity ratio of 3/1), gross interest expense on the excess will not be deductible. A taxpayer may request an Advance Pricing Agreement to allow higher interest deductions. Taxpayers may elect to calculate equity by adding the contributed stock capital tax account, the "net taxable income account" and the "reinvested net taxable income account" and dividing this number by two. Note that the reinvested net taxable income account was abolished in 2001 and so this is only relevant to taxpayers that have credit in such an account. An election to use this method must apply for at least five years.	For banking and insurance groups the rule only applies to interest expense derived from activities that are not part of the entity's core business.

Table III.B.1. **General interest limitation rules based on a financial ratio** *(continued)*

No.	Country	Applies to	Description of rule	Exceptions
13	New Zealand (thin capitalisation)	Banking sector	Banks registered with the New Zealand Reserve Bank and which otherwise are subject to the thin capitalisation regime (generally this requires either that they are foreign controlled, or they have foreign operations) must have average equity capital in New Zealand of at least 6% of their New Zealand risk-weighted assets. Both figures are calculated on the basis of the capital and assets of the New Zealand group and all New Zealand group members. Where this test is not met, a proportion of gross interest deductions on third party and related party debt will be denied based on the difference between the required equity capital amount and the actual average amount.	None.
14	New Zealand (thin capitalisation)	All sectors except banking	The rule applies where a company is at least 50% owned by a non-resident, or by non-residents acting together. Where the rule applies, the resident company can deduct interest subject to a maximum debt to assets ratio of 60%. There is no carry forward of disallowed interest expense.	Interest deductions are not denied if the debt to assets ratio of New Zealand group does not exceed 110% of the debt to assets ratio of its worldwide group.
15	South Africa (earnings stripping)	All sectors	The rule applies to interest which is (a) from lenders in a controlling relationship, including indirect loans via back to back arrangements, and (b) is not subject to tax in the hands of the recipient or included in the net income of a CFC. Where the rule applied, net interest expense is limited to a percentage of tax EBITDA. This percentage is determined using the formula: % = 40 x ((average repo rate for the year + 400 basis points)/10) Under this rule, disallowed interest expense may be carried forward.	None.
16	Switzerland	All sectors	Interest funding different categories of assets is permitted up to a safe harbour based on fair market values. The rule takes into account the total interest cost of a company, but only interest on related party debt is restricted. A range of safe harbour interest rates for related party loans is also published. Groups may apply an interest rate outside of this safe harbour if they demonstrate it complies with the arm's length standard. For foreign currency loans, the relevant market interest rate applies. Excessive interest expense is re-characterised as a deemed dividend.	For each category of asset, a safe harbour is provided.
17	United States (earnings stripping)	All sectors	Interest expense is treated as excessive to the extent it exceeds 50% of adjusted taxable income (i.e. tax EBITDA). To the extent this excessive interest is paid to foreign related parties (based on a 50% ownership test), or is paid to third parties on loans guaranteed by foreign related parties, it is disallowed for tax purposes. Disallowed interest expense may be carried forward indefinitely.	This rule only applies where the recipient of the interest (or the guarantor of loans from third parties) is exempt from US tax or is subject to a reduced rate of tax under a treaty. This rule does not apply where the debt to equity ratio of the company is less than or equal to 1.5/1.

Notes: a. Finland, Italy, Norway, Portugal, the Slovak Republic and Spain apply earnings stripping rules which include exemptions for banks and insurance companies.

b. In addition to the rules contained in this table, a number of countries apply limits to an entity's interest deductions based on an arm's length test.

Table III.B.2. **Rules to address interest funding non-taxable income**

No.	Country	Applies to	Description of rule	Exceptions
18	Canada	All sectors	Interest and other expenses are not deductible to the extent it may reasonably be regarded as incurred for the purpose of gaining or producing exempt income or in connection with property the income from which would be exempt.	The rule does not apply where funds are borrowed to earn dividend income.
19	Canada	All sectors	Where a Canadian company which is controlled by foreign shareholders makes an investment (equity or debt) in a foreign affiliate, the Canadian company is deemed to pay a dividend subject to non-resident withholding tax (or incurs a reduction in its paid-up capital that can be distributed to non-resident shareholders free of withholding tax).	The rule does not apply if: • The Canadian company makes a loan to the foreign affiliate and elects to receive imputed interest income on the loan; • The Canadian company acquires shares in the foreign affiliate in the course of an internal corporate reorganisation; or • The foreign affiliate's business is more closely connected to that of the Canadian company than to a business carried on by a non-resident parent or sister company.
20	Czech Republic	All sectors	Costs related to non-taxable income are not tax-deductible.	None.
21	Czech Republic	All sectors	Expenses associated with the ownership of shares in a subsidiary are non-deductible. Interest on loans taken out in the six months before shares are acquired will be deemed to be associated with the ownership of shares unless the parent company can demonstrate otherwise. Non-deductible costs are deemed to equal 5% of the value of dividends received, unless the parent can demonstrate that the expenses actually associated with the ownership of shares is lower.	None.
22	Finland	All sectors	Expenses funding non-taxable income are not deductible.	None.
23	Germany	All sectors	Interest and other expenses may not be deducted to the extent they bear a direct economic connection to tax-exempt income. Where dividend income benefits from the participation exemption, a standardised amount equal to 5% of the dividend income is treated as a non-deductible business expenses. Irrespective of this, connected business expenses actually incurred can still be deducted.	None.
24	Japan	All sectors	In applying the foreign dividend exclusion system, an amount equal to 5% of the dividend income will be deemed to represent interest and other expenses connected to the income. This will be deducted from the dividend income that benefits from the participation exemption.	None.
25	Mexico	All sectors	A proportion of an entity's total expenses, including interest, is treated as funding tax exempt income and is not deductible for tax purposes. This proportion is calculated by dividing the taxpayer's exempt income by its total income.	This rule does not apply: • to dividends and the profits of corporations, which are not considered as exempt income, or • to items that are not considered to be income under the income tax law.

Table III.B.2. **Rules to address interest funding non-taxable income** *(continued)*

No.	Country	Applies to	Description of rule	Exceptions
26	Netherlands	All sectors	Interest is non-deductible if it has a connection to the financing of tax-exempt participations. The non-deductible proportion of an entity's interest expense is determined using the formula (average participation debt/average total debt) x total interest. Average participation debt = acquisition price participations – equity. If the taxpayer is an active financing company, interest income and expense may be netted. For other companies, the rule applies to gross interest expense.	The rule is subject to a monetary threshold of EUR 750 000. Participations that qualify as an expansion of the operational activities of a group can in certain circumstances be excluded from the rule.
27	New Zealand	Banking	Offshore assets which are not subject to tax in New Zealand are deducted from equity in applying the thin capitalisation rules for banks. This reduces the bank's capacity to deduct interest expense.	None.
28	Portugal	All sectors	Interest and other expenses are not tax deductible if they are incurred for the purposes of earning non-taxable income.	None.
29	Slovenia	All sectors	Expenses related to managing and financing investments must be set against tax-exempt dividends and capital gains on equity holdings. These expenses are deemed to equal 5% of the value of dividends or profits received.	None.
30	South Africa	All sectors	Excessive interest expense used to fund acquisitions or reorganisations which give rise to tax-deferred income (e.g. tax-exempt dividend income). To achieve this, net interest expense is limited to a percentage of tax EBITDA. This percentage is determined using the formula: % = 40 x ((average repo rate for the year + 400 basis points)/10) Under this rule, disallowed interest expense may be not be carried forward. The rule is applied in the year the tax-deferred reorganisation occurs and the following five years of assessment.	None.
31	Switzerland	All sectors	The amount of dividend income and capital gains that benefit from a participation exemption are reduced by (i) amortisation, (ii) financing costs relating to the participation and (iii) an allowance for administrative costs deemed to be 5% of dividends. Financing costs include interest and costs economically equivalent to interest. These are allocated based on the ratio of the tax value of a company's assets that benefit from a participation exemption compared with the tax value of its total assets.	None.
32	United States	All sectors	In general, interest is not deductible for tax if it is funding certain income that is exempt from US tax. Generally, taxpayers can deduct claim a tax deduction for a portion of dividends. However, this deduction is reduced for dividends received on portfolio stock financed with debt, where the taxpayer holds a specified percentage of the stock. There are special ownership attribution rules relating to options held by taxpayers on 80%-owned banks.	Exemptions apply to small issuers.

Table III.B.3. **Selected other rules**

No.	Country	Applies to	Description of rule	Exceptions
33	Austria	All sectors	Interest expense is not deductible where it is paid to a related party and the interest income is not sufficiently taxed in the hands of the beneficial owner. An effective tax rate of 10% will be considered sufficient.	None.
34	Belgium	All sectors	Interest expense is disallowed if it is paid to foreign entities or permanent establishments which are not subject to income tax or are subject to a tax regime substantially more favourable than the general regime in Belgium.	An exception applies if the taxpayer can demonstrate that payments are with respect to normal business transactions and do not exceed normal limits.
35	Canada	All sectors	Interest on third party and related party loans is only deductible if the amount of interest is reasonable and the purpose of the borrowing is to earn business or property income.	None.
36	Czech Republic	All sectors	Interest expense is not deductible on loans where the interest rate is dependent on profits.	The rule does not apply to interest paid by public benefit entities or by stock exchange operators.
37	France	All sectors	Interest expense is not deductible where the interest is paid to a related party, and the lender is not subject to tax that equals at least 25% of the tax that would have been due under French tax rules.	None.
38	France	All sectors	Interest expense on loans to fund the purchase of shares in a company is not deductible unless the acquiring company can show that it effectively takes decisions with respect to those shares.	The rule does not apply if: • The total fair market value of participations owned by the acquiring company does not exceed EUR 1 million; • The acquisition was not financed by debt at the level of the acquiring company or at the level of a company in the same group; or • The debt/equity ratio of the group is equal to or higher than the debt/equity ratio of the acquiring company.
39	France	All sectors	25% of the net finance expenses of a company are not deductible. This applies to the consolidated position of a tax group.	This rule does not apply if the net finance expense if a tax group is less than EUR 3 million.
40	Ireland	All sectors	Interest is not deductible where it arises on borrowings from a related party or from a third party (which is financed back to back from a related party) and those borrowings are used: • to acquire shares in a company where either that company or the company from which it is acquired is a related company, or • to make a loan to a holding company which is used by that holding company to acquire shares in a company and either that latter company or the company from which it is acquired is a related company.	The rule does not apply to the extent interest expense is matched by interest or dividend income chargeable to tax in Ireland ("relevant income"), which would not have arisen but for the direct or indirect use of the loan in respect of which the interest relief is claimed. A company connected with the investing company may also claim part of the relief where the investing company does not have sufficient relevant income. An exemption also applies for interest on a loan from a related party used to subscribe for new share capital or to lend to another company to subscribe for new share capital, provided the new share capital is issued to increase the capital available to the issuing company for use in its trade or business.
41	Ireland	All sectors	Interest is not deductible on a loan from a related company that is used to acquire assets from a connected company, other than trading stock and certain other assets.	Where the interest is on borrowings used to acquire a trade which, prior to acquisition, was not within the charge to corporation tax, the interest is deductible up to the amount of the income from the acquired trade.

Table III.B.3. **Selected other rules** *(continued)*

No.	Country	Applies to	Description of rule	Exceptions
42	Mexico	All sectors	Interest expense is disallowed if it is paid to foreign related parties and the payments are not taxed on the foreign jurisdiction.	The rule does not apply: • to interest paid to non-resident pension funds if they are exempt from Mexican income tax and they were incorporated in a jurisdiction that shares tax information with Mexico; or • to interest paid to funds owned by a State, its subdivisions or local authorities if the fund is exempt from tax under a tax treaty between Mexico and that State.
43	Mexico	All sectors	Payments made to a related party are not deductible if they benefit from a preferential tax regime. A preferential tax regime is one that taxes income at an effective tax rate below 75% of the Mexican corporate tax rate.	This rule does not apply if the payment is made at arm's length.
44	Mexico	All sectors	Interest paid to related parties can be re-characterised as a non-deductible dividend in certain circumstances, including: • If the debtor executes a written unconditional promise of full or partial payment of the credit received, on a date determinable at any time by the creditor. • In the event of default by the debtor the creditor is entitled to intervene in the direction or management of the debtor company. • If the payment of interest is conditional on the generation of profits or if the amount of interest paid is determined by such profits. • Back-to-back loans. • The interest exceeds an arm's length price.	This rule does not apply to non-bank credit unions and savings-and-loan-co-operative entities.
45	Netherlands	All sectors	Losses of holding companies, which often represent interest costs, can only be set against "holding profits" and not against other profits.	None.
46	Netherlands	All sectors	Interest is not deductible where a loan is provided by a related party and used to fund: • a dividend or return of capital to a related party; • a capital contribution to a related party; or • an acquisition or expansion of a party who is related after that acquisition or expansion.	The rule does not apply if a debtor can demonstrate that the loan and the related party transaction are both for sound business reasons. This exception does not apply if the interest income is not taxed at an effective rate of at least 10% in the hands of the recipient.
47	Netherlands	All sectors	Interest is not deducted where it is paid to a related party on a loan of at least 10 years (or where there is no redemption date) and where the loan is interest-free or bears interest lower than 30% of the arm's length rate.	None.
48	Netherlands	All sectors	Interest is not deductible on any loan used to fund the acquisition of a target company in cases where the holding company and target company become part of a tax group.	The rule is subject to a threshold of EUR 1 million. Deductions are permitted up to a debt/acquisition price ratio of 60% in the first year. This ratio reduces by 5% points each year until it reaches 25%.
49	New Zealand	All sectors	Profit participating loans and debt which is stapled to shares is treated as equity for tax purposes. Interest paid on this debt is treated as dividend, to which imputation credits may be attached.	None.
50	Portugal	All sectors	Interest paid to shareholders that are not related parties is deductible up to a limit of Euribor+150 basis points.	None.

Table III.B.3. **Selected other rules** *(continued)*

No.	Country	Applies to	Description of rule	Exceptions
51	Slovenia	All sectors	Interest expense on related party debt is limited to the recognised interest rate, published by the Ministry of Finance.	None.
52	Slovenia	All sectors	Interest paid to lenders resident in a low-tax jurisdiction is not tax deductible. A low tax jurisdiction is one outside the EU where the general or average nominal tax rate is lower than 12.5%, are	None.
53	South Africa	All sectors	Interest on specific loans with equity-like features is re-characterised as dividend *in specie*. Features taken into account include: • convertibility of the debt into shares • repayment or interest payments being conditional on the solvency of the issuer, and • the reasonableness of the period for which the debt will remain outstanding.	The rule does not apply to interest on: • loans owed by small corporations • Tier 1 or Tier 2 capital instruments issued by a bank or bank holding company • regulatory capital issued by short term or long term insurers • units in a company held by a long term insurer, pension fund, provident fund or REIT that holds at least 20% of the linked units in that company, and more than 80% of the value of the assets of that company are attributable to immoveable property.
54	South Africa	All sectors	Interest paid on loans where the interest rate is dependent on the profits of the issuer is re-characterised as dividend *in specie*.	The rule does not apply to interest on: • loans owed by small corporations • Tier 1 or Tier 2 capital instruments issued by a bank or bank holding company • regulatory capital issued by short term or long term insurers • units in a company held by a long term insurer, pension fund, provident fund or REIT that holds at least 20% of the linked units in that company, and more than 80% of the value of the assets of that company are attributable to immoveable property.
55	Spain	All sectors	Interest deductions are denied on related party loans used to fund the acquisition of or contributions to the capital of group entities.	This rule does not apply if the taxpayer can demonstrate a valid economic reason for such operations.
56	Sweden	All sectors	Interest paid to related parties, including through back-to-back arrangements is not deductible for tax.	This rule does not apply: • If the beneficial owner of the interest income is subject to a tax rate of at least 10% (unless the principal reason for the loan is to achieve a significant tax advantage); or • If the company can show that the loan is made primarily for business reasons and the beneficial owner is located in a country within the EEA area or (subject to conditions) a country with which Sweden has a double tax treaty.
57	Switzerland	All sectors	Interest expense is disallowed where a special purpose vehicle is established to acquire a target company, the acquisition is wholly or partly debt financed, and the SPV and target are merged following acquisition.	None.
58	United Kingdom	All sectors	A company may not bring into account any income or expenses that have an unallowable purpose. An unallowable purpose is one which is not among the business or other commercial purposes of the company.	None.

Table III.B.3. **Selected other rules** *(continued)*

No.	Country	Applies to	Description of rule	Exceptions
59	United Kingdom	All sectors	Interest paid at more than a commercial rate of return or dependent on the results of the company is treated as a dividend distribution and is not deductible for tax purposes.	This rule does not apply to payments made to companies within the charge to UK corporation tax.
60	United States	All sectors	Taxpayers are able to claim foreign tax credits on their foreign source income. Interest funding foreign source income is allocated to this income, reducing the extent to which foreign tax credits may be claimed.	Disallowed and capitalised interest does not need to be allocated.

Note: A number of countries also apply general anti-avoidance rules (GAARs) or an abuse of law doctrine which may also restrict interest deductions in particular circumstances.

Annex III.C

Examples to Part III

Example 1 – Applying the fixed ratio rule to a banking or insurance group excluding banks and insurance companies

558. In Table III.C.1, a group consists of three entities all of which are located in Country X. A Co is a holding company with two subsidiaries, B Co and FI Co. B Co is a group service company with no independent business activities. FI Co is a solo-regulated bank or insurance company. A Co has negative EBITDA of USD 10 million and net interest expense of USD 20 million (most of which is incurred on interest-bearing regulatory capital instruments). B Co has EBITDA of USD 10 million and net interest expense of USD 5 million. FI Co has EBITDA of USD 20 million and net interest income of USD 100 million.

Table III.C.1. **Applying the fixed ratio rule to a banking or insurance group excluding banks and insurance companies**

	A Co USD	B Co USD	Local group USD	FI Co USD	Entire group USD
EBITDA	(10 million)	10 million	0	20 million	20 million
Net interest income/(expense)	(20 million)	(5 million)	(25 million)	100 million	75 million
Benchmark fixed ratio	-	-	25%	-	-
Interest capacity	-	-	0	-	-
Net interest income/(expense) of local group	(20 million)	(5 million)	(25 million)	-	-
Interest disallowance	20 million	5 million	25 million	-	-
Interest taxable/(deductible)	-	-	-	100 million	100 million

559. Country X applies the fixed ratio rule with a benchmark fixed ratio of 25%. The rule is applied to the net position of the local group, excluding regulated banks and insurance companies. Therefore, for these purposes the local group comprises A Co and B Co only. However, the local group has total EBITDA of zero. Therefore, the local group has no interest capacity under the fixed ratio rule and the full net interest expense of USD 25 million is disallowed (USD 20 million in A Co and USD 5 million in B Co). FI Co remains subject to tax on its net interest income of USD 100 million. Therefore, although the group as a whole has net interest income of USD 75 million, its net interest income subject to tax is USD 100 million. In part, this impact would be reduced if net interest expense on regulatory capital instruments and other loans funding the group's banking or insurance operations were excluded from the scope of the fixed ratio rule, but this would increase the complexity of the rule to apply and administer.

Example 2 – Applying the fixed ratio rule to a non-financial sector group including a bank or insurance company

Example 2a – Applying the fixed ratio rule to a non-financial sector group including all entities

560. In Table III.C.2, a group consists of four entities all of which are located in Country X. A Co is the group's main holding company. B Co is a manufacturing company. C Co is a sub-holding company and is the parent of FI Co. FI Co is a solo-regulated bank or insurance company. A Co has negative EBITDA of USD 10 million and net interest expense of USD 5 million. B Co has EBITDA of USD 50 million and net interest expense of USD 20 million. C Co has negative EBITDA of USD 10 million and net interest expense of USD 20 million (most of which is incurred on interest-bearing regulatory capital instruments). FI Co has EBITDA of USD 20 million and net interest income of USD 100 million.

Table III.C.2. **Applying the fixed ratio rule to a non-financial sector group including all entities**

	A Co USD	B Co USD	C Co USD	FI Co USD	Local group USD
EBITDA	(10 million)	50 million	(10 million)	20 million	50 million
Net interest income/(expense)	(5 million)	(20 million)	(20 million)	100 million	55 million
Benchmark fixed ratio	-	-	-	-	25%
Interest capacity	-	-	-	-	n/a
Net interest income/(expense) of local group	(5 million)	(20 million)	(20 million)	100 million	55 million
Interest disallowance	-	-	-	-	-
Interest taxable/(deductible)	(5 million)	(20 million)	(20 million)	100 million	55 million

561. Country X applies the fixed ratio rule with a benchmark fixed ratio of 25%. The rule is applied to the net position of the local group including all entities. However, as the local group has net interest income of USD 55 million, the fixed ratio rule has no impact. As a result of net interest income in FI Co, A Co, B Co and C Co are able to deduct all of their net interest expense without limitation, despite the fact that A Co and B Co have no direct connection to FI Co's banking or insurance activities.

Example 2b – Applying the fixed ratio rule to a non-financial sector group excluding banks and insurance companies

562. This example is based on the same facts as in Example 2a, but in this case Country X applies the fixed ratio rule to a local group excluding banks, insurance companies and entities directly connected to banking or insurance activities. Therefore, in Table III.C.3, the local group includes A Co and B Co, but does not include C Co and FI Co.

563. Country X applies the fixed ratio rule with a benchmark fixed ratio of 25% to the local group's EBITDA of USD 40 million. The local group therefore has total interest capacity of USD 10 million. Compared to its total net interest expense of USD 25 million, this means the local group incurs a total interest disallowance of USD 15 million. In this example, the group has allocated USD 5 million of this disallowance to A Co and USD 10 million to B Co, but other allocations could be used.

Table III.C.3. **Applying the fixed ratio rule to a non-financial sector group excluding banks and insurance companies**

	A Co USD	B Co USD	Local group USD	C Co USD	FI Co USD	Entire group USD
EBITDA	(10 million)	50 million	40 million	(10 million)	20 million	50 million
Net interest income/(expense)	(5 million)	(20 million)	(25 million)	(20 million)	100 million	55 million
Benchmark fixed ratio	-	-	25%	-	-	-
Interest capacity	-	-	(10 million)	-	-	-
Net interest income/(expense)	(5 million)	(20 million)	(25 million)	(20 million)	100 million	55 million
Interest disallowance	5 million	10 million	15 million	-	-	15 million
Interest taxable/(deductible)	0	(10 million)	(10 million)	(20 million)	100 million	70 million

564. Country X may exempt C Co and FI Co from the scope of the fixed ratio rule, or apply the fixed ratio to a second local group comprising these two entities. As, taken together, they have net interest income of USD 80 million, the fixed ratio rule would have no impact and so in this example the outcome would be the same. C Co is able to deduct its full net interest expense of USD 20 million without restriction and FI Co remains taxable on its net interest income of USD 100 million.

565. The outcome of this approach is that the net interest income in FI Co has in effect sheltered the net interest expense in C Co. However, given C Co is directly connected to FI Co's banking or insurance business this would appear to be the correct outcome. On the other hand, compared with Example 2, the net interest income in FI Co is no longer able to shelter net interest expense in A Co and B Co. Therefore, net interest expense in A Co and B Co is restricted to 25% of their combined EBITDA. This would be comparable to the outcome for a similar manufacturing group which does not own a bank or insurance company.

566. If the entities in Table III.C.3 above comprise the entire worldwide group, A Co and B Co may be able to obtain relief for their net interest expense if Country X applies a group ratio rule that excludes banks, insurance companies and entities directly connected to banking or insurance activities from the definition of a worldwide group. However, where the group also includes entities in other countries, this would depend upon the level of the group ratio taking into account the EBITDA and net interest expense of those entities.

ORGANISATION FOR ECONOMIC CO-OPERATION AND DEVELOPMENT

The OECD is a unique forum where governments work together to address the economic, social and environmental challenges of globalisation. The OECD is also at the forefront of efforts to understand and to help governments respond to new developments and concerns, such as corporate governance, the information economy and the challenges of an ageing population. The Organisation provides a setting where governments can compare policy experiences, seek answers to common problems, identify good practice and work to co-ordinate domestic and international policies.

The OECD member countries are: Australia, Austria, Belgium, Canada, Chile, the Czech Republic, Denmark, Estonia, Finland, France, Germany, Greece, Hungary, Iceland, Ireland, Israel, Italy, Japan, Korea, Latvia, Luxembourg, Mexico, the Netherlands, New Zealand, Norway, Poland, Portugal, the Slovak Republic, Slovenia, Spain, Sweden, Switzerland, Turkey, the United Kingdom and the United States. The European Union takes part in the work of the OECD.

OECD Publishing disseminates widely the results of the Organisation's statistics gathering and research on economic, social and environmental issues, as well as the conventions, guidelines and standards agreed by its members.

OECD PUBLISHING, 2, rue André-Pascal, 75775 PARIS CEDEX 16
(23 2016 49 1 P) ISBN 978-92-64-26832-6 – 2017

www.ingramcontent.com/pod-product-compliance
Ingram Content Group UK Ltd.
Pitfield, Milton Keynes, MK11 3LW, UK
UKHW051501290926
15471UKWH00008B/1332

9 789264 268326